Women in the Life
of Andrew Jackson

Also by Ludwig M. Deppisch

*The Health of the First Ladies:
Medical Histories from Martha Washington
to Michelle Obama* (McFarland, 2015)

*The White House Physician:
A History from Washington
to George W. Bush* (McFarland, 2007)

Women in the Life of Andrew Jackson

LUDWIG M. DEPPISCH, M.D.

McFarland & Company, Inc., Publishers
Jefferson, North Carolina

LIBRARY OF CONGRESS CATALOGUING-IN-PUBLICATION DATA

Names: Deppisch, Ludwig M., 1938– author.
Title: Women in the life of Andrew Jackson / Ludwig M Deppisch.
Description: Jefferson, North Carolina : McFarland & Company, Inc., Publishers, 2021 | Includes bibliographical references and index.
Identifiers: LCCN 2021009019 | ISBN 9781476679914 (paperback : acid free paper) ∞
ISBN 9781476642857 (ebook)
Subjects: LCSH: Jackson, Andrew, 1767–1845—Relations with women. | Presidents—Family relationships—United States. | Jackson, Rachel, 1767–1828—Family. | Donelson, Emily Tennessee, 1807–1836 x Family. | Generals' spouses—Tennessee—Nashville—Biography. | Upper class women—Washington (D.C.)—Biography. | Washington (D.C.)—Social life and customs—19th century. | United States—Politics and government—1829–1837. | BISAC: HISTORY / United States / 19th Century | HISTORY / Women
Classification: LCC E382.1.A1 D47 2021 | DDC 973.5/6092—dc23
LC record available at https://lccn.loc.gov/2021009019

BRITISH LIBRARY CATALOGUING DATA ARE AVAILABLE

ISBN (print) 978-1-4766-7991-4
ISBN (ebook) 978-1-4766-4285-7

© 2021 Ludwig M. Deppisch, M.D. All rights reserved

No part of this book may be reproduced or transmitted in any form or by any means, electronic or mechanical, including photocopying or recording, or by any information storage and retrieval system, without permission in writing from the publisher.

On the cover: Andrew Jackson (1767–1845), U.S. President (1829–1837), portrait by Thomas Sully ca. 1829
(© 2021 Everett Collection/Shutterstock);
left to right Mrs. Andrew Jackson (Library of Congress);
Emily Donelson (1807–1836), Andrew Jackson's niece portrait painted by R.E.W. Earl, 1830 (© 2021 Everett Collection/Shutterstock); Sarah Yorke Jackson, daughter-in-law and White House hostess for President Jackson (Library of Congress)

Printed in the United States of America

McFarland & Company, Inc., Publishers
Box 611, Jefferson, North Carolina 28640
www.mcfarlandpub.com

To my three grandsons, Nick, Joey and Jake.
Thanks for being around.

Table of Contents

Acknowledgments viii
Preface: The Contradictions of the Man 1
I—Elizabeth Jackson: His Mother 5
II—Rachel Donelson: His Wife 18
III—Rachel Jackson: A Complicated Decade 33
IV—Rachel Jackson: Their Marriage Thrives 46
V—Rachel Jackson: Her Unwelcome Public Life 58
VI—Rachel Jackson: Her Distress and Demise 71
VII—Emily Tennessee Donelson: His Niece 84
VIII—Margaret Eaton: Wife of His Secretary of War 91
IX—Rachel, Emily and Margaret: The Eaton Affair 102
X—Emily and Margaret: The Eaton Affair Denouement 116
XI—Emily Donelson: Presiding Lady Again 131
XII—Margaret Eaton: Trials and Triumphs After the White House 148
XIII—Sarah Yorke Jackson: His "Daughter" 160
XIV—Mary Ann Eastin: His Favorite Niece and Other Favored Young Women 174
XV—Andrew Jackson's Women: A Summary of Their Influence 186

Chapter Notes 191
Bibliography 221
Index 227

Acknowledgments

This is the third book written during my post-retirement career as a neophyte historian. The focus of the previous publications was American history, specifically the medical history of America's presidents and First Ladies. Previously, my decades-long profession was that of a practicing physician-pathologist and a medical school professor.

Researching and writing historical nonfiction has fulfilled my second career with both intellectual curiosity and delight. Research has been a great joy, but the actual writing is a chore. It can be burdensome, tiresome, and beyond frustrating.

Rejuvenated by the publication of *The Health of the First Ladies*, I searched for my next subject, which became more complicated than anticipated. Louisa Adams, the wife of President John Q. Adams, intrigued when I researched that book. However, an excellent biography of Louisa appeared, scuttling any hopes of another biography.

Subsequently, a second theme was considered: a study of the Surrogate First Ladies, those women who were not the spouse of an incumbent president yet fulfilled the social, ceremonial, and chatelaine duties of First Lady when a president's wife was dead, disabled, or disinterested in these responsibilities. This idea was likewise abandoned. Rosemarie, my very perceptive and wise wife, was unenthusiastic, opining, "Too many names," and "Too many women." I agreed that such a format, encyclopedic in its essence, would be boring for any reader.

Rosemarie fortunately was intrigued by my tales of Rachel Donelson Jackson, Emily Donelson, Margaret Eaton, and other ladies who influenced the career and behavior of Andrew Jackson, the seventh United States president. Jackson himself, with his successes, conflicts, and more than a few egregious foibles, is a transfixing American character, a personage who could have stepped out of the pages of a contemporary tabloid. My topic was set!

Acknowledgments

For forming this decision and her constant support and appreciation, my gratitude overflows for Rosemarie, the love of my life over many decades. Our children Carl and Barbara, and son-in-law Rich, have been more than understanding of my efforts during this multi-year effort. Thank you. The most splendid gift in aging has been the appearance of grandchildren. We are blessed with three grandsons, Nick, Joey, and Jake, who have offered both energy and happiness to this struggling writer.

It has been often said that success has many parents while failure is an orphan. The hoped-for success of this book has many parents, while any failure is the sole possession of the author. I am the orphan, the single individual responsible for any errors in the text.

Two most generous and preternaturally knowledgeable ladies deserve special acknowledgment. Marsha Mullin, Vice President, Collections and Research/Chief Curator of Andrew Jackson's Hermitage, has been a continual resource during the writing of the book. She answered my questions, pointed me towards resources unfamiliar to me, and reviewed the manuscript for factual errors. Any mistakes that escaped her very fine filter are entirely my fault. Moreover, she was beyond gracious during my visit to Nashville; all the requested materials from the Hermitage collections were prepared for review upon my arrival, and comfortable office space was available for my inspection.

Laura-Eve Moss, an editor of *The Papers of Andrew Jackson* project at The University of Tennessee, Knoxville, has been a constant companion from a distance. She has answered my always too-many questions, provided always helpful hints, and was extremely generous of her time when I visited the *Papers'* offices in Knoxville two years ago. Laura-Eve constantly supported my choice of, and the progress of, this project. Thank you.

Three talented friends copy edited the final manuscript. They are all from the University of Arizona in Tucson. Jeanne Clarke copy edited my two previous books and volunteered, despite an illness, to edit my third. Professor Cynthia Stokes and Erika Burkhart, Masters in Music Performance, spent long hours in refashioning my syntax and correcting my punctuation and capitalization mistakes. Erika also had the tedious responsibility of properly formatting the endnotes and the bibliography.

My thanks go out to friends who reviewed an earlier version of this manuscript: Michelle Marie Perrier, Michelle Gullion, Cyndee Fraily, and Debbie Quirk. You are much appreciated.

I cannot conclude my acknowledgements without thanking the

editors and editors and staff of McFarland & Company Publishers for their skill, support, and professionalism in bringing to print this, my third book, with this talented crew. Special thanks to David Alff, Krystal Hamby, Beth Cox, and Dylan Lightfoot. My apologies if I have excluded anyone.

Preface
The Contradictions of the Man

Andrew Jackson, the seventh president of the United States (1829–1837), was a towering figure during the first century of the American republic. His image projected all the heroic and manly virtues of those times. He was tall, ferocious in both word and action, courageous, persistent despite numerous injuries and illnesses, and constantly combative in defending his personal version of morality. He was twice elected president of the United States.

Robert Remini, the preeminent Jackson biographer, introduced his subject this way: "No American ever had so powerful an impact on the minds and spirit of his contemporaries as did Andrew Jackson. No other man ever dominated an age spanning so many decades. No one, not Washington, Jefferson, or Franklin Roosevelt, ever held the American people in such near-total submission."[1] A second, more recent, biographer, Jon Meacham, elaborated, "A source of inspiration to Lincoln on the eve of the Civil War, revered by Theodore and Franklin Roosevelt, and hailed by Harry Truman as one of the four greatest presidents—along with Washington, Jefferson, and Lincoln."[2]

Despite the negative judgments of some contemporary historians regarding his attitudes towards slavery and Indian tribes, Andrew Jackson continues to be rated highly by presidential scholars. He still is considered the 14th most effective (Siena 2010 poll), and the 18th most effective American president (C-Span 2017 poll).[3] Donald Trump, the forty-fifth president of the United States and frequently compared to its seventh, hung Jackson's portrait behind his desk in the Oval Office.[4]

He was an anti–British combatant in his early teens, their prisoner during the War of Independence, and an attorney and judge on the American frontier; all were achieved at an early age. Later, he became a

Tennessee entrepreneur, a relentless opponent of the Creek Nation and all of the Southern Indian tribes, a first Representative from Tennessee to the United States House of Representatives, the military hero of the Battle of New Orleans, and the most important advocate for the annexation of Florida into the Union.

Yet, several biographers have questioned the "unidimensional" Jackson image. His personality was far more complex. Andrew Burstein in 2004 addressed his passionate personality: "In our time, Andrew Jackson ... no more the sharp-eyed, romantically gazing, stormy-haired presence on the ... twenty dollar bill." "To some, an unsurpassed war hero who walked among ordinary people.... To others ... a rude and overblown man of meager understandings."[5]

Andrew Jackson's attitude towards women was that of a traditional Southern gentleman, i.e., courtly and protective. He was, "...naturally chivalrous and something of a gallant in the approved ... fashion that was the mark of a gentleman."[6] His defense of a woman's honor was swift and dramatic, with words, fists, and ultimately, with dueling pistols. In 1806 he killed Charles Dickinson in such a duel over insults to his wife Rachel.

It is little known even today that Andrew Jackson's character and behavior, that of a masculine icon, were greatly influenced by women. Elizabeth Hutchinson Jackson, his mother, was a widow when Andrew was born and infused his maturing personality with the traits of her Scots-Irish heritage. Rachel Donelson Jackson, the love of his life during their union of over thirty-five years, provided him with conjugal solace, medical sustenance, and a prosperous home environment. Perhaps her greatest gift to her husband was the kinship of her very large, talented, and influential Donelson family.

Emily Donelson, his niece, was his White House Hostess for most of his eight-year Presidency. Young Emily was the sole woman who defied the overbearing Jackson. Although accomplished in her responsibilities, she, in her obstinacy, caused her uncle great personal pain and significant political complications by her conflict with the wife of Secretary of War John Eaton. The wife, Margaret (Peggy) O'Neale Timberlake Eaton, was the centerpiece of The Petticoat Affair, an historic scandal that consumed the early Jackson administration.

Sarah Yorke Jackson became his daughter-in-law when she married the president's adopted son. She was both a bulwark of strength and solace in his debilitated retirement. Mary Eastin Polk was another niece, and as Emily Donelson's close friend, was often a guest in the White House. Her marriage to Lucius Polk, of the prominent Tennessee family, may have buttressed Andrew Jackson's political legacy.

Preface: The Contradictions of the Man

These six women orbited Andrew Jackson. They reciprocally influenced and were influenced in turn by his towering figure. "Influence," as represented in this book, is not unidirectional. The theme is not limited to the effects, or lack thereof, that these women had upon Jackson, on either his behavior or his successes. The reciprocal effect of Jackson upon these ladies also is explored. Three of these women lived for varying periods of time after the president's death in 1845: Mary Eastin Polk briefly, and Sarah Yorke Jackson and Margaret Eaton for decades. The residue of their Jackson connection lingered. To date, these reciprocal relationships have never been studied exhaustively. This book intends to further explore the record of one of our most memorable presidents.

A word about usage: The terms "Old Hickory," "The Hero," and "The General" are occasionally used in the text to identify Andrew Jackson. "Hero" and "General" refer to his military exploits. Historically, "Old Hickory" was a sobriquet indicative of General Jackson's toughness, determination, and leadership, qualities acknowledged by his soldiers during his orderly 1813 return march from Natchez to Nashville. "Old" because at age forty-six, he was so considered by his much younger troops; "Hickory" because the wood of the hickory tree was noted for its hardness and toughness.

"The Eaton Affair," "The Petticoat Affair," and "The Eaton Malaria" are terms used synonymously in Chapters IX, X, XI, and XII to refer to the political scandal that embraced the first three years of the Jackson presidency.

I

Elizabeth Jackson
His Mother

"Never tell a lie, nor take what is not your own, nor sue anybody, for slander or assault and battery. Always settle them cases on your own."[1]

Scots-Irish Heritage

The story of feminine influence upon Andrew Jackson originates in the lowlands of Scotland where Jackson's forebears toiled. His mother, Elizabeth Jackson, was the initial, and after his wife, the most important woman who both molded his character and influenced his future behavior. Unfortunately for him, Elizabeth died during a mission of mercy that left Andrew an orphan at fourteen. His father, also named Andrew Jackson, predeceased Elizabeth by more than a decade; the senior Andrew died before his son and namesake was born. Any recollection of his father passed along to Andrew only through the reminiscences of Elizabeth. Jackson's parental formation, other than genetic, was exclusively maternal.

The future president's cultural inheritance emanated from the Scottish Lowlands. It was refined during his ancestors' century-long experience in the Ulster Plantation of Northern Ireland, where grinding labor and an impoverished environment hardened personalities and tempered optimism. His cultural heritage was likely distilled and fulfilled through his Scots-Irish forbears who emigrated to America's Appalachia during the 1700s.[2] Indeed, some have acclaimed Andrew Jackson as the quintessential American Scots-Irish hero and champion. Among United States presidents of similar heritage, "…(he) remains in a class by himself. Andrew Jackson was an original, an unusual and fearless leader who dominated the American political process more fully than any president before or since."³ Another historian employed hyperbole in linking Jackson with his roots: "This ill-treated Ireland, this trampled-upon Ireland, has produced the greatest soldier and the greatest statesman, whose name as yet appeared upon the records of valor and wisdom."⁴

By the sixteenth century, the Scottish Lowlands had witnessed centuries of political conflict between the Scots and the English, together with religious clashes that pitted the Presbyterian Church of Scotland against both Catholicism and the established Anglican Church of England. Additionally, the Lowlands suffered from its geographic isolation from the then modernizing nations of Western Europe. Its backward agricultural methods, its miserly infertile soil, and a medieval feudal system together made continued settlement more than undesirable.⁵ The Scottish Lowlands, poverty-stricken and generally lawless, still lingered in the Middle Ages at the onset of the seventeenth century.⁶ Layered upon this bleakness was the radical religious teachings of the Protestant reformer John Calvin. Calvinist Reformed Protestantism was introduced into the Scottish Lowlands in the 1500s, cultivated and championed by Presbyterian John Knox. This powerful movement swept away the unpopular Catholic Church, still remnant in the region.⁷

The harsh environment was responsible for the most distinctive characteristics of these people: dourness, hardness, and durability, all traits necessary for survival under duress.⁸ The Scots cohered for defense in extended family units, even as clans. Kinship was valued. "This hardness combined with a tendency towards violence which sometimes was not far removed from cruelty. The Scot had ruthless enemies to fight, and the customs of his country had not taught him to gloss over his encounters with the lacquer of chivalry."⁹

Opportunity beckoned for these hard-pressed people after King James VI of Scotland, the son of the beheaded Mary, Queen of Scots, succeeded the childless Queen Elizabeth I of England. He became King James I of England, thereby uniting the English and Scottish crowns and nations. In 1610, King James I formed a Protestant plantation on the shores of northern Ireland. Through a series of maneuvers, the Irish nobility and aristocracy that previously inhabited its six northern counties departed, leaving this land destitute and unpeopled. King James named these counties *The Ulster Plantation*, the geopolitical Northern Ireland of today. As James Leyburn explains, "The Scotch-Irish came into existence because England tried to settle the Irish problem, a perennial nettle to royal politicians.... By the time of Queen Elizabeth (ruled 1558–1603) the Irish 'problem' was no longer a sporadic one; it had become a steady drain on the royal exchequer, as on English manpower."[10]

A mass migration to Northern Ireland to escape a miserable Lowlands life followed. Tens of thousands of humble Scots with ambition and character who wanted a better life crossed the North Channel of the Irish Sea. Most intended to resettle permanently in Ulster. Families headed out from the denuded Scottish hills for the coastline where boats would take them to the Ulster Plantation. They traveled with few possessions. "They would be traveling not simply in families, but more likely in groups of families."[11]

The shores of Ulster lie within twenty-five miles of Scottish territory.

The migrants found plenty of adventure which called for bravery upon their arrival in Ireland, "for the Irish yielded ground most grudgingly to the newcomers ... who had to fight for every acre they occupied. Nor did the struggle ease with passing time. The Irish continued to resent the intrusion, and with each generation that was born, the fight began anew."[12]

By 1715, one-third of Ulster's population of 600,000 consisted of Scots. However, a majority of the indigenous Ulster population remained hostile to these migrants. As a protection against the hostility, many new settlements were walled and fortified.[13] Moreover, the Scottish immigrants were intense adherents of the Church of Scotland, i.e., the Presbyterian Church. The established English Church in Ireland, the Anglican Church, was predominant and attempted to control the Presbyterians.[14] Consequently, the Ulster Scots inevitably developed a defensive and intolerant outlook, called by some "a siege mentality."[15]

With time, the prospect waned that Northern Ireland would be a land of opportunity for generations of Scots. Material prosperity of the immigrants was sporadic at best. Most of the settlers had arrived either as tenants who rented their land from a more privileged class or as landless agricultural laborers who worked the land for the aforementioned tenants.[16] An expanding population, an increasing scarcity of land, the precarious fertility of the arable land that was available, and the aforementioned religious grievances made the conditions of life more than unpleasant. However, there was another opportunity for the Scots-Irish.

Another English-speaking land, America, although reached only by a months-long sea journey, presented new hope and promise. A substantial immigration of the Scots-Irish commenced at the end of the seventeenth century. As part of the British Empire, the American colonies offered no barriers of either language or emigration restrictions to the Ulster Scots. In addition, the linen trade had previously established a transatlantic trade route between ports in Ireland and America. Philadelphia, a thriving city situated on the Delaware River, was a very important port. "Ship-owners and sea captains who hauled hundreds of tons of flaxseed annually from Pennsylvania to Ulster were eager for a paying cargo for the return voyage, and they actively encouraged migration."[17] From 1717 until the American Revolution, this migration was a powerful dynamic that attracted at least 200,000 and as many as 400,000 migrants from Ulster to America.[18]

Previously, the attraction of America had been inviting for settlers from England. By 1717, colonists from England had lived in the New World for a century. Some of their colonies were flourishing; most were optimistic. Reports of opportunities for enterprising settlers circulated widely in the Old World. William Penn had advertised the attractions of his Pennsylvania colony during personal journeys to Europe. In 1717 the fourth successive year of drought ruined Ulster crops; the magnet of a new start in America became stronger; serious preparations began for a long sea journey.[19] Meanwhile, subsistence-living for the Scots-Irish became an endless succession of "dark and drublie days."[20]

These migrants carried with them the characteristics of their heritage—practicality, earthiness, and a religious sense that men and women were destined to participate in separate spheres of activity. Their ingrained Presbyterianism taught them that salvation depended solely upon themselves. Both their religion and the usual darkness of their situation inculcated their personalities with hardness, dourness, stubbornness, pride, and touchiness. A sense of humor was rare. The Scots-Irish fought their own battles and were frequently violent and ruthless in combating enemies.[21] Family kinship, thrift, and ferocity in battle were additional character traits. Unfortunately, their culture did not include an appreciation of music, literature, or any of the "fine arts."

Both of Andrew Jackson's parents were Scots-Irish whose families had lived in the Ulster Plantation for generations. Andrew Jackson was a first generation American. He was "...sprung from poor Irish emigrant parents driven from their native land by its inexorable oppressors (the English).... No man living ever did so much to humble England as Andrew Jackson, and these pages will show us how his zeal was sharpened, how his anger was pointed, by the lessons taught him by his ill-treated parents."[22]

The principal American ports of entry for Scots-Irish immigrants were located along the Delaware River. Philadelphia was the most important, but the cities of Chester and New Castle also welcomed many Scots-Irish. From these entry points, most migrated westward and then southward, through the Great Valley of Virginia and into the mountains of the Carolinas.²³ A second, less used, portal was the South Carolina seacoast city of Charleston.

Elizabeth Hutchinson, the mother of Andrew Jackson, probably was born in Carrickfergus, now a large town of nearly 40,000, in County Antrim, Northern Ireland.²⁴ It sits on the north shore of Belfast Lough, eleven miles from Belfast. Belfast Lough empties into the North Channel of the Irish Sea.

There is little verifiable information either about Elizabeth's ancestors or her own birth. Remini suggested that her forbearers immigrated to Ulster after the 1690 English victory in the Battle of the Boyne in Ireland.²⁵ King William's defeat of deposed King James II of England assured the dominance of Protestantism over Catholicism in the United Kingdom.²⁶

Elizabeth's birth date has not been firmly established either by The Hermitage, the Andrew Jackson Papers project, or any of Andrew Jackson's biographers. One unverified date from a history website lists November 1737.²⁷ She was one of five daughters and one son born to Cyrus Hutchinson and Margaret Lisle Hutchinson. Sisters Margaret (married McKemie), Sarah (married Leslie), Jane (marred Crawford) preceded her while Mary Molly (possibly Martha) (married Leslie) followed. The sisters were described as "comely, thrifty, well-bred, and sprightly—besides which they could read and write." Any information about the fate of Robert, their only brother, is unknown.²⁸

Andrew Jackson, the father of future president Andrew Jackson, was the youngest son of Hugh Jackson. Andrew senior married Elizabeth Hutchinson in the parish church of Carrickfergus on February 7, 1759.²⁹ Hugh Jackson was a well-to-do linen weaver and draper.³⁰ Linen, a textile made from the fibers of the flax plant, was a major product of the Ulster Plantation and all of Ireland. Linen was laborious to manufacture, but Hugh Jackson was clever enough to prosper. He was wealthy enough to settle his four sons as farmers in the neighborhood.³¹ However, none of the four had sufficient capital to purchase land, and consequently, they were compelled to rent plots from the well-to-do. Each of the bothers occupied a large farm and paid rents to the "Lord of the Soul."³² One of the brothers, Hugh Jackson, the namesake of his accomplished father, sought an alternative to farming and left Ulster to join the British army. He fought during the American French & Indian War in the uplands of the Carolinas. Upon his return to Ulster, he intrigued his brothers with tales about the fertile lands and the ease of property ownership in the Carolinas.³³

The senior Andrew Jackson was known for his hospitality and his strict adherence and attachment to the faith as professed by the Kirk of

Scotland, the established Presbyterian Church of Scotland. He lived near Castlereagh, a hundred and twenty-five miles from Carrickfergus.[34] However, this Jackson was a poor man who had difficulty extracting a living from the soil of his rented farmland. Elizabeth, his wife, was a poor man's daughter. Linen-weaving was the employment of her and her sisters. They worked late into the Ulster night to make their production quota.[35]

For many Scots-Irish, the idea of America emerged as a very welcome alternative to the undesirable reality of their Ulster life, even though the difficulty and length of the transatlantic journey dwarfed the hardships encountered by their ethnic forbearers in their previous migration to Ulster from Scotland. The Atlantic voyage lasted between six and ten weeks.[36]

Four of Elizabeth's sisters, and most likely their brother, had already made the arduous Atlantic crossing around 1750.[37] In 1763, the conclusion of the seven-year French & Indian War (in Europe, termed The Seven Years War) freed the American frontier from the French and much of the Indian danger. So, the Jacksons departed Ireland for good in 1765.[38] They sailed as a family: Andrew, Elizabeth, sons Robert and Hugh; James Crawford, Jane, his wife (who was Elizabeth's sister), and Crawford's two brothers.[39]

The details of their Atlantic crossing and their port of arrival are clouded due to the sparseness of documentary evidence. Just as Elizabeth's birth date is clouded in uncertainty, so to incomplete records leave uncertain other aspects of Elizabeth's early American history. Both the location of the Jackson family's arrival in America and the site of Andrew Jackson's birth remain controversial. Most biographers conclude that the Jackson family landed in Philadelphia or in one of the Delaware River ports.[40] A minority opinion claims Charleston, South Carolina, as their port of entry. These harbors presented the first vision of the New World to most of the Ulster immigrants.[41]

Their subsequent overland trek from an Atlantic seaport to the Carolina hills is undocumented. They may have followed the route of Elizabeth's sisters who, after their Pennsylvania disembarkation, settled briefly near Lancaster, Pennsylvania, among other Scots-Irish immigrants, before they travelled south towards the Carolinas.[42]

The Jacksons, and the Hutchinsons before them, settled in the Waxhaw border region of North and South Carolina. The area was the home of the Waxhaw Indian tribe, who were related to the more numerous and enduring Catawba tribe. After several wars between 1711 and 1715 in which the natives were eventually defeated by white settlers, the Waxhaws disappeared, either by amalgamation into neighboring tribes or by decimation during a 1741 smallpox epidemic.[43]

I—Elizabeth Jackson: His Mother

The European Waxhaw settlement dates back to May 1751, when six or seven families, all Scots-Irish Presbyterians, arrived to clear the rich land between two creeks, which were named Waxhaw and Cane. Their headwaters arose in present day Union County, North Carolina, and they subsequently flowed westward through Lancaster County, South Carolina, into the Catawba River. The area, often referred to as the "Garden of the Waxhaws," had become nearly unoccupied after the decimation of the Waxhaw tribe. Most newcomers of the 1750s arrived from the western areas of Virginia and Pennsylvania. By 1755 the Scots-Irish settlers had built a meeting house, still in existence today and known as the Old Waxhaw Presbyterian Church. It was the first church in the upcountry of South Carolina.

The senior Andrew Jackson probably owned the land that he farmed in America, an economic improvement upon his previous tenancy on a rental farm in Northern Ireland. His son Hugh was three and son Robert was less than a year old when the family arrived in Waxhaw. The Waxhaw farms of the Hutchinson sisters and their husbands were convenient for assistance, but not proximate. Elizabeth's sister, Jane Crawford, and her family lived in the center of the Waxhaw community. Peggy Hutchinson and her husband George McCamie had settled a mile east of the Crawford home. A third sister, Sarah Hutchinson, and her husband John Leslie owned a farm located a mile farther east of the McCamie homestead. For various reasons Andrew Jackson settled his family on Twelve Mile Creek, seven miles from the heart of Waxhaw.[44] The Jacksons' two-hundred-acre farm was located on the border between North and South Carolina.

Elizabeth's husband died in 1767, some months before Andrew Jackson's birth. "He injured himself while working—family tradition said he was trying to lift a log heavier than one man can handle—and he was forced to bed." He died shortly after his accident. Additional information regarding the circumstances is lost.[45]

Elizabeth, in the third trimester of her pregnancy, and without the support and protection of a husband, abandoned the Jackson family farm. Accompanied by her first-born Hugh and her infant son Robert, Elizabeth fled to the security of a nearby sister's house where she gave birth on March 15, 1867, to Andrew Jackson, her third born son and the future seventh president of the United States. Neither Elizabeth Jackson nor her three sons ever returned to their Waxhaw home on the banks of Twelve Mile Creek.[46]

The proximity of the North Carolina–South Carolina border and uncertainty over the identity of the sister whose house was Andrew's birthplace resulted in some uncertainty over the location of his birth.

Both Carolinas have vied for the honor of claiming President Andrew Jackson as a native son. Biographer James Parton claimed that Elizabeth went to the home of Margaret Hutchinson McKemie where she delivered Andrew. The McKemie home was placed in Union County, North Carolina. However, Andrew Jackson himself believed that South Carolina was the state of his birth. "'Fellow citizens of my native State!' he exclaims, at the close of his proclamation to the nullifiers of South Carolina."[47]

Meacham's biography chose not to resolve the controversy.[48] According to Remini, the confusion results from Elizabeth's actions subsequent to the death of her husband. If she went to her sister Jane Hutchinson Crawford's house and delivered there, then Jackson was born in South Carolina. In contrast, there is oral history within the Leslie branch of the family: Elizabeth, on the way to the Crawfords, stopped at her sister Margaret's home where she went into labor suddenly and gave birth precipitously. If so, Andrew Jackson was born in North Carolina.[49]

All other biographers conclude that Elizabeth gave birth in the home of sister Jane Crawford, who lived just over the boundary line, in South Carolina.[50] The Hermitage, the site of Andrew Jackson' home and the Andrew Jackson Foundation, responds to this frequently asked question by replying that there is evidence for both sides, but that Jackson himself believed he was born in South Carolina.[51] Finally, The Andrew Jackson Papers Project at the University of Tennessee concluded that Jackson's own belief that South Carolina was his native state has settled the controversy.[52]

Elizabeth and her sons move into her invalid sister, Jane Crawford's, home was permanent. Jackson's mother not only managed the Crawford home but also raised Jane's eight children in addition to her own three sons.[53] The Crawford house thus became the Jacksons' home. This modus operandi was almost certainly never formalized but simply evolved: Elizabeth assumed the role of housekeeper and second mother to the eight Crawford children in exchange for her and her own three boys' maintenance.[54]

In her youth, there "burned a seal for accomplishment that seemed to make handicaps resolve themselves in her favor." As a young woman, Elizabeth Hutchinson Jackson was depicted as possessing "snapping blue eyes," red hair, and a "brisk little body." But, in her maturity, she had grown stout; however, she was credited as being a woman of "extraordinary interior strength."[55] Elizabeth, "Though small in stature ... was strong and resilient in spirit. She adapted to life's changes and disappointments and put others' needs before herself. Working hard and pushing forward through challenges was the model she set for her sons."[56]

Andrew's debt to his mother was deep and significant. Her character, formed and refined by her hardened Scots-Irish heritage, both molded Andrew's personality and guided his behavior perhaps more than any other person with the exception of his wife Rachel Donelson. Mother Elizabeth greatly influenced Andrew Jackson, both before and long beyond her death. The influence of Elizabeth Hutchinson Jackson upon Andrew, her youngest son, was profound, and in many cases, indelible.

What the future president inherited from his father was nebulous and probably evanescent. His many "Waxhaw uncles and aunts apparently did not take a good deal of interest in him. They had their own children, their own problems, their own lives." However, the proximity to his uncles James and Robert Crawford, who accompanied his parents on their transatlantic journey, surely affected the young Jackson. He lived with his mother in James' home; he may also have spent some time with Robert. Uncle Robert "is credited with giving Andrew his first gun and contributing to his love of horses."[57]

Andrew's mother was a fervent Presbyterian, the strict Reformed Protestant creed that was part of the Scots-Irish heritage. Elizabeth faithfully took Andrew and his older brothers each week to the Waxhaw meeting house for services. From dawn to dusk, she worked every minute of each day in some useful activity. The exception was Sunday; the Sabbath was devoted to the worship of the Lord. Her religious zeal was so fervent that she desired her youngest son to become a Presbyterian minister. But Andrew frustrated his mother's hope for the clergy. The son's humility and piety were lacking, and his boyhood years were often dominated by fighting and swearing. Despite these inclinations, Elizabeth still was able to instill a strong religious streak in her rambunctious son which persisted through his entire adult life. Later, Rachel Jackson also became a devoted observer of Presbyterianism, and thereby a religious model for her husband. Jackson greatly respected Rachel's beliefs and constructed a chapel on the grounds of The Hermitage to accommodate her worship. Finally, it may be possible that his devotion to community, military, and state and national service may have had its source at the spring of Elizabeth's religiosity.[58]

Stephenson's affidavit testified to her fervor: "…the mother of the General, sustained as fair a character for virtue and piety, as any lady that I ever knew. …member of the Presbyterian church, and I have frequently heard the old people speak in terms of high commendation of her piety and worth."[59]

Andrew received a better education than brothers Hugh and Robert. Their mother eyed her youngest son as a future Presbyterian minister. He attended the common school behind his uncle McCamie's cabin, now officially located in North Carolina. Commonly, a school venue in the region was a little cabin in the woods where a young master in his teens or twenties received a small fee to teach boys and girls their letters and rules for arithmetic during part of the year. Literacy was high in Ulster communities, where up to eighty percent could read and write. Both before and after school, and during recess, the schoolboys usually raced or fought.[60]

Around 1776, young Jackson moved in with his uncle, Capt. Robert Crawford, at his big log house near Waxhaw Creek. The reason was Andrew's admittance to another school, an academy where Latin and Greek—the passports to serious learning, reading, and mathematics—were taught. The school was the Waxhaw Meeting House, located three miles from Capt. Crawford. Elizabeth did not enroll either of his brothers in the academy. In 1776 a "dominie," a schoolmaster capable of teaching Latin and Greek, named William Humphries arrived to open the school. All of Andrew's classmates attended because their parents, like his mother, wanted their sons to have careers in the ministry, medicine, or the law. Unfortunately, this school closed in 1779. Jackson's formal education ended after a term taught by a novice instructor named Stephenson, and possibly another term at Liberty Hall in Charlotte.[61]

Elizabeth inculcated her sons with her unalterable hatred of the English. Her Hutchinson ancestors had been abused by the English regime, both in the Lowlands of Scotland and in the harsh countryside of Ulster. "Often would she spend the winter's evenings in recounting to them the sufferings of their grandfather at the siege of Carrickfergus, and the oppressions exercised by the nobility of Ireland, over the laboring poor, impressing upon them as a first duty, to expend their loves, if it should become necessary, in defending and supporting the natural rights of man."[62]

The destruction of the tiny Jackson family at the hands of the English military could only amplify Andrew's hostility, an emotion that drove him to successfully battle the British during the War of 1812 and later English influence during the Seminole War in Florida. During his early teenage years, the future president experienced the deaths of both of his brothers and the demise of his beloved mother either directly or indirectly at the hands of the English. During the early 1780s, as the American War of Independence was winding down elsewhere in the colonies, the Waxhaws exploded with repeated and vicious battles with the American rebels, the British military, and the colonial Tories who supported the British.

To avoid the hostilities, the Jacksons, firm supporters of independence, were forced, often with their relatives, to flee their homes for the safety of the forests. The three Jackson siblings fought against the English army; the two older siblings died for their service. Hugh, the oldest brother at age sixteen, perished due to heat stroke following the Battle of Stono Ferry, near Charleston, in 1779. The two-hour battle was not a win for the patriots. "Huey Jackson was dying. He had been sick, and his commander ordered him to stay out of the battle ... he had gone into battle anyway and had collapsed from exhaustion after it was over. He barely made it home, died almost at once, and was buried quickly in the church-yard."[63]

The following years, 1780–1781, continued to be disruptive ones for the Waxhaw Scots-Irish, including the Jackson and Crawford families. Repeated incursions into their territory by the English army, especially the mounted dragoons of Sir Banastre "Bloody" Tarleton, and later by the Irish American Tories, terrified and uprooted the patriot population. Elizabeth and her tiny family, together with their kin and their neighbors, fled to the relative security of North Carolina. They sheltered for four months during the autumn and winter of 1780-1781. Then Elizabeth reluctantly permitted her two surviving sons to ride with the American forces. Initially Robert and Andrew were forbidden to bear arms; their military duties were limited to support and supply, although they were permitted to drill with the troops. Eventually both brothers were allowed to carry a rifle.[64]

Disaster awaited the Jackson brothers on April 11, 1781, as they were eating in a forest cabin. A mixed force of English regulars and Tory volunteers surprised them and their colleagues; overwhelmed, they surrendered. The officer-in-charge, a Tory, arrogantly insisted that the thirteen-year-old Andrew clean his muddied boots. The fiery future president refused, answering, "I am a prisoner of war and claim to be treated as such."[65]

The startled officer brought his drawn sword down towards the head of the recalcitrant prisoner. Jackson's fingers and wrist of his left arm were slashed, but his skull was only dented. He escaped being impaled by the Tory saber. Andrew and Robert Jackson, their cousin Thomas Crawford, and several other prisoners were taken to the military jail in Camden, South Carolina. After his arrival Jackson's wound stopped bleeding, but the accompanying pain was excruciating, and the loss of blood produced a searing thirst.

The prison conditions were beyond unhealthy; large rooms

confined the 250 American prisoners. Smallpox was rampant, and both brothers contracted the easily transmissible infection. The characteristic sign of this disease is a "pox," the appearance of widespread, blistering pustules over the patient's skin. A serious pernicious complication of smallpox was a pneumonia that accounted for most deaths of patients who perished from the disease. Elizabeth Jackson heroically traveled the forty-five miles to the Camden prison from Waxhaw and somehow participated in a prisoner exchange that freed her two sons. She procured two horses and placed the dying Robert on one, while Andrew walked the forty-five miles home in a drenching rain. Robert became the second Jackson fatality at the hands of the English; he succumbed to his disease two days after reaching home.[66]

Elizabeth nursed Andrew back to health. When her son was out of danger, she travelled one hundred sixty miles over four days to reach the English prison ships, berthed in the Charleston, South Carolina, harbor. Hers was a mission of mercy to tend to the health of her kin, her two Crawford nephews who were detained there. She died in Charleston from ship fever in the fall of 1781.[67]

Ship fever is an old name for epidemic typhus, which was common in the crowded conditions aboard prison ships. Charleston Harbor was a recognized "fever pit" during the Revolutionary War. Webb alternatively ascribed her death to cholera, another infection associated with this term.[68] Andrew Jackson never saw his mother again after she left on her mission of mercy. She died in Charleston helping other boys and was buried in obscurity. Her clothes were all that were returned to her son. Andrew long sought the location of his mother's grave but to no avail.[69]

John Eaton, Jackson's first biographer, quoting Jackson, recalled that Elizabeth's last words of advice to him: "…was never to institute suit for assault and battery, or for defamation, never to wound the feelings of others, nor suffer my own to be outraged."[70] Booraem related an alternative final instruction to Andrew as she departed for the prison ships in Charleston Harbor. She began, "Make friends by being honest, keep them by being steadfast. Andy, never tell a lie or take what is not yours." Then she confirmed her intention with this admonition, "Never sue for slander. Settle them cases yourself."[71]

Elizabeth bequeathed her iron-clad determination to Andrew. It allowed no obstacle to stand in the way of necessary action. She determined to keep her family together until the war split them up, and later to rescue the two surviving sons from the Camden prison. She was a resourceful woman who made a good bit out of little. Andrew Jackson projected strength and exercised perseverance in adversity during his long public career. Both virtues can be ascribed to his mother's influence, brief though it was.[72]

She was "...a strong minded woman who had a powerful influence on her son." Her son did not speak of her often in later life. He remarked mostly on the courage and strength she displayed in losing her husband, facing up to the rigors of harsh frontier life, and raising three fatherless boys.[73]

Rachel Jackson later wrote in a letter to a friend, "Elizabeth—she encountered many hardships while on this earth, but is now at rest I trust with the spirit of the good and just—it is probable from this cause My Husband obtained the fortitude which has enabled him to triumph with so much success over the many obstacles which have diversified his life."[74]

Jackson's image of the revered Elizabeth Hutchinson Jackson was a likely factor in his later chivalrous attitude towards women. He "imbibed a reverence for the character of women and treated them courteously—far beyond what was expected of him as a proper gentleman."[75] Many years later, during the contentious 1828 presidential campaign, after the followers of John Quincy Adams issued a scurrilous defamation against Elizabeth, Jackson said to a friend, "...and my pious mother, nearly fifty years in the tomb, and who, from her cradle to her death had not a speck on her character, has been dragged forth ... and held to public scorn as a prostitute who intermarried with a Negro, and my eldest brother sold as a slave in California."[76]

Jackson's mother left no written word of her decisions, her insights, or her emotions. Only her son's future behaviors and his few recollection of her words can add to an historian's retroactive consideration of her influence.

II

Rachel Donelson
His Wife

"Besides her answering love and constant attention to his needs, Rachel provided Andrew with a large family who embraced him, supported his ambitions, and loved him as one of their own."[1]

The Interim

Andrew Jackson, an orphan, passed through his teenage years without any demonstrable female influence of significance. Little information is recorded about any contact with women from the moment of his mother's death when he was fourteen until his introduction to Rachel Donelson when he was twenty-one. After his admission to the North Carolina bar in the late 1780s, Jackson rode the judicial circuit in rural North Carolina with his attorney brethren. During his time as a practicing lawyer, any female attachment was transient, if at all.

The story of his social, physical, and professional journey after the death of his mother in the fall of 1781 to his establishment in Nashville in 1788 is only fragmentary. Most of what is known is available in Hendrik Booraem's *Young Hickory: The Making of Andrew Jackson*.[2]

During this period Jackson traveled widely, twice or more visiting the port city of Charleston, South Carolina. Becoming cognizant of his academic deficiencies, he enrolled in a coeducational school in Bethel, North Carolina, for a brief time in order to practice writing English and Latin.[3] Thereafter for several years, he studied the law in North Carolina. Later as a practicing attorney, he rode the back roads of the state on horseback as he sought cases and clients. Occasionally, Jackson returned to his native Waxhaws, where he stayed at the homes of his uncles.[4]

Jackson's future direction was influenced by his two-year-older cousin Will Crawford. Will advised Andrew to study law, since "A law license was the passport to the world of opportunities." At that time North Carolina had no age or educational prerequisites for a law degree. The only requirement was passage of an oral examination administered by judges that tested the basic procedures and terminology of the law. Accepting Crawford's advice, the seventeen-year-old Jackson rode off to North Carolina in December 1784 to study law. After several years of hard work and studious application, Jackson was successfully examined by State Superior Court Judge John Williams.[5]

For several years, the young attorney, not yet twenty, rode the 400-mile court circuit with a convoy of lawyers. Gambling, socializing, and deal-making with his lawyer pals provided the entertainment; there was no hint of womanizing. His close friend, John Overton, later a Tennessee judge, commented many years later about then-presidential candidate Andrew Jackson's behavior, both while a young attorney in North Carolina and, subsequently, while he was the target of Rachel Donelson Robards husband's anger in Nashville:

> *The whole affair* [with Robards] *gave Jackson great uneasiness.... Continually together during our attendance on wilderness courts, while other young men were indulging in familiarities with females of relaxed morals, no suspicion of this kind of the world's censure ever fell to Jackson's share.*

From then on, promiscuity could never be called a personality trait of Andrew Jackson. Confirmation of his behavior is derived from the following observations: "Of Jackson's progress with the girls at Bethel, there is not a trace of evidence," and "There are few traditions about his success with girls in the Waxhaws."[6]

John McNairy, a close companion and a fellow circuit rider, was offered a judgeship in Davidson County, Tennessee, which lay across the mountains from North Carolina. At the time, Tennessee still remained the Western District of North Carolina. After McNairy accepted the position, he persuaded Andrew to accompany him to Tennessee. In the spring of 1788, they made the trip together with a large party of friends. Probably the young Jackson saw this as a way to make his fortune and to establish his reputation. He concluded that an attorney in a newly settled region could acquire and sell land based on opportunities provided by his court contacts.[7]

Young Rachel Donelson

The McNairy-Jackson party reached Nashville in October 1788. Then the town was inhabited by a few hundred settlers. Its frontier landscape was interrupted only by a courthouse, two stores, two taverns, a distillery, and a number of houses, cabins, tents, and miscellaneous other abodes.[8] Jackson soon located lodging as a boarder with Mrs. Rachel Donelson, the widow of one of the founders of Nashville, Colonel John Donelson. The widow and her immediate family occupied a large blockhouse; her boarders, including the young attorney, resided in an adjacent cabin. Living with her mother in the blockhouse was the married Rachel Donelson Robards.[9]

When the twenty-one-year-old Rachel was introduced to the twenty-one-year-old migrant attorney in her mother's home in 1788, both their futures were decided. Without doubt, she became the most influential woman in his life after the death of his mother.

The history of the Donelsons contrasted with that of the Jacksons. Andrew was the solitary remnant of the Jackson family while the Donelsons were legion. Rachel was one of eleven children. Andrew was a first generation American while the Donelsons had been settled in America for generations. He arrived as a newcomer in Nashville where her family had been prominent for the past eight years. The Donelsons had acquired wealth and position; Andrew Jackson possessed neither.

Rachel was the daughter of John Donelson and Rachel Stockley; they had married in 1744. When newlyweds, Rachel's parents moved to Pittsylvania County, Virginia, from the settled Eastern part of the State. Their new home was located in the south-central part of the state in the foothills of the Appalachians, adjacent to the North Carolina border.[10]

Rachel's father John Donelson was born in Somerset County, Maryland, in 1718. Donelson was a third generation American of Scottish-Welsh heritage. As a young man, he moved to Virginia where, at age twenty-six, he married the fourteen-year-old Rachel Stockley. After John and Rachel moved to Pittsylvania, Donelson became a prominent landowner in the county. He

> ...acquired an iron foundry, and a plantation, worked by some thirty slaves ... appointed county surveyor in 1767, represented Pittsylvania in the (Virginia) House of Burgesses for five years, and joined the county militia as colonel at the outbreak of American Revolution in 1775. The Donelsons were prosperous and well-respected minor gentry and might have lived out their lives in Virginia if John Donelson had not gone over the mountains to survey western lands.[11]

Donelson was well educated for his day, especially in the practical phases of statesmanship, military service, plantation management, exploring, surveying, iron manufacturing, boat building, navigation, and trade.[12] He reportedly acquired some formal education at the College of William & Mary in Williamsburg, Virginia.[13]

While in Virginia, John was a member of the Church of England

(Anglican Church). In the years during and following the Revolutionary War, the Anglican Church lost favor in the American Colonies because of its association with the British Crown.[14] His mother, Catherine Davies, was the sister of the famous Presbyterian clergyman, the Reverend Samuel Davies, who preached widely in Virginia and later became the president of Princeton University. The Donelsons became Presbyterians.[15]

Donelson accepted a commission in the Pittsylvania County militia in 1775. Later, he served as a colonel in the Cherokee Expedition, which took him west over the Appalachian Mountains. Donelson, his sons, and his sons-in-law ardently supported the American Revolution.[16]

British colonies Virginia and North Carolina were bordered by the Atlantic Ocean on the east; its southern and northern borders were carefully designated by latitude from Maryland and South Carolina. However, their western boundaries were, in theory, almost limitless. The original colonial grants for the two colonies ran from sea to sea; at the time, no one had determined how far away the western sea might lie.

The adventuresome father became afflicted with a wanderlust when he enlisted with a surveying crew that trekked from his Virginia home through the Cumberland River area of middle Tennessee. The area, with its broad bottomlands, navigable rivers and streams, and abundant salt licks, invited settlement by those pioneers who dared.[17] At age 54 John Donelson decided to sell his land in Virginia, uprooted his large family, and traveled to the Tennessee frontier. The Donelson family subsequently established their homes along the Cumberland River. John Donelson later was acclaimed with James Robertson as the founders of the city of Nashville. The pioneer Donelson was murdered in 1785 by unknown killers on the road between Kentucky and Nashville.[18]

Rachel's mother, Rachel Stockley Donelson, was a native Virginian of Ulster Scottish-English stock. This Rachel was a native of Accomack County on the Eastern Shore of Virginia. Little is known of her forebearers. Even her date of birth is not known with certainty.[19] "Like early records of the Donelson family, many of the birth, marriage and death records of the Stockley family are not to be found." Her journey from the beautiful and historic Eastern Shore of Virginia to a new home in the frontier county of Pittsylvania has to be only the first of her several odysseys on the American frontier.[20]

For over thirty years, Rachel Stockley Donelson maintained a comfortable home in Pittsylvania County and enjoyed a prosperous lifestyle as the wife of Colonel John Donelson. She bore and raised eleven children. Rachel, the Donelson's youngest daughter, was born in Pittsylvania County in 1767.[21] Her biographers confusingly have asserted differing birth positions for Rachel among her Donelson siblings. She is listed as either eighth, ninth, or tenth in order of birth. Fortunately for historians, they do agree that Rachel Stockley Donelson gave birth to a total of eleven children.[22]

Rachel was described as a "brown eyed baby girl with curly black hair."[23] During her childhood she became the pet of the Donelson household. Her doting father frequently took her with him on trips. Fortunately, the young girl, "...possessed a good nature and genuine sweetness which kept her from being spoiled...."[24] Rachel was taught to read and write, but her spelling was described as somewhat "irregular." She developed into an eager and interested reader. "The education which she received during her childhood in Virginia ... was superior to that of many girls of her time."[25]

Journey to Tennessee

In 1779 when the adolescent Rachel was twelve years old, the entire close-knit Donelson family uprooted its comfortable and peaceful life in Virginia. Colonel Donelson, aware that he and his family were marked as active patriots, concluded that their material, and even their personal, well-being would be jeopardized in the event of a British victory. The patriarch's previous surveying expeditions across the mountains located an opportunity for his family in the fertile Cumberland Valley of Tennessee. Donelson decided that the prospect of fortune and opportunity in the West outweighed the inevitable dangers of the lengthy trip required to get there.[26]

James Robertson, a seasoned explorer of the trans-Appalachian wilderness, planned the expedition to the Cumberland with Colonel John Donelson. The expedition comprised many families besides the Robertsons and the Donelsons. According to their plan, the travelers would be divided into two groups—the first, a caravan over land to be led by Robertson, and the second, a river journey to be commanded by Donelson. Robertson's party consisted only of men; its mission was to trek as quickly as possible over the hazardous mountains to establish a presence in the Cumberland. Its members were pioneers whose purpose upon arrival was to construct huts, plant corn, and secure the area until the arrival of Donelson's main party. Today, their direct route by road measures 285 miles. In contrast, Donelson had decided on a raft voyage of over one thousand miles.[27]

Donelson's water route was via a complicated network of rivers—the Holston, the Tennessee, the Ohio, and finally, the Cumberland. His party contained families including men, women, and children. Many of Robertson's relatives, his wife and young children, his widowed sister and his kin and neighbors from North Carolina groups, together with Donelson's complete family, were entrusted to the Colonel's leadership.[28]

John Donelson took command of the flotilla as it commenced its hazardous, multi-river journey. This water journey had never been attempted previously by white settlers; the greater part of the route was vulnerable to attacks by hostile Indians, mainly of the Cherokee tribe. In addition, the flotilla's progress would be at the mercy of the vagaries of the weather. The flotilla's departure from Fort Patrick Henry was delayed until December 22, 1779. However, the twin effects of low water in the Holston River and a protracted spell of freezing cold soon stranded the travelers for two months, until late February 1780. The Donelson's flotilla, after an adventuresome four-month journey, finally landed at its destination, Big Salt Lick on the Cumberland River, on April 24, 1780.[29]

The Adventure, the Colonel's fittingly named lead flatboat, was about 100 feet long and 20 feet wide. The thirty flatboats of the river convoy followed in *The Adventure*'s wake. Rachel, not yet thirteen, travelled on her father's boat and often helped to steer it. She was described favorably, as "black eyed, black haired brunette, as gay, bold, and handsome as ever had danced on the deck of a flat boat."[30]

James Robertson and John Donelson together established Fort Nashborough on the Cumberland River. The settlement eventually became the City of Nashville. Thus, the father of Rachel Donelson was instrumental in the construction of the urban platform upon which his future son-in-law's personal, political, economic, and military history was built. Donelson's co-founder James Robertson was a leader, an excellent woodsman and farmer, as well as an experienced Indian fighter and negotiator. He had first crossed the Appalachian Mountains into these unexplored regions with Daniel Boone in 1769.[31]

The frontier Nashborough settlement was a major irritant to the Indians who previously hunted unhindered throughout the Cumberland Valley. Their hostile attacks upon the white settlers commenced and continued; the danger persuaded the patriarch of the Donelson family to uproot his clan once again. His entire family moved to Bowman's Station in Kentucky.[32] By 1781, tribal attacks upon the river settlements had reduced their population dramatically. Nearly half of the 256 men who had signed the Cumberland Compact a year earlier had been killed by Indians or had relocated to a safer region.[33]

The family's initial residence in Tennessee was brief, since by late 1780 Colonel Donelson already re-established his relatives and their enslaved people on newly purchased Kentucky property. The entrepreneurial Donelson continued to acquire additional land in Kentucky through 1784.[34] Singing and making music, usually with a fiddle, was the centerpiece of most social gatherings in their new homes. Young Rachel had a clear, pleasant voice and became a stylish, untiring dancer.[35] Her beauty, her natural charm, and vivacity, as well as her family's position, made Rachel attractive to the young men of their Kentucky community.

Four years in Kentucky passed. The 1783 Treaty of Paris officially concluded the War of American Independence. During the following year, 1784, peace prevailed along the American frontier. With this brightened outlook, the Donelson clan made plans to return to the Cumberland River Valley of Tennessee. The decision was one vote shy of unanimity. Teen-aged Rachel was reluctant to undertake yet another exhausting journey and preferred to remain in Kentucky.[36]

The major reason for her decision was a flourishing romantic attachment to a handsome suitor. In 1783, Lewis Robards was twenty-six when he, his widowed mother, and his younger brothers and sisters moved to Kentucky. The Robards family was both more socially prominent and wealthier than the Donelsons. Robards was a veteran, having served under George Washington, and was mustered out of the Revolutionary Army as a captain after the decisive American victory at Yorktown.[37]

Rachel Donelson married Lewis Robards on March 1, 1785, in Mercer County, Kentucky. The groom was twenty-seven, the bride but eighteen.[38] The newlyweds soon received an important visitor, Colonel John Donelson. Rachel's father had concluded business in Virginia, and returning to Kentucky, discovered that his family, except for his daughter, had already set out for Tennessee. After a brief visit, Donelson also set out for Tennessee. Unfortunately for many, he was murdered somewhere on the trail between Kentucky and the Cumberland. His 1785 homicide was never solved.[39]

Rachel's marriage became both an unhappy and demeaning experience. Although happily welcomed into the Robards family by her new mother-in-law, troubles with Lewis soon left her despondent and uncertain. He, "…became sullen and suspicious…. He saw in her good-natured interest in every living thing about her, cause for an insane jealousy. Their days became embittered by his unjust accusations and their life together grew entirely impossible. Finally the end came when he openly voiced his suspicions about his wife and a young man in the neighborhood." As a result, Rachel's existence as Lewis's wife became shrouded with shame, unhappiness, and ignominy.[40]

After three unbearable years of living with Lewis Robards, Rachel summoned Samuel Donelson, her brother, to escort her away from Robards and Kentucky in order to return to her supportive Donelson family in Tennessee. The twenty-one-year-old's first attempt at marriage had failed after three miserable years. Her Nashville homecoming occurred in the summer or early fall of 1788.[41]

Robards, the rejected husband, had a high opinion of his self-worth. As a military man and a significant land owner, abandonment by his young wife undoubtedly was a disaster to his manly pride. His reaction, surprisingly, was remorse and apology. "Divorce, to all practical purposes, was unknown, and, had it been considered, there was little place for it in pioneer society."[42] Rachel agreed to a reconciliation, but only on the condition that Robards buy land near the Cumberland homes of the extended Donelson family. He accepted her condition and eventually fulfilled her demand. He reunited with Rachel sometime in 1788 or 1789. The couple lived together in the home of Rachel's widowed mother, the matriarch of the Donelson family.[43]

Andrew Jackson arrived in Nashville in late 1788. From that time his future and that of the community were inextricably linked. When Jackson arrived, Nashville and other settlements along the Cumberland contained five thousand souls or perhaps a few more. But the place was still an outpost of civilization, and so exposed to Indian hostility that it was not safe to live five miles from its central stockade.[44]

Jackson boarded at the widow Donelson's home with John Overton, another young attorney who became a lifelong friend and a sagacious political ally. The two lived in a single room and slept in the same bed. Adjacent to their cabin was a large blockhouse, the home of Rachel Donelson, where her daughter Rachel and son-in-law Lewis Robards resided.[45]

It was roommate John Overton who previously effected the reconciliation between Lewis and Rachel Robards. Overton, before moving to Nashville, completed his study of the law in Kentucky, where his landlady was none other than Elizabeth Lewis Robards, Rachel's future mother-in-law. He became a close friend of Mrs. Robards, and he inevitably observed the problems of the young married couple. Because of this relationship, Overton worked towards the reunion of Rachel and Lewis in Nashville.[46]

The close proximity of the unhappy, but socially outgoing, attractive twenty-one-year-old Rachel and the handsome, gregarious, but feisty twenty-one-year-old Andrew predictably led to a mutual but restrained familiarity. Conflict with the jealous Lewis was unavoidable.

Robards' ingrained paranoia and suspicion smoldered as a result of his wife's talks with Jackson. Rachel's innocent conversations with the new Donelson boarder continued, stoking Robards' jealous anger. Many years later, in correspondence, John Overton, an observant bystander, dismissed Robards' suspicions as groundless.[47] The interactions between the boarder and the daughter were deemed completely innocent. However, the husband, fearing being identified as a cuckold, began to berate his wife and to openly criticize her behavior with Jackson. Jackson, the accused, rose to Rachel's defense. Robards, paranoid and angry, then forbade the two to even speak to each other. However, a subsequent mundane conversation between Rachel and Andrew further enraged the seething husband.

Jackson, uncharacteristically diplomatic, tried to cool the heated Robards. He approached the volatile husband in the Donelson orchard to mildly rebuke the husband over his harsh treatment of his wife. Robards, in response, became violently combative; he threatened to physically punish Jackson by whipping him. Jackson, again uncharacteristically, avoided an immediate violent confrontation. Instead, he responded by saying that he had not the bodily strength to fight Robards. But he offered an alternative neither legal nor physical. Jackson applied his mother's implied solution, to settle the matter with a duel. Robards refused to accept the challenge, and Jackson retired to his cabin.[48]

Robards, Rachel, and Jackson soon left the widow Donelson's home and dispersed. Rachel, accepting her mother's advice, went to live in her sister's Nashville home. Jane Donelson Hays was the wife of Colonel Robert Hays. Andrew, listening to John Overton, sought lodging elsewhere in Nashville. Last, Lewis Robards, experiencing both rejection and embarrassment, departed for his Kentucky plantation.[49]

Abandonment, Natchez and Their Aftermath

Once again Rachel determined to distance herself from the obsessive and unstable Lewis. She concluded that this time her separation must be permanent. In 1789, the grounds for divorce in North Carolina (Tennessee, prior to its statehood, was legally the western part of this state) were limited—adultery, desertion, and extreme cruelty. Even though Lewis Robards was known to visit his plantation's slave quarters for sex, fornication with an enslaved person was not considered adulterous. Therefore, at that time, no legal grounds existed for Rachel to obtain a divorce.[50]

What happened next is muddled partly due to incomplete record-keeping during the 1790s on the American frontier and partly a

II—Rachel Donelson: His Wife

result of the intensely political and personal presidential campaigns of 1824 and 1828. The Jackson-friendly version follows:

> In late 1790, a rumor reached the Cumberland that Robards was planning to return to Nashville in order to snatch Rachel back to his Kentucky plantation.[51] In reaction to this threat during the 1790–1791 winter, the abandoned Rachel and her mother Rachel had intense discussions with their extended Donelson family. The resulting decision was for the abandoned wife to leave Nashville and to travel to the Mississippi River Port of Natchez which remained under Spanish rule. There the frightened woman would be placed under the protection of friends of the Donelson family. Her eldest sister, Mary Donelson Caffrey, may have lived then in the Natchez area.
>
> In Patricia Caldwell's account, Colonel Stark, a family friend, agreed to staff and stock a flatboat, and to captain it during its lengthy water journey to Natchez by way of the Cumberland, the Ohio, and the Mississippi Rivers. Before departure Stark insisted on male help both to ward off hostile Indians and to steer the flatboat. Strangely, the services of all Rachel's numerous brothers, brothers-in-law and even grown nephews were unavailable for this task.[52]
>
> But most conveniently, Jackson was available and volunteered to be the additional boat hand. His motivation for this undertaking is conjectural. One possibility was his innate chivalry, to protect a woman in distress. This behavior was lifelong and a trait likely instilled by Elizabeth Jackson. Caldwell proposed that the young attorney, assuming the blame for the jealous Robards' angry outbursts, "felt honor-bound to offer his services." A likely explanation was Jackson's increasing affection for the passenger, a lovely and very sociable young woman, now permanently separated from her husband. Jackson's role in the planning, organization, and provisioning of the expedition remains unknown. There is no record of payment for his service,
>
> Ann Toplovich, more recently, offered a somewhat different version of events. Using new sources, she probed the legal, chronological, and historical accuracy of the above tale. Instead, she concluded that Andrew and Rachel eloped to Natchez in 1789 where they lived in an adulterous union until 1791. Their return to Nashville in 1791 was occasioned only because legal and inheritance matters made it a propitious time to do so.[53]

Rachel and Andrew did return to Nashville in 1791. The more friendly version attributed their homecoming to a report that the Virginia legislature (Robards' Kentucky then was a region of Virginia) had granted a divorce to Robards. The unconventional relationship over the following three years (1791–1794) between the adventuresome Jackson and the spirited youngest daughter of Colonel Donelson would be consequential to their personal, and to his political, histories. Their conjugal relationship, if not bigamous, was certainly adulterous.

The rumors of a divorce were false. It was true that Lewis Robards did petition the Assembly of Virginia for a divorce on the grounds of his wife's adultery. However, his petition resulted in a December 20, 1790, decree that allowed Robards *to sue for divorce, but not to actually obtain a divorce.* John Overton recollected decades later that the people of Nashville understood at the time that the divorce was granted and that the Jacksons were legally man and wife. Moreover, Overton contemporaneously visited the Robards Kentucky home, and as their guest, "never understood otherwise than that Captain Robards divorce was final."[54]

Meanwhile, to further confuse the nature of the marital situation, Lewis Robards, while his divorce was still up in the legal air, bigamously married Hannah Wynn in December 1792. During the succeeding August or September, Robards, either in shame or to obviate legal consequences, returned to court in Kentucky (now a state and no longer under Virginia's jurisdiction). Hugh McGary was his witness who attested to the sordid allegations regarding Rachel and Andrew's flight to Natchez. On September 27, 1793, Robards was granted a complete dissolution of his previous marriage on the grounds that his wife deserted him and "hath and doth Still live in adultery with another man." In November 1793, Lewis and Hannah legally and quickly remarried in Mercer County, Kentucky.[55]

In September 1791, Andrew and Rachel returned to Nashville, where they lived with the widow Rachel Donelson for three years. Life was both good and happy for the young couple. The extended Donelson family warmly welcomed Andrew, who was in their unanimous opinion a far more agreeable match for Rachel than the unworthy Lewis. The Donelsons treated the couple as "man and wife."[56] John Overton, Jackson's lifelong sage adviser, pressed his friend to formally marry, or "remarry," to clarify their marital situation for the public. The Jacksons agreed and were wed in Nashville on January 18, 1794.

Why such confusion? Mary French Caldwell, Rachel's biographer, indicted Lewis Robards, her estranged husband, for deceit. Caldwell suspects that Robards wanted Rachel to suffer for some time in ignorance about the conclusion of their unfortunate marriage. She further speculates that the vindictive, rejected husband wanted Rachel's alleged sexual wantonness to be paraded in public without any possibility of cross-examination in a Virginia divorce court.[57]

Unsubstantiated rumor and self-serving local tradition claimed that the couple already were married when they returned to Nashville. But it never occurred. "Not one scrap of paper has been found to prove that Andrew Jackson and Rachel Robards were married in the neighborhood of Natchez. Determined and continuous search for such evidence has been made since William B. Lewis spent several weeks in Mississippi in 1827 and returned to Tennessee only to remain silent on the subject."[58]

Nevertheless, the Jacksons' union was uncontroversial for three decades until Old Hickory immersed himself in the political swamp of presidential politics. "A less spectacular career would not have aroused the jealousies which resulted in the repeated attacks upon their one vulnerable spot—the unfortunate circumstances of Rachel's first marriage and her divorce."[59]

The Jacksons Marry at Last

On January 18, 1794, the marriage between "Andrew Jackson AND Rachel Donelson Alias Rachel Roberts [sic] was solemnized in Davidson County Territory of the United States South of the River Ohio." Robert Hays, Rachel's brother-in-law, the husband of Rachel's older sister Jane, performed the ceremony as Justice of the Peace for Davidson County.[60]

"Besides her answering love and constant attention to his needs, Rachel provided Andrew with a large family who embraced him, supported his ambitions, and loved him as one of their own." In every possible way the Donelsons, then comprising more than sixty, considered Rachel's husband as one of them.[61] Rachel provided her orphaned husband with the kinship and family that he sadly lacked and needed. The Donelson family connections significantly influenced his years in Nashville.

Robert Hays was neither the first, nor the last, nor the most frequent member of the Donelson clan to abet, accommodate, or attend Jackson. During these years, his closest connection was with Stockley Donelson, Rachel's fifteen-year-older brother. Stockley was one of the largest and most persistent land speculators in Tennessee. His land dealings often brought him trouble, debt, and finally penury. In an August 3, 1792, letter, he implored his brother-in-law to intervene as his attorney in a dispute over a land title.[62] Less than a month later, this speculator, entangled in another legal wrangle, announced the appointment of "my Trusty friend Andrew Jackson ... my True and lawful attorney in fact for me to Transact all manner of business for me...."[63]

On March 2, 1794, Stockley, then in Knoxville, wrote his brother-in-law a long letter,

"...Nothing has for a long time given me more reel [sic] Satisfaction than your Expressions of Friendship which I have every reason from experience to believe the Most Sincear [sic]...." But Stockley continued, bemoaning at length his financial straits and requesting once again that Jackson accept his power of attorney, this time attached with a monetary liability.[64] This Donelson surpassed all speculators in Tennessee land schemes; Andrew Jackson also became involved in the speculative fever. With John Overton he rapidly acquired much land.[65] Letters from Stockley in 1795 and 1796 reveal property buying and selling that further involved Jackson in his brother-in-law's business.[66]

In December 1794, perhaps to protect himself and his wife from any legal issues arising from Tennessee's free-wheeling frontier economy, Jackson appointed brother-in-law Robert Hays as his lawyer with power of attorney. Loyalty and gratitude to the family probably was paramount in this decision; Hays, as mentioned above, officially married Rachel and Andrew.[67]

Moreover, Andrew did business with Rachel's third oldest brother, Captain John Donelson. In 1793, Jackson paid this brother-in-law one hundred pounds for a tract of land "on south side of Cumberland river in Jones Bent...." This property, known later as Poplar Grove, became the first home of the Jacksons; they occupied the land the following year.[68] Finally, a fourth brother-in-law, Samuel Donelson, dealt with Andrew "in land, slaves, and horses and shared his enthusiasm for racing."[69]

Rachel bestowed a second major gift upon her new husband. Practiced in the skills of homemaking after experience in the Robards' home and in Nashville under her mother's tutelage, she successfully established a milieu that allowed him both comfort and respite. Within the relaxed atmosphere of his home, Jackson was able to meet, greet, and negotiate with associates in political, business, legal, and judicial matters.

Rachel was not an ambitious woman, but she was a gracious hostess. She combined a keen interest in people with a kindly and warm manner that endeared her to many. A good listener and a sprightly conversationalist, she became an insatiable reader of books, magazines, and newspapers. Their home was often alive with children and young people, both of the Donelson family and of their acquaintances. She was affectionately called Aunt Rachel or Aunt Jackson.[70]

Home became the political headquarters of Andrew Jackson. It was in Rachel's pleasant household where his most important decisions were made and where the brilliant men he gathered about him made plans.[71] "He had a very happy home. Mrs. Jackson, besides being an excellent manager and mistress, was also a kind and jovial soul. She had a wonderful memory, which contained a great store of anecdotes and tales. She could remember the Cumberland settlements from their infancy...."[72]

Andrew Jackson's horizons expanded in the decade after he returned to the Cumberland. His stature in the community and in the state was heightened during the Tennessee State Constitutional Convention in Knoxville (1796) and during his intermittent congressional service as a representative and senator in Philadelphia (1796–1798). Rachel Jackson, in contrast, remained homebound and became very unhappy with the many absences of her husband. "In the coming years she was to learn to endure his long absences spent in the service of his country—but never was she persuaded, by the thought of fame and wealth, to desire his participation in distant affairs a moment longer than honor and duty demanded."[73]

Their domestic situation became complicated about this time when they moved to a larger home called Hunters Hill. The future president's motive for relocation may have been self-centered, "...so he set himself to the task of providing a more suitable home in which his Rachel could play hostess to their rapidly increasing stream of friends and acquaintances." Rachel's involvement in the decision to move is unknown, but his motivation indicated his complete confidence in his wife's ability to make it a successful one.

While away, Jackson was considerate of his lonely wife, writing from Philadelphia in January 1798, "If I live to return I will bring you some medicine that I have Not a distant doubt but it will Effectually cure you."[74] From Knoxville in September 1799 he wrote, "Sorry to read from that letter, that you are not well, but I sincerely hope that you are much better than when I left you.... My love how precious health is, and how careful we ought to be, to acquire it."[75] The specificity and severity of Rachel's illnesses generally are unrecorded.

In both the above letters, Andrew also mentioned his own ill health, perhaps medically insignificant, but important as an indicator of his significant future problems. In the first, he referenced "a severe attack of the Rheumatic in my left Knee." In the second, he wrote, "... Except a touch of the Rumatick—and a head ache today which I Suppose preceded from a Cold I caught riding in the night, last night."[76] Jackson's myriad medical problems, both infectious and traumatic, troubled Rachel for the remainder of their life together. Andrew repeatedly withdrew both to the comfort of the restful Hermitage and to the solicitous healing arts of his loving wife.[77] Together these recuperative powers again and again restored Old Hickory to the military and political battlefields. If these salutary resources from Rachel had not been available to him, the alternative outcome that might have occurred will be left to the speculations of dabblers in alternative history.

The years 1802–4 became a transitional period for the Jacksons. They moved to the iconic Hermitage, outside of Nashville. He discarded his judicial responsibilities; instead he focused his considerable energies upon both building a military reputation and improving the couple's financial situation.

The introduction to Volume I of *The Papers of Andrew Jackson* contains this apt summary:

> At the age of thirty-six—the year (1803) this volume closes—Andrew Jackson had achieved a measure of success as a social and political leader, a gentleman farmer-businessman, and a respected lawyer and judge. His character was firmly shaped by then and reveals itself in all its admirable and less admirable qualities throughout his correspondence. As his detractors were quick to point out, he was often irascible, proud to a fault, painfully defensive on the subject of his or Rachel's honor, and occasionally very demanding of his friends. But what his critics often missed were complementary traits that bound his friends and followers to him. His own loyalty was legendary ... his honesty was unquestioned. Whereas other Tennessee leaders were accused of land fraud, Jackson never was.... Jackson's sense of family was extravagant even in a time of close family ties, and his tenderness toward Rachel and his generosity to her young nieces and nephews are traits of character and conduct rarely seen outside his correspondence.[78]

III

Rachel Jackson
A Complicated Decade

> "You without provocation made the attack, and in an ungentlemanly manner took the Sacred name of a Lady in your polluted lips, and dared me publickly to challenge you, and ever since you gave the insult, has cowardly evaded an interview."
> —Andrew Jackson to John Sevier, 9 October, 1803.[1]

The 1803–1813 decade marked a time of trial and transition for the Jacksons. Andrew's instinctive anger and aggression resulted in frequent physical brawls, duels, a gunfight, and damaging bodily injuries. Their financial situation was at times chaotic, and his personal and political reputation was crippled, at least temporarily.

The introduction to Volume Two of *The Papers of Andrew Jackson* succinctly summarizes these troubled years:

> In 1804, at thirty-seven, Andrew Jackson retired from public-office with a solid record of achievements and a sound reputation. Ten years later, he was again in public service and on the threshold of national fame. But the intervening years had bought setbacks and disasters, leaving a tarnish on his reputation that neither discourse, nor future achievements could completely remove. The decade was one of the most troubled and controversial in Jackson's long life. His strong-willed nature and intensity embroiled him in almost constant turmoil. Yet, it was also the period when Jackson began to demonstrate those qualities of leadership that would win him the presidency in 1828.[2]

However, the bleakness of the decade had its high points. Their refuge, The Hermitage, was purchased and was destined to become the center of the Jacksons' social, political, and economic lives. They adopted two boys: Andrew Junior, officially and Lincoya, a Creek Indian infant, unofficially.

Rachel became ever more the buttress of her husband's emotional, medical, economic, and social health. Additionally, her Donelson siblings and their offspring were among her husband's most faithful supporters. Rachel's support became a vital and necessary influence for a future president.

Move to the Hermitage

In 1804, economic necessity forced the Jacksons to sell their Hunter Hill home. They subsequently moved to a 420-acre property about ten miles from Nashville, which was purchased in August of that year from Nathaniel Hays. Four years previously, a log house had been constructed on this land. The log house was fairly substantial, a building with two floors that contained a limestone chimney. Its ground floor comprised a single room, measuring twenty-six by twenty-four feet. This structure became the Jacksons' third home.[3] It was eventually replaced. Sometime in late 1816 or early 1817, Jackson began definitive planning for the construction of a brick mansion that was completed in 1821. Rachel selected the exact site on their expansive estate for the new home.[4]

This residence became the fabled Hermitage, the iconic home of Rachel and Andrew Jackson. Collins English Dictionary defined its name as *a retreat; any place where a person may live in seclusion*.[5] The who, why and when of its historic designation remains neither certain nor documented. However, its naming most likely occurred during the early spring of 1805, when "...it is certain that Jackson's earnest desire to retire to private life made the name an appealing one." Speculatively, Aaron Burr, the owner's erstwhile friend, may have had an influence. Hermitage was the name of the New Jersey home of Burr's current romantic interest. The beautiful widow Theodosia Prevost, who later became Burr's wife, resided at the New Jersey Hermitage. It was at about this time that Aaron Burr befriended the Jacksons and almost embroiled the Tennessean in his secession scheme. However, the first explanation above is more cogent. The first time that Jackson used The Hermitage in a letter of his occurred in 1805, prior to his meeting with Burr. Researchers at both *The Papers of Andrew Jackson* and The Hermitage concur that the notion was an expression of its owner's desire that his home serve as a rural retreat.[6]

Rachel as Chatelaine of the Hermitage

Rachel not only determined the exact site of the new building but also managed the mansion and its plantation. During her husband's frequent absences, first for business ventures, then for military campaigns, and finally for political pursuits, Rachel had overall responsibility for its cotton crop and its nearly one hundred enslaved people. The Hermitage also became a part-time home to a crowd of little boys who came to live there for months at a time.[7] Moreover, it served as a hub for socializing and recreation for Rachel's numerous nieces and nephews. Rachel, in addition, presided as social hostess to welcome her husband's frequent political and commercial guests.

Rachel as Caregiver

Mrs. Jackson used the comfortable ambience and relative seclusion of The Hermitage to nurse Andrew back to health. Over the next twenty years, Jackson frequently retreated to her and their home to heal from injuries and infections. Rachel was able to heal her husband's hurts but not to halt his hurrying to danger. She was unsuccessful in taming her husband's capacity for violence; she failed to control his penchant for combat, for physical confrontation, or his willingness to settle disputes on the streets and the dueling fields rather than in the courts of law. Surely Rachel felt fear and frustration whenever Andrew's temper became ignited. She certainly made attempts to moderate his tantrums, but the frequency and the measures used are unknown There is one recorded instance when she successfully restrained Jackson's anger, and this occurred years later. While steaming down the Mississippi River towards New Orleans in the 1827-28 winter to commemorate his famous 1815 victory, Jackson became incensed when he saw that another steamer was bothering his boat. In response, he issued a challenge to the captain of the annoying steamer. When informed of her husband's behavior, Rachel called him below deck before he could cause any mayhem.[8]

Jackson as Warrior

Andrew Jackson's temper was a signal characteristic of his Scots-Irish forbears, a trait that he would eventually moderate but never lose. His mother's antipathy for the British may have contributed to his easy anger. Her final words to her son "...was never to institute suit for assault and battery, or for defamation," suggesting that the resolution of a dispute should be physical, not legal.[9]

Consequently, the Tennessean resorted to a gun rather than a written brief as a solution. He fought two duels, issued challenges to duel on several additional occasions, acted as a second for one of the duelists more than once, and was wounded in a gunfight with a future United States senator on the streets of Nashville.

August 11, 1788, is the date of Jackson's first duel. It took place while on his initial trip to Nashville, prior to his first meeting with Rachel. Andrew was one of two opposing attorneys at a trial in Jonesborough, Tennessee. His arguments were thoroughly outclassed by his opponent, the seasoned lawyer Waightstill Avery. Avery was somewhat dismissive of Jackson's courtroom performance, leading the embarrassed loser to rip a blank page from a law book and challenge the winner to a duel. At first Avery refused to take the challenge seriously. However, the intemperate Jackson repeated his challenge the following day, writing, "My character you have injured, and further you have insulted me in the presence of a court and a large audience. I therefore call upon you as a gentleman to give me Satisfaction…." The following day, the two attorneys met on the agreed field of battle where both deloped, i.e., fired into the air. Honor was satisfied and injury was avoided. At the time the event created little comment because neither attorney shot at the other.[10]

Dueling was evidence of the military-mindedness of Southern males and their cult of honor. And as Elizabeth Jackson had advised, it avoided the irresolution of courts of law. Challenges to a duel resulted from political differences, unhappy business relationships, presumed insults about family or friends, or about one's physical, moral, or mental traits.[11] Paradoxically, "In Tennessee an amended dueling act emphasized a provision that admission to the bar depended in part on the applicant's swearing a no-duel oath." Parenthetically, possibly of no surprise considering the professional predilections of lawyers towards dispute and combat, one author assumed that "about ninety percent of duels fought in Tennessee were between attorneys."[12]

John Sevier was a much-respected pioneer figure in the settlement of the state of Tennessee. He was a leader in the formation of its government. Sevier had commanded military forays against the Indian tribes that threatened the safety of settlers in the state. For these successful efforts, he was elected and re-elected as governor numerous times. The relationship between the governor and Jackson was initially a cordial one. In 1798, Sevier appointed Jackson to the State Superior Court.[13]

Any semblance of cordiality was destroyed and was replaced by a vicious antagonism after Andrew Jackson was elected Major General of the Tennessee Militia. In 1802, during a hiatus as governor, Sevier's candidacy for this position had been challenged by Jackson. The governor, with his previous military experience, considered his challenger an upstart with no previous formal military background. Sevier was justifiably outraged when Archibald Roane, at the time his successor as governor, cast the deciding vote to appoint the upstart Jackson to the position of Militia Major General.

In 1803, Major General Jackson accused the ex-governor of corrupt land dealings. He did so in writing, in which he accused Sevier of bribery and the destruction of bank records. Adding to their enmity, Jackson supported his patron Roane over Sevier in their recent race for the Tennessee State House. To Sevier's delight and Jackson's dismay, Sevier was elected to his fourth gubernatorial term. The bitterness of Sevier was matched by the fury of Jackson; the result was a verbal confrontation in public on the town square of Knoxville, then Tennessee's state capital.[14]

During their verbal clash, Sevier was enraged that a mere lawyer had the audacity to defame him, challenge him, and attempt to humiliate him, the acknowledged leader of the state. His anger became uncontrolled, leading to an extremely personal insult, "I know of no great service you have rendered the country except taking a trip to Natchez with another man's wife."[15]

This triggered Jackson's immediate response, "Great God! Do you mention her sacred name?" He then challenged the Governor to a duel.[16] During the following week, the two principals exchanged a series of vituperative letters. In an October 2 message to Sevier, Jackson fulminated against "...gasgonading conduct ... ebulutions of a base mind" as he requested an interview (a duel).[17] Sevier responded immediately, castigating his rival for "Your Ungentlemanly and Gasgonading conduct of yesterday and indeed at all other times heretofore have unmasked yourself to me...."[18]

Eight days of near comedic back and forth proposals followed, regarding where and when the "interview" was to take place. The governor was cautious about fixing a date and location, since his executive duties were time-consuming, and his position demanded that the event take place beyond Tennessee's state borders. The impulsive challenger was by nature insistent on concluding the matter "here and now." Jackson impatiently concluded the interchange on October 9, writing, "After this note I will bid you adieu.... I would advertise you as a coward and paltroon." He ended the correspondence with a final fusillade, "You without provocation made the attack, and in an ungentlemanly manner took the Sacred name of a Lady in your polluted lips, and dared me publickly to challenge you, and ever since you gave the insult, has cowardly evaded an interview...."[19]

Their feud never culminated in a formal duel. Instead, an embarrassing and, for Sevier, somewhat humiliating near-gunfight outside Knoxville provided the denouement for the quarrel.[20] These events occurred entirely in Knoxville and its vicinity. Rachel was 181 miles away in Nashville and geographically powerless to moderate her husband's temper. This argument, like his previous gentlemanly duel, fortunately did not result in any traumatic injury for the future president.

Jackson's fiery temper continued to flare back in Nashville. His predilection to settle controversies by a duel in a forest clearing, rather than by verbal argument in a law court, remained unabated. The restraining hand of Rachel, if raised at all, was apparently ineffective. On July 26, 1805, the general was Thomas Overton's second in a duel with John Dickinson. Thomas was the nephew of John Overton, Jackson's close friend. In a lengthy memorandum regarding arrangements to settle the challenge, Jackson displayed remarkable familiarity with the procedures and traditions of dueling. Thomas Overton was severely, but not fatally, wounded in his arm and chest during the fray.[21]

Later, in a letter dated January 12, 1806, Thomas Swann challenged Jackson to a duel. Swann demanded satisfaction for the general's abusive and menacing language directed toward him. Jackson dismissed the challenge, considering Swann neither a gentleman nor his equal. Instead, he caned his accuser at Nashville's Wine's Tavern the following day.[22]

Andrew Jackson fortunately escaped physical injury from the artifice of a duel with Avery, the unconsummated duel with Governor Sevier, and his violent caning of Thomas Swann. However, misfortune accompanied his duel with Charles Dickinson. It occurred on the morning of May 30, 1806. The consequent injuries were both physical and political. He suffered greatly from a bullet lodged within his left lung, and his Tennessee reputation was nearly destroyed by the allegation that he wantonly killed an unarmed man. Jackson's political stature was re-established only after his 1814 military successes against the Creek Indians and his 1815 smashing victory over the British in New Orleans. However, the gunshot wound never healed completely; it became a constant physical and emotional reminder of the duel for the remaining thirty-nine years of his life.

The antagonists' confrontation took place during the morning of May 30, 1806, in Logan County, Kentucky, just across the Tennessee State line. It was the culmination of a dispute that had lingered unresolved for many months.

The Dickinson-Jackson duel has been described at length by many noted Jackson biographers.[23] The exposition that follows attempts to

III—Rachel Jackson: A Complicated Decade

include Rachel Jackson in the narrative. This author hopes that the following summary is neither too long nor too tedious.

The affair began innocently enough in November 1805 over a wager between Captain Joseph Erwin and son-in-law Charles Dickinson with Andrew Jackson. Erwin's horse Ploughboy was scheduled to run a match race against Jackson's Truxton. Shortly before the date, Ploughboy became injured and was forced to withdraw. The Erwin-Dickinson camp quickly paid the forfeiture bond. Unfortunately, a dispute about the payment led Dickinson lackey, Thomas Swann, to spread the rumor that Jackson had accused Dickinson and Erwin of double dealing. Further, Swann challenged Andrew to a duel, which the latter dismissed with contempt (see Swann challenge above).

It is not clear whether, or to what extent, aspersions against Rachel's honor precipitated the general's challenge to Dickinson. "Rachel's name did not appear in the correspondence that led to the duel, but it was bandied about verbally by the Erwin faction."[24] About the time of the suspended race, "...a report reached her husband's ears that Charles Dickinson had uttered disparaging words about Mrs. Jackson." It was reported that Dickinson, when drinking, had taken the "sacred name" of Rachel into his "polluted mouth" and pronounced it in "a most lascivious way." Jackson confronted Dickinson who at first denied it, but then ascribed any affront to drunkenness. The apology was accepted, and the two parted. After a second report that Dickinson uttered offensive words about Rachel in Nashville, Jackson advised Erwin to reign in his son-in-law.[25] According to biographer Brands, Jackson asserted that Dickinson had committed the most mortal of sins, aspersing the honor of Rachel. Again, there is no contemporary documentation, and the degree to which "the Rachel Factor" determined Jackson's ensuing behavior remains unclear.[26]

The heated dispute quieted down after his mentor, James Robertson, calmed Jackson and after Dickinson left on a business trip to New Orleans. The calm was temporary. After Dickinson's return, the argument reheated when both combatants accused the other of cowardice. Whatever the reason, Dickinson wrote a letter, published on May 21, in which he castigated Jackson as a "worthless scoundrel, a paltroon [sic]... too great a coward."[27] Two days later Andrew, as expected, responded by challenging his accuser so "that I will obtain speedily that *satisfaction due me for the insults offered*."[28] The months-long hostility between the two combatants ended in the deadly May 30 duel.

The challenger was accompanied by his second, Thomas Overton, who was returning Jackson's support and assistance of the previous year. He was also accompanied by a physician, Dr. Francis May. Meanwhile

Dickinson traveled with a coterie of boisterous friends who enjoyed his bluster over his shooting prowess.[29] In contrast, Overton and Jackson soberly discussed duel strategy. Their plan was to permit Dickinson to fire first. Jackson, if not mortally wounded, would steady himself, aim from a stable stance, and kill his antagonist.[30]

Indeed, Dickinson's shot hit his opponent in the left chest, but both Jackson's steadfast demeanor and a heavy coat masked the serious injury. Dickinson, dismayed but gallant, stood facing his opponent to meet his fate. Jackson's first attempt was a misfire. However, according to dueling tradition, he was allowed to squeeze the pistol's trigger until a true firing occurred. The bullet struck Dickinson just below the ribs, mortally wounding the young man. "The bullet had passed clean through his body, leaving a gaping hole. Charles Dickinson bled to death." Jackson, Overton, and Dr. May immediately galloped away from the scene. Soon the general's blood-soaked clothes alerted May that Jackson had suffered a significant injury. Wounded, he convalesced at The Hermitage under Rachel's care, but his injury was far more severe and troublesome than was first anticipated. The wound healed slowly; it was nearly a month before the patient was able to move without debilitating pain.[31]

The resultant lung infection persisted until Jackson's death in 1845. He suffered periodically from severe chest pain and episodic coughing of blood. The multiple recurrent episodes of hemoptysis likely produced a chronic and enervating anemia. Its most likely cause was a bronchopulmonary fistula, a traumatic connection between the lodged bullet and a major airway. The bullet, close to his heart, was never removed.[32]

Dr. May did not possess a degree from an accredited medical college; his training was probably as an apprentice to a qualified physician. He was a friend of Jackson's since at least 1804 and later accompanied the general for several weeks on his campaign against the Creek Indians. May's medical practice commenced in Nashville in 1790, but he was forced to temporarily abandon it and flee to Knoxville after he killed Frank Sappington, another physician, in a duel.[33]

No record exists of Rachel Jackson's conversations with her husband before or after the deadly confrontation on May 30, 1806. However, the unfortunate lack of primary source material did not prevent Rachel's biographer, Mary Caldwell, from speculating that her "restraining hand must have had something to do with his patience" in allowing the dispute with Dickinson to linger for months. When her wounded husband was returned to The Hermitage, Caldwell further presumed that "Rachel, in this hour of trial, was at once a tower of strength and a gentle healing influence. She not only encouraged him to regain his health and take up his life again, but she kept him from becoming too depressed and bitter."[34]

Many citizens of Nashville were appalled that the general had killed an apparently defenseless man. "Coming on the heels of his quarrel with Sevier, the duel did him great harm and saddled him with a reputation as a fearful, violent, vengeful man. For the next few months, Andrew Jackson was virtually a social outcast in western Tennessee."[35] Furthermore, "…it is certain that at no time between the years of 1806 and 1812, could General Jackson have been elected to any office in Tennessee that required a majority of the voters of the whole state … there existed a very general impression that he was a violent, arbitrary, overbearing, passionate man."[36]

The Jacksons' Recovery

Jackson's political troubles were accompanied by business losses. For the next several years, his focus was upon the repair of his financial situation. Tenacity and indefatigable stubbornness, traits ingrained during his upbringing, together with the social skills inherent in his wife's breeding as a Donelson and as the hostess of a plantation, combined to rehabilitate Andrew Jackson after Dickinson's death. "…the Jacksons entertained widely and generously. They were known as a very social family—who bought to their home a great number of people, from the rich and affluent to the poor and itinerant."[37] The notorious Aaron Burr was one such guest. In the years 1805–1806, the former vice-president made four visits to Nashville and twice stayed at The Hermitage.[38]

Andrew Jackson's rehabilitation was buttressed by Rachel's formidable family of ten siblings, consisting of three sisters and seven brothers. Both her oldest brother, Alexander, and youngest, Leven, remained unmarried. Her eight married siblings were as fecund as their Donelson parents; combined they produced a total of sixty-two children.

Unfortunately, the marriage of Rachel and Andrew was barren. Rachel's inability to become pregnant was certainly not familial. Moreover, history does not record any disease that would have made her incapable of child-bearing. A probable cause for the couple's childlessness was her husband's smallpox infection when he was a teenager. In the past, prior to widespread vaccination, smallpox infection was an acknowledged cause of infertility.[39] Of interest, the father of our county, George Washington, was similarly infertile. Washington also contracted smallpox during his teenage years.[40]

Rachel's eagerness for a child was satisfied by the Jacksons' adoption of one of the twin boys born to her brother Severn and his wife Elizabeth on December 4, 1808. Elizabeth Donelson allegedly was too ill to raise twins. "It was probably this as well as Rachel's pathetic desire for children that persuaded the biological parents to allow the Jacksons to take one of the twins." The adopted infant, unsurprisingly named Andrew Jackson Junior, was received by the Jacksons three days after his birth. Thereafter, young Andrew was raised as the Jacksons' son and became the heir of the general's estate. Junior's lineage was acknowledged by society from then on. The method of the child's adoption, whether through an agreement with his parents or in some other way, was never specified.[41]

Jackson and the Ties of Kinship

Jackson relied to a varying degree upon Rachel's three brothers-in-law and seven brothers, in business, legal, and even military matters. Brothers-in-law Thomas Hutchings (Catherine Donelson) and Robert Hays (Jane Donelson) were both justices of the peace who assisted Andrew in legal matters. Hutchings signed an affidavit, swearing that Jackson's liquor still indeed had burned down. This legal procedure reduced the general's financial loss in this matter.[42] Later, Hays signed an affidavit that corroborated his brother-in-law's version of events in the Andrew Jackson–Thomas Swann dispute. A third sister, Mary Donelson, married John Caffrey; they moved to Mississippi. John Caffrey and Mary Caffrey were members of Colonel John Donelson's flatboat flotilla to Tennessee. He may have acted as brother-in-law Jackson's mercantile agent in Natchez.[43]

The Hutchings' son John was Jackson's business partner for many years, beginning in 1802. Their partnership, later joined by John Coffee, operated general stores in Lebanon, Gallatin, and Hunters Hill, Tennessee, plus a distillery and a cotton gin. Later at Clover Bottom, Tennessee, they established another store, a tavern, a horse racetrack, and a boat landing.[44]

Robert Hays was a Revolutionary War officer and an original member of the North Carolina Society of the Cincinnati. A land grant for his war service took him to Tennessee, where he met and married Jane Donelson. Hays became the conduit to Rachel and family members through which Andrew transmitted personal and other information during both his 1796–7 congressional service in Philadelphia and his 1813–4 campaign against the Creek Nation.[45] Hays was recalled as a colonel during the Creek War to serve under his brother-in-law's command. In December 1812, Jackson ordered Hays to return to Nashville to a safe assignment, mustering volunteers into service.[46]

Jackson acted as an attorney for Rachel's bothers, Alexander and Leven Donelson, and engaged in a land transaction with yet another, Severn Donelson.[47] A fourth brother, Samuel, was Jackson's partner in a short-lived mercantile business in 1795. Samuel was an attorney and had political ambitions. However, he was only forty-five when he died in 1804 at The Hermitage. Thereafter Samuel's three sons became Jackson's wards. The middle son, Andrew Jackson Donelson, was favored by his uncle. This Donelson later became Andrew's secretary, both before and during his presidency. His importance to the story of Jackson's women, as the nephew of one, the husband of second, and the opponent of a third, will become evident later.[48]

Rachel's brother William engaged in a legal transactions with her husband; in 1790 Andrew issued a surety bond for William to be the guardian of his younger brothers, Samuel, Severn, and Levin Donelson.[49] Three children of still another brother, John, were destined to serve their uncle. Alexander (Sandy) and John (Jack) were soldiers in the campaign against the Creek Nation.[50] Their youngest sibling, Emily Tennessee Donelson, became Andrew Jackson's White House Hostess. Their father, John Donelson, was one of Jackson's closest friends. Rachel's generous gift to her husband of her Donelson family continued to be a critical factor in his life.

Children were at The Hermitage constantly; young nieces and nephews visited for short or extended periods. "Several times the General served as guardian for children whose father had died. First there were the four children of Edward Butler," and shortly thereafter the children of Butler's brother, Colonel Thomas Butler. Then the general raised and schooled the three sons of Samuel Donelson after the death of their father. Some years later Andrew Jackson Hutchings, the son of Jackson's partner, became Jackson's ward at the age of six. Mary Lewis, daughter of William B. Lewis, and Mary Eastin, the granddaughter of Rachel's brother John, were also Jackson's wards.[51]

Denouement of the Decade

Andrew Jackson could not entirely control his impulsive anger, either before or after he survived the Dickinson duel. He found himself in court on two occasions, once in January 1806, and the second in May 1807. On January 27, 1806, the court found him guilty of assault and battery upon Timothy Baird. His sentence was a fine. The circumstances of this fracas are undocumented.[52]

A more serious event occurred on March 6, 1807, during a confrontation between Andrew Jackson and Samuel Dorsey Jackson, connected by commerce and not by family. "The two Jacksons had enjoyed a business and social relationship since 1799." The fight apparently was over money. However, the opponents' recall of events differed significantly regarding its details, but both versions agreed that the general unsheathed his sword and ran it through Samuel's coat. "A violent scuffle ensued ... was soon put an end to by the bystanders." Subsequently, Andrew was indicted for assault and battery upon this unrelated Jackson. When the case came to trial on November 9, 1807, the jury acquitted him of all charges.[53]

Rachel was fortunate that neither her nursing skills nor her uxorial assurance were required after these two incidents. Her husband was not injured in either brawl. However, a brawl in the center of Nashville nearly a decade later (1813) would leave her Andrew seriously wounded. A series of untoward events both preceded and resulted in a violent public gun and knife fight between brothers Jesse and Thomas Hart Benton and Old Hickory, his close friend John Coffee, and another one of his innumerable nephews, Stockley Hays.

Previously, Jackson foolishly had allowed himself to be drawn into a dispute between his junior officer, William Carroll, and Jesse Benton. Loyalty, being an elemental characteristic of his Scots-Irish inheritance, compelled General Jackson to support his military subordinate when asked. With reluctance he agreed to serve for the second time as a second; this time he was Carroll's second in a duel that occurred in the morning of June 14, 1813. Both combatants survived, but were wounded: Carroll, minimally in the thumb, and Benton, embarrassingly, in both of his buttocks.[54]

Thomas Hart Benton, Jesse's older brother, had also loyally served under Jackson's command. However, he became infuriated by his general's involvement in his brother's duel. Benton's anger was stoked further by rumors that Jackson blamed him for fomenting unrest against their former commander, General James Wilkinson. In response Benton openly, publicly, and repeatedly condemned Jackson for conducting the Carroll/Benton duel, "...in a savage, unequal, unfair, and base manner."[55]

Jackson was incensed; "...what really infuriated Old Hickory was that they were repeated in public places over and over, in every major town in Tennessee. Jackson had just recaptured popular favor, and he was not about to see his reputation endangered by Benton's reckless charges."[56]

III—Rachel Jackson: A Complicated Decade

In early September, Jackson and his allies strolled down Nashville's main street with the sole purpose of physically confronting the Benton brothers. They were successful; a violent brawl broke out on the steps of the Nashville City Hall. Jesse shot the general in the left shoulder, seriously wounding him. The shoulder was shattered, and the blood loss was severe. Many Nashville physicians attended the wounded patient, and all but one recommended the amputation of the affected limb. Before sliding into unconsciousness, Jackson defiantly contradicted the medical consensus: "I'll keep my arm!" And he did.[57]

The bullet was finally extracted from the then president's shoulder in 1832, nearly twenty years later, by Navy surgeon Thomas Harris. The doctor was visiting Washington, D.C., and Jackson seized the opportunity to have the projectile excised by this skilled surgeon.[58] The lead bullet, lodged in his left shoulder joint, was the source of chronic lead poisoning that afflicted the patient for almost two decades; the symptoms of plumbism (lead poisoning) disappeared with the bullet's removal.[59]

The acute injury was devastating as well. "The wounds were dressed with poultices of elm and other wood cutting, as prescribed by the Indians. Jackson was utterly prostrate from the great loss of blood; it was three weeks before he could leave his bed, to health; and to confidence in the world about him."[60] His long-time mentor, James Robertson, regretted: "as to the loss the public will sustain for the want of your service in my opinion is incalculable." Robertson's conviction that Jackson would be unfit for service in the coming Creek campaign was based upon information received from his son, Dr. Felix Robertson, who was thoroughly aware of the seriousness of the wound caused by Benton's pistol. Scarcely a month after the fight, Jackson was in the field.

The conclusion of the Complicated Decade was thereby punctuated with an exclamation point!

IV

Rachel Jackson
Their Marriage Thrives

"...still pale and weak, with his arm in a sling, Jackson took command of his West Tennessee forces at Fayetteville."
—Remini, *Andrew Jackson*. Volume One, 192

"I can now scarcely write with a pain in my left side."
—*Andrew Jackson Papers IV*, 115:
May 9, 1817 letter Andrew Jackson
to Isabella Butler Vinson

Constant Military Absences

Soldiering in the service of his beloved country between 1813 and 1820 kept Andrew Jackson from both his beloved wife and his treasured Hermitage for long periods of time. His departure from his comfortable home in 1813 was forced by the Creek Indian Nation. Although still recuperating from his gunfight with the Bentons, Jackson, as Major General of the Tennessee State Militia, was compelled to avenge the Creeks' August 30, 1813, savage massacre of two hundred fifty men, women, and children at Fort Mims, Alabama Territory. War parties of this Indian tribe had continued to raid white settlements on the Tennessee frontier and elsewhere in the South leaving death and destruction.

On October 7, 1813, "...still pale and weak, with his arm in a sling, Jackson took command of his West Tennessee forces at Fayetteville," Tennessee.[1] He returned to Nashville, victorious but haggard, nine months later in the spring of 1814. The Creek Nation was decisively

IV—Rachel Jackson: Their Marriage Thrives   47

defeated in battle, and Nashville was overcome with manic joy and hyperbolic adulation for their hero, General Andrew Jackson.[2]

Old Hickory's respite at his home was abbreviated. The United States Secretary of War, John Armstrong, soon ordered him to return to military duty. The American effort in the War of 1812 was faltering, and its southern border was threatened by the remnants of the Creek nation, the British Army, and the military forces of the Spanish Empire. Jackson arrived at Fort Jackson, Alabama, on July 10, 1814, to assume control of the American forces.[3] In a whirlwind of military successes over a period of fewer than seven months, his army forced the remnant Creeks into an unequal peace treaty, captured the Spanish controlled cities of Mobile and Pensacola, and triumphed over the renowned British Army in the iconic 1815 Battle of New Orleans.[4]

Rachel and their son, Andrew Junior, at the insistent urging of the triumphant general, traveled the long distance to New Orleans where the family reunited in March of 1815. They were fêted in New Orleans and celebrated upon their return to Nashville that May. Jackson was required to appear in Washington to submit his reports of the concluded, successful campaign. He traveled there with Rachel and Junior, where he undoubtedly enjoyed the Capital's continuous applause and adulation.[5]

The general's fame as an American hero became so enormous that there was a clamor for a biography. His aide-de-camp John Reid took up the commission. Reid completed four chapters before his unexpected death in 1816. John Henry Eaton, Jackson's friend and military associate, was asked to complete Reid's work, thereby becoming Andrew Jackson's first biographer. Eaton and Jackson became intimately associated for the next twenty years.[6] Eaton finished the book, which was published as *The Life of Major General Andrew Jackson* in 1817. The biography was revised and republished in 1824 and in 1828 as Jackson campaign biographies during those years' presidential contests.[7]

Rachel Jackson remained alone at The Hermitage without her husband. He had been dispatched to the American South to negotiate land treaties with the Native American Creek, Cherokee, Chickasaw, and Choctaw tribes. Jackson successfully wrested millions of acres of tribal land for the United States government. The treaty with the Choctaws was not signed until October 1818, but as it required further negotiation with Jackson, it was not finalized until October 1820. These treaties commenced the process of Indian expulsion from the southern states to reservations west of the Mississippi River.[8]

Spanish Florida remained a safe haven for those Creek warriors who remained unsubdued and for hostile fighters of a fifth Indian nation, the

Seminoles, who occupied the territory. Both tribes used the sanctuary of a foreign country to harass American settlers in Georgia and Alabama by raiding their villages. Who was responsible for securing the country's southern border? Major General Andrew Jackson, of course. In January 1818, he departed for Fort Scott on the Georgia-Florida border from where he intended to commence his campaign which would be labeled the First Seminole War.[9] The war was successful, decisive, and swift. On June 2, 1818, he wrote President James Monroe that the war was over, and that he was returning to his Nashville home.[10]

The physical fighting in the Florida peninsula ceased, but the political brawling in its aftermath had only begun. Once again Jackson was compelled to leave The Hermitage; on this occasion he needed to defend before Congress his actions during the war. His enemies sought to censure his behavior in both the Senate and the House of Representatives. The General successfully defended his reputation and defeated both resolutions of censure. He spent six weeks in his defense; he departed for Nashville on March 9, 1819.[11]

Rachel at the Hermitage

Rachel Jackson furnished support, both critical and necessary, during this period of Andrew's long absences. Her presence was the beneficent and secure harbor of both his hearth and health. Rachel's words and thoughts concerning her influence upon her husband during this decade are almost non-existent, either in print or in hearsay accounts.

Jackson gradually but increasingly viewed himself as an elite Southern male; he clearly enjoyed the companionship of Rachel, who "as a mother, hostess, and plantation mistress, epitomized the ideal of genteel womanhood" in the South.[12]

Rachel remained the undoubted matriarch of the mansion, both as its social mistress and as its household matron. However, the degree to which she was responsible for the management and the production of The Hermitage plantation in his absence is unclear. One role entrusted to her was that of a trusted conduit for Jackson's instructions to the overseer of the plantation. Several letters were orders to be transmitted in his name to the overseer, who was usually Mr. John Fields. One letter directed Fields to send a wagon of pork as part of a transaction, to keep "all hands under him ... constantly employed at gathering a crop until it is in ... have as much land cleared as he can, take care of my stock, and see that you [Rachel] are comfortable."[13] Overseer Fields seemed to have trouble controlling the plantation's enslaved people. His hard drinking was the alleged cause of this problem.[14] Later, in 1816, Jackson fulminated against Field's replacement, Harrison Saunders, "...and you will charge him to sell nothing without your express orders...."[15]

On occasion, Andrew left decisions entirely to Rachel's discretion. A December 1811 letter asked her to select a location for the overseer to construct a home for newly purchased enslaved people. A March 1813 correspondence discussed the sales price of a slave but left the amount up to Rachel.[16]

The extent of Mrs. Jackson's estate management is unclear. Brady credited Rachel "for keeping an eye on their businesses. Making sure that all of their cotton, as well as that of their customers, was ginned and baled was her responsibility, as was seeing to the grinding of wheat into flour and its safe storage in barrels sealed against bugs and mice."[17]

However, another observer minimizes Rachel's role in managing The Hermitage plantation: "Although many of the more romanticized biographical writings about Rachel suggest that plantation management in Jackson's absence was one of her duties, reviewing letters doesn't really hold this up. There isn't much discussion of the farm or 'to-do' lists. Rachel complained once about the enslaved workers being vexing, but that was probably the ones with domestic duties. She may have had some authority over spinning and weaving, poultry, or dairying but there isn't a lot to go on."[18]

Jackson wrote to his nephew, Stockley Hutchings, with marital advice five years after Rachel's death. Therein he acknowledged his wife's value to his estate. However, his accolades were couched in generalities without a specific listing of her managerial achievements. He wrote,

> ...recollect the industry of your dear aunt and with what economy she watched over what I made, and how we waded thro the vast expense of the mass of company we had, nothing but her care and industry, with good economy could have saved me from ruin, if she had been extravagant the property should have vanished and poverty and want would have become our doom. Think of this before you attempt to select a wife.[19]

Mother, "Sister Rachel" and "Aunt Jackson"

Rachel was the mother of Andrew Junior, their adopted son; a foster parent to Lincoya, a Creek infant discovered amongst the Creek battle-dead; and the maître d'hôtel for the numerous Donelson clan.

Rachel and Junior were frequently unwell during Andrew's absences. The infectious diseases of the American frontier afflicted the family as well as the plantation slaves; she summoned a physician to treat them all. The distant father often expressed tenderness, love, and concern for his son, closing his letters to Rachel with "kiss our son for me."[20] Writing in 1813, "I have only to add a renewal of my prayers to the Sovereign of the universe for the superintending care and protection of you and our little Andrew"; and he instructed his wife, "Say to *my son* if he will learn his Book well his sweet papa will bring him a *pretty* from New Orleans."[21]

The gentle Rachel was compliant in fulfilling her husband's demands dispatched from a distance. There is no record of either a complaint or a rebuttal as she fulfilled his wishes regarding the estate or of raising Junior, whom Jackson expropriated as *my son*. Her workload was increased when the general arbitrarily assigned a Creek Indian waif to her care and nurturing.

Lincoya, named as such by Jackson, was discovered amidst the Creek warriors and women slaughtered by the Jackson army at their village of Tallushatchee. The ten-month-old boy was found in the arms of his deceased mother. U.S. Army Lieutenant Richard K. Call, destined in the future to be a frequent visitor to this story, was horrified by the slaughter: "Heart sick, I turned from the revolting scene."[22] All the surviving Creek women, now prisoners, refused to care for the infant, with the excuse that all his relatives were dead. The boy was brought to General Jackson's tent, where he resolved to raise the orphan. His motives for such generosity are speculative. Only after his decision did Andrew inform Rachel, "Keep Lincoya in the house—he is a Savage that fortune has thrown in my hands when his own female matrons wanted to kill him.... I therefore want him well taken care of, he may have been given to me for some Valuable purpose ... tell my dear little Andrew to treat him well...."[23]

Lincoya was welcomed by the matron of The Hermitage. Rachel received the boy with care and affection, and "...the boy grew up in the Jackson family, treated by the General and his kind wife as a son and a favorite." Lincoya received an education equivalent to that provided for the planters' sons in the neighborhood. At an appropriate age, Jackson introduced him to Nashville tradesmen so that he might choose a skill that would provide him an independent life. Saddle-making was his selection of a trade. However, Lincoya contracted tuberculosis and was nursed by Rachel. He tragically perished from the disease at the age of seventeen. Three years after the waif's "adoption," Andrew Jackson expressed gratitude for his wife's tenderness and charity: "...how thankful I am to you for taking poor little Lincoya home and clothing him."[24]

The affectionate Rachel was also Aunt Jackson to her many young

IV—Rachel Jackson: Their Marriage Thrives

Donelson nephews and nieces who enjoyed her warmth, congeniality, and hospitality at The Hermitage. The kinship, loyalty, assistance, and support of Rachel's Donelson family continued to confer great service to the future president. The influence of his wife's family remains an important theme of this book. The benevolent kinship for Andrew of Rachel's generation of Donelsons was catalogued previously.[25]

The nephews, nieces, and grandchildren, members of succeeding generations of Donelsons were about to make significant appearances in this story. Alexander Donelson was the oldest son of Rachel's brother John, and in turn the oldest brother of Emily Tennessee, John Donelson's youngest child. His first appearance in the *Jackson Papers* was as the sender of an October 1811 letter to *Dear Uncle*, wherein he encouraged Jackson to consider a move to Northern Alabama. He closed the correspondence with "My love to Aunt."[26]

Alexander possessed his uncle's warlike temperament. While in Nashville he joined Jackson's defense in the notorious knife and gun battle with the Benton brothers. Thomas Hart, the older Benton, wrote that Alexander Donelson drew a dagger, "made at me and gave me five slight wounds."[27] Shortly afterwards, Alexander, together with his brother Jack, enlisted as soldiers in Jackson's command to fight in the Creek Indian War. It was a deadly decision; he was killed in battle in January 1814. Rachel mourned his death, "Oh my unfortunate Nephew he is gone [sic] how I Deplore his Loss his untimely End."[28]

Andrew Jackson Donelson was the oldest surviving son of Rachel's brother Samuel Donelson. Samuel died when young Andrew was five; thereafter his uncle not only directed his social and educational development but also managed his professional career. Aunt Rachel cherished this Andrew; her affection was evident in an October 1818 letter, "…when I tell you how gratified it is to me that in all your deportment thus far you meet our highest expectations, and may you go on and proper in every laudable undertaking is the sincere wish of a *Second Mother*…."[29] Andrew continued to rely on Jackson's advice regarding his possible expulsion from the United States Military Academy at West Point, and how to act during a disturbance by his fellow cadets. He frequently asked the older Andrew for money. He later became indispensible as Jackson' private secretary.

Andrew Jackson Hutchings was the grandson of Rachel's sister Catherine Donelson Hutchings and the son of John Hutchings, who was a business partner of Andrew Jackson. Upon the death of his parents in November 1817, this Andrew, the Jackson grandnephew, became the ward of Rachel and Andrew. Little Hutchings, as the family affectionately called him, came to live at The Hermitage where he then was raised. The general saw to his schooling through college. The young namesake caused his benefactor apprehension through the years with his immaturity and adolescent antics. However, he finally settled down on his inherited Alabama farm and delighted President Jackson by following the Donelson tradition of cousin marriage. He wedded Mary Coffee in 1833. Mary, a favorite of the president, was the daughter of John Coffee, one of Jackson's closest friends.[30]

Rachel, the Caregiver

She was the nurse guiding her husband's recovery from the severe injuries and debilitating infections that resulted from the foolhardy altercations and martial adventures during this period. His military campaigns forced him to trek through unhealthy terrain where both safe water and nutritious food were lacking. The general's physicians' treatments probably magnified his symptoms, rather than lessening them. Calomel (mercurous chloride) and sugar of lead were therapeutic weapons of the early nineteenth century doctor's armamentarium. The oral ingestion of calomel had a corrosive effect upon Andrew's digestive tract, leading to rapid and progressive dental caries, and possibly to his abdominal colicky pain, chronic dysentery, and unrelenting diarrhea.[31]

Dr. Francis May treated Old Hickory during the aftermath of the bloody 1806 Dickinson duel. Nearly a decade later, May accompanied Jackson during the early part of the Creek campaign. He introduced the general to treatments with sugar of lead. The doctor wrote, "...they had to stop the General frequently and wash him from hand to foot in solutions of sugar of lead to keep down the inflammation, and ... he was better." Both analysis of hair samples and characteristic symptoms document that Jackson in fact developed lead poisoning. However, its cause was Benton's bullet in his left shoulder joint rather than the lead maltreatment of May.[32] Dr. James Craine Bronaugh was the army surgeon who replaced May; he was the General's military aide from late 1816 until at least 1821. Whether his professional advice was effective or ineffective is unknown.[33]

Biographer Robert Remini concluded that the 1813–1814 Creek War permanently shattered the general's health. For eight months his body was devastated by a relentless chronic diarrhea, likely caused by bacterial infested water used for drinking and bathing. The typical obstinacy and determination of the Scots-Irish compelled him to overlook physical suffering. Instead he marched onward against his Creek foes. "For months he could barely move his arm because of the shattered bone ... when the attacks (dysentery) were particularly severe ... he doubled over a branch of a tree; in camp he pressed his chest against the back of a chair ... when eating was unthinkable, he swallowed weak gin and water."[34]

After a short respite at The Hermitage, the hero of New Orleans journeyed to Washington to deliver his military report upon the War of 1812's conclusion. The real reason for this trip, taken despite his suffering, was to savor the applause of the political élites for General Jackson's military triumphs during the war. Unfortunately, Jackson collapsed during these celebrations and nearly died. The incumbent President James Madison became so alarmed that he summoned the illustrious Doctor Phillip Synge Physick from Philadelphia to consult. During this crisis, Jackson's left arm and shoulder continued to cause great pain. It was several weeks before the discomfort subsided.[35]

Andrew remained under his wife's care until a May 1817 departure. His mission this time was the negotiation of a land treaty with the Cherokee tribe. When he left, he still complained about left-sided pain. He added, "I can scarcely write with a pain in my left side ... with copious repletion I am getting better." While away, he informed Rachel, "I have enjoyed only tolerable health, since I left you, troubled with my bowels, which perhaps has kept me free of the pain in my side and breast."[36]

Jackson's pattern of alternating periods of home rest with much needed respite, interspersed with distant campaigns under unhealthy and dangerous circumstances, continued. January 1818 witnessed his departure for Florida to conduct the First Seminole War. He was gone for five months. A June letter to Rachel voiced a mixture of self-pity and bravado: "I have been so much exposed wading through waters that I have a bad cough. I am somewhat emaciated, but still able to march on foot 25 miles a day." The war was won quickly. In a letter that announced the victory to President Monroe, he announced his intention to resign from the U.S. Army, and then amplified, "I am at present worn down with fatigue and a bad cough with a pain in my left side which produced a spitting of blood, have reduced me to skeleton. I must have rest, it is uncertain whether my constitution can be restored to stand the fatigues of another campaign; should I find it so I must tender my resignation."[37]

The exhausted general returned home and remained under his wife's observation and care for some months. What was the loving and dutiful Rachel to make of her husband's continual adventures? Jackson surely knew that distant campaigns and tribal negotiations would harmfully affect his many medical maladies; but, for whatever motivation, be it patriotism, political advancement, his ego's search for fame and applause, he exposed himself to harm anyway. Rachel certainly was worried, concerned, and even frightened whenever her husband embarked on yet another escapade. Her personal admonitions remain private, and her written letters were destroyed by The Hermitage fire in 1834.[38]

The ill general remained under Rachel's supervision and care for some months. In a series of letters to fellow Chickasaw Commissioner Isaac Shelby, his nephew and ward Andrew Jackson Donelson, and his president, James Monroe, he wrote of his "bad state of health" and catalogued his symptoms—weakness, cough, pain on his left side and in his breast. He balanced his complaints with a bit of optimism, to wit that he was "again acquiring a little Strength, so that I can again attend to business." Rachel's contribution to his optimism included the solace of being home, healthy and restorative nutrition, enforced rest, and general nursing care. Supplemental treatment in the form of medicinals or herbs and doctors' visits are not documented.[39]

Prudence again was cast aside when, in October 1818, he embarked on a month-long excursion to conclude a land treaty with the Chickasaw Nation; his effort was a success. Once again, in January 1819, a trip was necessary. Jackson's political enemies in Washington attempted to censure him for his 1818 activities in Florida. He charged towards the national capital to personally confront his accusers in both the Senate and the House of Representatives. This battle was successful, but it required a three-month absence from Rachel and resulted in a major medical meltdown. His physical collapse was serious and considerable. For a while Old Hickory was not expected to survive. His symptoms were those previously experienced but more severe in intensity—weight loss, lack of appetite, chest pain, and the coughing of blood.[40] He explained what happened to his evermore frequent correspondent, his nephew, "...brought on one of the most violent attacks I ever experienced. Nothing but the skill of Doctors Bronaugh & Samuel Hogg and their arduous attention saved me, from which I am so far recovered as to be able to walk to my room & write a little.... I am very much debilitated."[41]

However, Jackson was unable to seize an opportunity to recuperate. President Monroe asked his former general to accompany him partway on his pre-election tour of the western states. The elder Andrew complained to the young Andrew Jackson Donelson, "The President reached me whilst recovering from a severe illness; before he proceeded on his tour, having regained my strength, duty combined with inclination, urged me to escort him through the north-western part of my Division."[42] Predictable results followed: "...yesterday was the first day in twelve that I could sit up long enough to write a letter..." and "I was taken very ill and confined to my bed for ten days..." he bemoaned in letters.[43] Jackson's debility stretched into 1820, while his physical problems began to intrude upon his psyche. On his fifty-third birthday he wrote, "This is my birthday, but I am so afflicted with pains, that I have some doubts whether I ought or ought not to rejoice, that I was born—or at least whether it would have been better for me not to have lived to see the 15th of March 1820—but I conclude, that it is best, as it is in the lords [sic] will I am here...."[44]

During her husband's frequent absences from 1813 until 1820, Rachel Donelson Jackson succeeded as the mother of two young boys, as the full-time manager of their Hermitage home, and as the infrequent supervisor of The Hermitage estate, as the chatelaine of her extended family, and as nurse and comforter of her sometimes erratic husband. From October 1813 to the end of 1820, a span of eighty-six months, Andrew Jackson was away from his wife, in war, in land treaty negotiations, in reviews of southern military defenses, or in Washington, for thirty-seven and one-half months, or nearly forty-four percent of the time.

Rachel, a Pious Presbyterian

Religion became an increasingly important element in the life of Rachel Jackson. It is likely that the intensity of her religious devotion enabled her to overcome the loneliness and worry resulting from her husband's persistent absences. Her faith was probably the buttress that fortified her to fulfill Andrew's needs and wants with love and to enable her to complete her multiple roles with generosity and geniality.

Colonial Anglican Protestantism, the North American transplant of the official Church of England, used external forms and rituals to promote outward conformity among its adherents. In contrast, evangelical Presbyterianism, transplanted from Scotland by way of Ulster, featured emotional preaching with stirring imagery to stimulate the spiritual rebirth of each believer. Evangelicals embraced an introspective religion of emotion and sensibility. Rachel, like many Southern women, were prominent supporters of the itinerant ministers who preached the Presbyterian message across the region. "A prominent Presbyterian clergyman argued that religion brought women security and influence as well as spiritual uplift."[45] Besides her cultural history, genealogical attachments further cemented Rachel to Presbyterian practice. "On the paternal side she was the granddaughter of Catherine Davies, who was the sister of Reverend Samuel Davies. This eminent Presbyterian minister succeeded Jonathan Edwards as President of Princeton University." Moreover, Colonel John Donelson, her father, previously served as a vestryman for a Presbyterian congregation.[46] Rachel saw everything through the lens of her religious beliefs. She had repented her sins, especially her adultery, and had been forgiven. Attending church, reading the Bible, and praying became integral to her daily and weekly life. Her letters to her husband showed her newfound fervor, her desire that he was healthy was her nightly prayer, that "... my blessed redeemer is making intercession with the Father or us to meet again (and) restore you to my bosom."[47]

Advancing age added to her piety, which appeared extreme to some. For many believers, aging enhances religious attachment as the prospect of death and final judgment approaches. For Rachel it was more than ordinary, but rather, "a rousing, evangelical. Piety that permeates her entire life."[48] Biographer Patricia Brady characterized her fervor with this passage: "Rachel's faith was the bedrock of her life. Joining with a congregation in prayer, being toughened by emotional sermons, discussing the Gospel with other believers—these things kept her going. Camp meetings were still a feature of evangelical life in Tennessee, and she had begun attending each summer for the refreshment of her spirit...."[49] Since her husband was often absent, free time and possibly spousal loneliness led Rachel to Bible study and the company of ministers and the devout women of the First Presbyterian Church.[50]

Her letters to her husband and to close friends overflowed with florid spirituality; additionally, they were prolix with biblical references. An 1813 letter to Andrew contained the following passage: "But my blessed redeemer is making intercession with the Father.... Gracious God help me pray for your happiness." Letters to bereaved friends included the following thought: "Angels wafted her on their Celestial wings to that blooming garden of roses that have no thorns where Honey has no Sting," and, "She seemed as if she slept in Jesus and all those God will bring with him At his Coming, in First Thessalonians iv Chapter 13 14 verses...."[51]

Andrew Jackson was certainly not an example of Presbyterian piety. The general was very famous, and widely caricatured, for his instantaneous and sometime-violent temper. His anger was combustible; it resulted in physical brawls and even in the death of a young man in a duel. He bore an overbearing, condescending, and superior attitude against the five Indian Nations of the American South; his Indian opponents suffered many deaths and forcibly relinquished vast stretches of their historic tribal lands. Moreover, he was boastful, egocentric, and

IV—Rachel Jackson: Their Marriage Thrives

the master of many enslaved people. Was he influenced at all by the religious practice of his mother Elizabeth or his wife Rachel?

Through osmosis from his two closest female relatives, a degree of spirituality did permeate. Certainly in his letters to Rachel, "I thank you for your prayers ... when the protecting hand of providence if it is his will, will restore us to each other's arms ... and the god of Battle and Justice will protect us..." and "I have only to add a renewal of my prayers to the Sovereign of the universe for the superintending care and protection of you and our dear little Andrew...."[52] It surfaced sometimes in his actions. While in Washington and in Congress during the winter of 1823–24 and away from Rachel, he spent Sundays in church. Knowing how much his church attendance would please her, his many letters to The Hermitage so informed Rachel. However, he deviated from her strict sectarianism by visiting a church of a different denomination each week.[53]

Mrs. Jackson was reluctant to accompany Old Hickory on his travels. However, when she did, her respectful husband dutifully bowed to her hermetically sealed Tennessee religious perspective.[54] Andrew Jackson, as the military hero of New Orleans and as the temporary governor of Florida, used his authority to terminate behaviors both in New Orleans and in Pensacola that affronted her sensibilities. "Undoubtedly at Rachel's urging, Jackson ... cracked down on all demonic and heathen activities she pointed out to him. The gambling, vice, and Sabbath-breaking had to be stopped if such a god-fearing woman as Rachel were expected to stay in Florida."[55]

In 1823, Jackson donated a parcel of his Hermitage land to build a neighborhood church. He and his Presbyterian neighbor, a church elder, contributed most of the money for the neat little brick building. It was completed in January 1824. The Hermitage church was dedicated and held occasional services when traveling preachers were available. To Rachel's regret, a full-time minister was difficult to find.[56] "But what delighted her Presbyterian soul more than anything else was the opportunity to go church and pray whenever the spirit moved her. Not a day or night but there is a church opened for prayer. Glory to God for the privilege." Andrew reported that his wife spent her time on Sundays at church and on Thursdays at a prayer meeting.[57]

V

Rachel Jackson
Her Unwelcome Public Life

> "Shortly I have to experience another trial, I must go with him or be unhappy as I was last winter and how could I bare [sic] it, I shall have to go with him."
> —Rachel to Latitia Dalzell Chambers,
> 12 August 1824, *Jackson Papers V*, 432.

Rachel Jackson, the wife of the increasingly popular Andrew Jackson, was very dismayed by her husband's magnetic gravitation towards national prominence and political influence. She found public life unwelcome; she preferred instead the private life of a plantation mistress comfortably surrounded by her husband, her son, and her Donelson family.

While the general was away campaigning during the War of 1812, Rachel, with great sorrow, responded to his letter that informed her of the death in battle of Alexander Donelson, a favorite nephew. Her February 10, 1814, response not only mourned the loss of Alexander, but also expressed her wifely fear, "Let me Conjure you by every Tie of Love of friendship to Let me see you before you go againe [sic]. I have borne it untill [sic] it had thrown me into feavours [sic]." She pleaded for Jackson to return home, "I am very unwell...."[1]

Mrs. Jackson dreaded every occasion that threatened to remove her husband from her loving care. Her distress sometimes led to emotional and hysterical scenes prior to a departure. Rachel acknowledged that Andrew placed his duty to the country above early retirement at The Hermitage.[2] She was sadly aware of this preference despite his obvious, yet paradoxical, sense of peace and tranquil restoration at his beloved Tennessee home.

Rachel accompanied her spouse infrequently on his numerous journeys. Nevertheless, she overcame her reluctance. She travelled with

Old Hickory to New Orleans and Washington, D.C., in 1815; to New Orleans and Pensacola, Florida, as the governor's wife in 1821; and again to Washington during his unsuccessful presidential campaign of 1824–5. She explained her decision to escort Jackson on this, her last journey, in a letter to a friend: "Shortly I have to experience another trial, I must go with him or be unhappy as I was last winter and how could I bare it, I shall have to go with him."[3]

The young Rachel Donelson had been an energetic and fearless pioneer during her family's long river journey from Virginia to the Tennessee Cumberland, during the subsequent forced retreat of the Donelson clan to Kentucky to escape marauding Indian warriors, and later fleeing from Nashville to Natchez, Mississippi, by flatboat in order to avoid a threatened abduction by her estranged husband.

New Orleans (1815)

For two decades, Rachel, now middle-aged, devoted her energies to her time-consuming domestic and familial responsibilities while comfortably settled in Middle Tennessee. Travel was neither coveted nor necessary, until General Jackson, yearning for domestic tranquility and conjugal affection summoned his wife, together with their adopted son, to New Orleans. The hero of New Orleans, after two arduous years of warfare, was in a state of physical and emotional exhaustion and needed his wife.

Rachel arrived in New Orleans with Andrew Jackson Junior a few days before the March 13, 1815, local announcement of a conclusion to the War of 1812. "Rachel was now an extremely stout, dark complexioned, 47-year-old woman *religious to the point of fanaticism,* yet warm and gently beguiling." Jackson's war campaigns forced his wife to help manage their plantation. Her appearance may have reflected her many hours of outdoor toil in the southern sun. Rachel, homely both in dress and speech, presented a sharp contrast to her tall, thin, and elegant husband.[4] The General previously had admonished his spouse, "You are now a Major General's lady—in the service of the U.S., and as such you must appear, elegant and plain, not extravagant—but in such stile [*sic*] as strangers expect to see you."[5]

In 1815 New Orleans was a small but strategically significant city that controlled trade between the American Midwest, the Caribbean, and even distant Europe. Its population was increasing and probably exceeded ten thousand at the time of her visit. But its people certainly appeared foreign, and indeed exotic, to this plain Southern American

Presbyterian woman. New Orleans was distinctly Creole with many recent migrants from Cuba and Haiti. French was the prominent language, Roman Catholicism was its preeminent faith, and its cultural behaviors were very flamboyant, sensual, and even erotic.[6]

Almost immediately when attending a ball, Rachel was astonished by New Orleans' glamour. She wrote to her brother-in-law Robert Hays of "...the splendor, the brilliant assemblage, the magnificence of the supper and ornaments of the room." She continued, "I have seen more already then in all my life past. It is the finest country for the Eye of a stranger...."[7]

Foremost Jackson biographer Robert Remini captured one amusing incident, first recorded in Vincent Nolte's memoirs. Rachel was persuaded to attend a grand ball given in her husband's honor. At first, she could barely comprehend the brilliance of the table settings at the dinner. Afterwards, Andrew and Rachel led the way to the ballroom where they danced county-style. "To see these two figures, the general, a long, haggard man, with limbs like a skeleton, and Madame la Generale, a short, fat dumpling, bobbing opposite each other like half-drunken Indians, to the wild melody of *Possum up de Gum Tree* and endeavoring to make a spring into the air, was very remarkable, and far more edifying a spectacle than any European ballet could possibly have furnished."[8]

Vincent Nolte was an Italian-born German who had survived Napoleon, and then established himself as a commodities broker in New Orleans. He supported Jackson during the city's famous battle, but his allegiance was fissured by a dispute over his compensation for supplying the general's Army with cotton and wool. Nolte's estrangement from Jackson undoubtedly was a factor in his future negativism towards the general.[9]

His recollections many years later of Andrew and Rachel Jackson were scathing: "After supper we were treated to a most delicious *pas de deux* by the conqueror and his spouse, an emigrant of the lower classes, whom he had from a Georgian planter [sic], and who explained by her enormous corpulence that French saying, 'She shows how far the skin can be stretched.'"[10]

Washington (1815)

Jackson was called to the capital city to provide a report to the government regarding his actions in Louisiana. Therefore, in early October 1815, Andrew, Rachel, little Andrew with his nurse, Rachel's nephew Lemuel Donelson, Jackson's military aide John Reid, and household servants departed for Washington. Jackson's military adjutant, Robert Butler, looked after The Hermitage, including the Jacksons' business affairs and the other boys resident at the plantation for the duration of the Jacksons' absence. Little is known regarding Rachel's behavior and activities in Washington, D.C., or her motive for accompanying her hero-husband there. Brady speculated about her reasoning, "Rachel was always proud when her husband was properly appreciated."[11]

Their return west was delayed by illness until December 24, 1815. Rachel recovered from a heavy cold in early December, but Andrew was hassled by an arm infection until their departure for Tennessee.[12]

New Orleans/Pensacola (1821)

For the next five and a half years, Mrs. Jackson was content to tend to her husband's needs, care for her adopted son, minister to the desires of any Donelson relatives who were guests at The Hermitage and assist in the supervision of the plantation.

The quiet of The Hermitage was especially salutary for Andrew despite repeated absences: "His health responded to the devotion of his wife."[13] It had remained precarious from the cumulative effects from both his protracted negotiations in the field with the Southern Indian tribes and from his military efforts in Florida's unhealthy swamplands during the First Seminole War.[14]

The General repeatedly considered both retirement from public life and the resignation of his Army commission. However, he procrastinated over the latter. First, financial implications delayed a final conclusion, but the major motivation for a delay was the possibility of a war with Spain. Jackson finally resigned from the United States Army on June 1, 1821, after his acceptance of a new role as Governor of the Territory of Florida.[15]

The generous Rachel was rewarded with a generally very satisfying multiyear interlude at her Hermitage home until 1821, when President James Monroe appointed her husband to be the first Governor of the Florida Territory. Jackson was charged to govern the semi-wilderness that he previously conquered during the First Seminole War. The Jacksons traveled from Nashville to New Orleans in the latest style, aboard a river steamboat. From New Orleans they sailed to Pensacola, Florida, where they arrived in the early summer of 1821.

During the spring of 1821, the newly appointed governor revealed both his wife's reluctance to travel south with him, and his rationalizations that her participation in his new office would be very salutary for her. Letters to Andrew Jackson Donelson, Rachel's nephew, and then to John Coffee, his close friend and comrade-in-arms, expressed his thinking and his determination: "Your aunt appears very reluctant to go to that climate ... your aunt does not enjoy a good state of health and I have a hope that the Journey may improve it...."[16] "...And the great reluctance of Mrs. J, added to her bad health, increases my regret."[17]

On April 14, 1821, Governor-Appointee Jackson, Rachel, their adopted son Andrew Junior, Rachel's niece and nephew, Narcissa and Stockley Donelson Hays, together with Dr. James C. Bronaugh from Jackson's military staff, departed for New Orleans, and then traveled on to Florida. Stockley and Narcissa were the children of the recently deceased Robert Hays and Rachel's sister, Jane Donelson Hays.[18]

Rachel's voluminous family continued to be both a gift and a responsibility to her husband. At this point a brief hiatus may be useful to unthread a few tangles of the closely knit Donelsons. Jane Hays was the third youngest of Rachel's three sisters; she married Nashville Justice of the Peace Robert Hays, and together they raised eight children. Stockley was the oldest, and Narcissa was the third of five daughters. Robert Hays had died several years previously; Stockley (33) and Narcissa (25) may have accompanied Aunt and Uncle Jackson to Florida in a search for new opportunities. Andrew Jackson Hutchings, then nine years old, was left at The Hermitage.[19]

Hutchings was one of at least six relatives of Rachel Donelson Jackson to share in Andrew Jackson's patrimony, that is, his name. This legacy was but one of Rachel's innumerable gifts to Andrew through her membership in the fecund Donelson family. The namesakes included two nephews, Andrew Jackson Junior, the son of brother Severn and the Jacksons' adopted son, and Andrew Jackson Donelson, the son of her brother Samuel; and two grandnephews, the aforementioned Andrew Jackson Hutchings and Andrew Jackson Coffee, the grandson of Rachel's brother John and the son of John's daughter Mary.

Andrew Jackson Donelson and his wife Emily Donelson named their son Andrew Jackson Donelson. After this Andrew Jackson Donelson died, Andrew Jackson Donelson and his second wife Elizabeth Randolph named their son Andrew Jackson Donelson.[20]

The author hopes that the previous paragraphs may be considered a helpful explanation of the complexities of the Donelson family, rather than an unnecessary and unhelpful detour in the flew of the narrative.

On her second visit to New Orleans, "Rachel was a far different woman from the country mouse who six years before had been so dazzled by its citizens' sophistication and glamour. During the intervening six years Rachel had developed a coherent worldview that saw her though any situation." When Andrew was away, her free time was spent in Bible study and in the company of ministers and the devout women of the First Presbyterian Church. Religious prejudice was stoked while confined in such a closed and dogmatic furnace: "...Catholics were not among the godly as far as Evangelical Protestants were concerned...." This attitude affected her attitude and behavior toward the natives of New Orleans and Pensacola, French Catholics in the former and Spanish Catholics in the latter.[21] Unsurprisingly, her very unfavorable recollections of New Orleans were expressed in an 1821 letter to Eliza Kingsley: "Great Babylon come up before me. Oh, the wickedness, the idolatry of the place! unspeakable the riches and splendor."[22]

The Jackson party embarked on the overland route from New Orleans towards Pensacola, then the Spanish capital of Florida. The incoming governor, in order to secure an orderly and complete transfer of the Florida Territory from Spanish to United States sovereignty, halted his progress in Montpelier, Alabama, while he negotiated the withdrawal of Spanish troops with the outgoing Spanish governor. While he waited, the impatient United States governor on June 28, 1821, dispatched Rachel, their son, and the rest of his personal party, to take up residence in Pensacola. His ceremonial arrival with the American military under the U.S. flag was delayed until July 17.[23]

Rachel oversaw the repairs and furnishings of the governor's residence situated on the little town's main square. Pensacola, with a population of only seven hundred including enslaved people, made Nashville look like a metropolis. Rachel was "able to appreciate the town with its white sand, abundant fruit trees, beautiful flowers growing wild, views of the water, and fine sea breezes."[24]

However, her complaints of heat, rain, mud and a lack of her type of Christian society surpassed any pleasure from the town's picturesque ambience. While awaiting Jackson's assumption of civil authority, she became scandalized by the natives' wanton non-observance of the Sabbath. Sunday drinking, gambling, and partying were widespread. When her husband arrived, Rachel persuaded Jackson to terminate what she determined as ungodly, unchristian, demonic, and heathen activities. In response the governor ordered the Sabbath to be strictly observed. Fiddling and dancing on the Lord's Day were prohibited. Gambling houses were demolished. Legal enforcement included a $200 fine for each offense and the posting of a $500 good behavior bond. Under Jackson's administration, Sundays in Pensacola became very quiet and quite solemn.[25]

The Jacksons' tenure in Florida was brief. Jackson served as governor of the Florida Territory for slightly more than eleven weeks. The brevity of his time as the occupant of the territorial governor's home raises the question, "Why did he accept the position?" Perhaps Jackson owed a debt to President Monroe, who was always friendly toward him. Perhaps his pride welcomed the opportunity to parade as a conquering hero while assuming American control of Florida, completing the mission he had begun in Pensacola in 1814. However, once Jackson had cemented United States' sovereignty and constructed a framework for the territory's future effective administration, he soon became bored with executive routine and looked for a plausible rationale to return home. The always accommodating Rachel provided it.[26]

Previously, the future president was apprehensive about his wife's health in Florida. However, after their arrival, Jackson, in a self-congratulatory mood, wrote Coffee, "...added to this Mrs. J. was in declining health, I was advised it would be the means of restoring not only hers but of my own.... But Mrs. J's health is much improved and I have great hope that she will be perfectly restored."[27] Once settled in Pensacola, her health was characterized as "good" for the most part.[28]

Yet, in a contradiction to this personal assessment, Jackson instead cited Rachel's physical well-being as the reason for his apparently precipitous departure from Florida. He informed President Monroe of his plans to return to Tennessee only two days previous to his leaving for The Hermitage.

Characteristically self-laudatory, his October 5 correspondence with Monroe explained that he had organized the government of the Floridas which was "now in full operation," and that a respite was appropriate "from the laborious duties with which I have been surrounded." However, "This becomes necessary, as Mrs. Jackson is anxious to return home, *and the situation of her health requires that she should pass through the newly settled country before the inclement weather sets in...*" (italics by the author).[29]

Home Again. The Hermitage, from Late 1821 to Late 1824

The general and his family reached Nashville in mid–November 1821, less than a month after their departure from Pensacola. Home at last, the Jacksons enjoyed their very fine, comfortable, new home, completed after two years of work. "After having lived so long in their conglomeration of log buildings, they now enjoyed a house of some elegance. It was described by Andrew as a gift to his Rachel but also a symbol of his arrival as a National personage."[30]

They very quickly re-established themselves in the newly built Hermitage. The interval turned into a period of renewal and happy compatibility for the couple, now in their mid-fifties. For Rachel, she "again felt a release from the alien and inassimilable world against which she had striven for thirty years. She and Andrew undertook to make their home comfortable for the decline of their days."[31] For Andrew, "Now that his health had failed and he realized how much he needed to rest at home, he readily slipped into the routine that Rachel programmed for him to speed his recovery."[32] Unfortunately, their aspirations eventually, and perhaps inevitably, diverged; Rachel desired a tranquil retirement while Andrew was drawn again to the rancor and turbulence of national politics.

A large two-story brick house replaced the original log house as the Jacksons' Hermitage in 1821. In 1804 Andrew was forced by financial reverses to sell their original home, Hunters Hill, and to move to newly acquired land which became the site of the iconic Hermitage. The couple lived in a log cabin on the property while Jackson used the profits form his cotton crop to acquire more land, growing their frontier farm into a Southern plantation. Construction of a suitable house began in 1819 and was completed in time for the Jacksons' occupancy when they returned from Florida. Rachel purchased most of the Hermitage furniture during her most recent visit to New Orleans.[33]

This was Andrew's present to his wife. Rachel selected the site of the home, and despite objections from his close aide, Andrew adhered to her decision.[34] The brick mansion was large, measuring nearly ninety feet across and almost one hundred feet in depth. It contained two floors. From a small porch, a long hall on the bottom floor ran the entire length of the house with two parlors situated on the east side of the house. The front room on the west was the Jacksons' bedroom. Behind the bedroom was the dining room. The kitchen was located behind in a separate building adjacent to the rear of the house. Several bedrooms for children and guests were on the second floor. The two stories were connected by a sweeping staircase at the rear of the main hall. In 1831, during Old Hickory's first term as president, the building was extensively remodeled, and wings were added to the home. A devastating fire destroyed much of the mansion in 1834, and it was constructed once again.[35]

Jackson, again tired after another stint of extreme exertion in Florida as its governor, was bedridden with cough, pain, and diarrhea. Correspondence with Andrew Jackson Donelson, his nephew and ward (soon to become his secretary), documented the course of his recovery.

My health is improving, but I find it very difficult to get clear of the cough, every change of weather gives me a new cold & excites my cough—I have found some difficulty in keeping me bowels open—when my bowels are open, the cough measurably subsides."; "I have been lately taken with a violent Lax, what ultimate effect it is to produce upon my health I cannot say..." "My cough has considerably abated, but I am afflicted still with the pain in my left shoulder and neck, with the oppression of the cough in the morning...."[36]

Jackson's medical condition eventually improved. His recovery was hastened both by his friends and Rachel's relatives who visited frequently, and especially by Rachel's kindness and tender care. As a precursor to his national political persona, it was indeed propitious that both Jacksons loved to entertain; The Hermitage provided the venue.[37]

Jackson as Senator (1823–4)

The increasing prospect of a Jackson campaign for the presidency in 1824 encouraged his Tennessee backers to prospectively enter his name in nomination to the United States Senate. Jackson subsequently was elected United States Senator from Tennessee by the state legislature, meeting in the then capital city of Murfreesboro, Tennessee, on October 1, 1823.[38]

The new Senator then traveled to Washington, where he arrived on December 3, 1823. That Rachel did not accompany him was no surprise. That Andrew sought and accepted this position also should not surprise the reader. He rationalized his decision in a lengthy letter to Rachel written shortly after his Washington arrival: "This seperation [sic] has been more severe to me than any other, it being one that my mind was not prepared for, nor can I see any necessity for—still my country (did); & no alternative was left for me but to okay...." Jackson attempted to ameliorate Rachel's unhappiness by mailing his many inquiries about her health, by assuring her of his own, and by declaring that he attended a Presbyterian Church on Sunday.[39]

He was very aware of the suffering and emotional unhappiness of his wife, since a month before his trip, he wrote his long time friend Judge John Overton, "Mrs. J. is more disconsolate than I ever knew her before, & I do assure you I leave home with more reluctance than I ever did in my life—it was so unlooked for, unwished for, & so inconsistent with my feelings—But I have no doubt but providence will protect her & myself as well absent as present...."[40]

While away in the nation's capital, the senator sought to assure his wife of his good health, not only through his own letters, but also through the letters of his former aide, now Senator John Eaton, when he was too busy to write himself. In one letter, Eaton endorsed Jackson's decision to serve in Washington by writing, "If the Genl. had remained at home, I am satisfied he would not have enjoyed such health. His farm would have annoyed him ... exposure and wet would have been met with: but here nothing of that is found."[41]

During this separation from Rachel, the most important person in his life, two other women, Peggy (Margaret) O'Neale Timberlake and Emily Tennessee Donelson, make their introductions into his orbit.

Senator John Eaton, Jackson's co-senator from Tennessee, was responsible for renting the rooms where he and the Jackson party lived: The O'Neale's boarding house and saloon in central Washington. Senator Jackson wrote to his wife, "We are in the family of Mr. O'Neale whose amiable pious wife & two daughters, one married the other single, take every pains in their power to make us comfortable and agreeable.... I never was in a more agreeably & worthy family—When we have a leisure hour in the evening we spend it with the family—Mrs. Timberlake ... plays on the piano delightfully, & every Sunday evening entertains her mother with sacred music—to which we are invited."[42] He further described Mrs. Timberlake (Peggy O'Neale, who later married John Eaton) as "the martyred daughter whose husband belongs to our Navy."[43]

Old Hickory undoubtedly was very familiar with Emily Tennessee Donelson, the thirteenth and youngest child of his wife's brother and neighbor, John Donelson. Emily was probably one of the nieces who stayed with Rachel while her aunt was "indisposed" in January 1824.[44] In his letters from Washington to his favorite nephew, Andrew Jackson Donelson, in Tennessee, Senator Jackson began by requesting that he be "presented affectionately to Miss E."[45]

During 1823–4, Donelson, a West Point graduate and a practicing Nashville attorney, committed more and more time to assist his uncle with Jackson's personal and political affairs. "Of the prominent Tennessee families in the early nineteenth century, the Donelsons almost certainly possessed the most complicated and intertwining family genealogy. First cousin marriages were seemingly the norm, and not the exception, in the family and were intended to strengthen kinship ties." Not only was Emily kin, but also she was young, available, intelligent, and quite pretty.[46]

On September 16, 1824, Donelson married Emily, who was his not yet seventeen-year-old first cousin.[47] Their wedding took place on the grounds of The Hermitage. The patriarchal Jackson rewarded the newlyweds with the deed to 348¼ acres of land adjoining The Hermitage, and an enslaved man, John Fulton. The gift of the land kept Donelson conveniently close to The Hermitage to work on Old Hickory's forthcoming presidential campaign.[48]

In Andrew's absence, Rachel had kept the plantation and household going very much as usual. In a December 1823, letter, he advised his wife, "I hope Mr. Parson (the overseer) will in all thing of what you desire, I have confidence in him, & I am sure he will okay you in all things you may require."[49] Senator Jackson finally reached home in early June 1824.[50]

Washington (1824–1825)

Jackson's respite in Tennessee was a short five months, before the senator returned to Washington, this time with Rachel. The winter of 1824–1825 was a season of political tumult in the nation's capital city. The 1824 presidential campaign was not decided until a vote in the House of Representatives in 1825.

Andrew Jackson had been a stealth candidate for the Presidency, and his candidacy was largely ignored in 1822 and 1823. However, his presidential nomination by the Pennsylvania State Legislature in March 1824 popularized his national image and made him a fine target for his political opponents. The criticisms cascaded. His personal behavior was the main focus of adversaries' critique. His temperament was exceedingly martial and vituperative and far from presidential. His denunciations were enumerated, and included, among other charges, the mortal duel with Charles Dickinson; his punitive enforcement of martial law during the New Orleans campaign; and his executions of British citizens Arbuthnot and Armbrister during the First Seminole War.[51]

Rachel Jackson dreaded this trip. In an August letter to her close friend, Latitia Dalzell Chambers, she mourned, "Shortly I have to experience another trial, I must go with him or be unhappy as I was last winter and how could I bare it, I shall have to go with him."[52] The Jacksons left The Hermitage in a fine carriage with a saddle horse in early November and arrived in Washington on December 7, 1824, twenty-eight days later.[53] Accompanying the couple were newlyweds Andrew Jackson and Emily Donelson. Previously, in April, Uncle Jackson had alerted his nephew that he was wanted to accompany the Jacksons to Washington that fall.[54]

The party lodged at Gadsby's Tavern; this was formerly William

O'Neale's property that had been sold due to financial difficulties. Senator John Eaton, for unstated but for suggestively implied reasons, had purchased it from O'Neale and then subsequently sold the property to Gadsby. Jackson's former military aides, the aforementioned Eaton and Richard Keith Call, also were guests at Gadsby's, conveniently situated to be at the call of their former commander.

Mrs. Jackson decried Washington's bustle when compared with The Hermitage. She bemoaned that fifty to one hundred persons called on her every day. She preferred her privacy, writing, "The play-actors sent me a letter, requesting my countenance to them. No. A ticket to balls and parties. No, not one.... Indeed Mr. Jackson encourages me in this course."[55] Rachel spent her time on Sundays at church and on Thursdays at prayer meetings with a religious friend. The balance of the time she spent in receiving and paying visits. She enjoyed the Presbyterian church in Washington and did not worry about remarks regarding her elegance or lack thereof.[56]

Other than personal disinterest, her health was a second reason for Rachel's inability to keep up with the capital's pace. At age fifty-seven, she was "a little inclined to corpulency." Her physical state was seldom good enough to permit her to engage in Washington's social whirl. Both heart and bronchial troubles were probable for a plump woman of her years.[57]

Mrs. Jackson's letter to Eliza Kingsley summed up her reactions. She was excited to be boarding in the same house as the Marquis de Lafayette, the hero of the American War of Independence, who was paying a visit to the United States on the fiftieth anniversary of its independence. Interestingly, she expressed more tolerance of Washington society than she had previously of New Orleans: "The extravagance is in dressing and running to parties, but I must say they regard the Sabbath, and attend preaching, for there are churches of every denomination.... Don't be afraid of my giving way to those vain things. The apostle says, I can do all things in Christ, who strengthened me."[58]

In the 1824 presidential election, Andrew Jackson defeated his three competitors—Secretary of State John Quincy Adams, Secretary of the Treasury William Crawford and Speaker of the House Henry Clay—with a plurality of both the popular and the Electoral College vote. Since his total in the latter was a plurality, and not a majority, the selection of the president was decided by the U.S. House of Representatives. Speaker Clay, excluded from the contest, assigned his votes in the House to Adams, thereby electing the latter. In return, the new president nominated Clay to become his Secretary of State. This became known in history as "The Corrupt Bargain."

Her steady temperament and wifely reassurance probably calmed her husband, assured his outward civility, and cooled his anger after the corrupt bargain between Henry Clay and John Quincy Adams withheld the presidency from Andrew Jackson. The Jackson party left Washington and reached home on April 13, 1825.[59]

VI

Rachel Jackson
Her Distress and Demise

> "To me the Presidential charms by the side of a happy retirement from Public life are as the tale of the candle and the substantial fire, the first of which it is sad is soon blown out by the wind but the latter is only increased by it."
> —Rachel Jackson, May 18, 1825[1]

> Jackson "...now saw in her pitiful condition the human price of his bid for the presidency."
> —Robert Remini, December, 1828[2]

The final four years of Rachel Jackson's life (1825–1828) coincided with her husband's determined campaign for the presidency of the United States. The campaign was protracted, savage, and vehement during which both Jackson's ferocious and turbulent past and his wife's character were pilloried in public with scorn and hyperbole.

The four years began with the Jacksons' return to The Hermitage after the disappointing 1825 resolution of the disputed 1824 presidential election. The period concluded in the final months of 1828 with Old Hickory's election victory and Rachel's unwelcome death. Both husband and wife were in good health upon their Tennessee return, and Rachel couldn't have been happier. She blissfully believed that "Tennessee is the best Country in the United States."[3]

The Campaign

In early 1825, Jackson renewed his candidacy for the presidency in the 1828 national election. The defeated candidate, paradoxically the leader in both the 1824 popular and electoral college vote, was outraged that the "Corrupt Bargain" between incoming President John Quincy Adams and his nominated Secretary of State Henry Clay had stolen the presidency from him.[4] The candidate ignored his wife's wishes that he avoid politics completely.[5] Andrew was tempted to openly campaign, but "Rachel's faltering health convinced him to shy away," at least for awhile.[6]

For nearly forty years, American presidential candidates adhered to the tradition that it was improper for them to openly announce their candidacy. Instead, they employed the fiction that they would run only if the "people" clamored for their candidacy. Old Hickory subscribed to this tradition. Accordingly, Andrew Jackson declined all invitations to appear outside Tennessee in order to avoid the appearance of being an active candidate. However, he did accept them from within the state, appearing at a rally in Fayetteville, Tennessee, on July 5, 1826. The supporters of his rival, President Adams, attacked his presence there, complaining he indeed was campaigning. "Hypocritical," "demagogic," and "subterfuge" were a few of the epithets hurled against Jackson.[7] Perhaps warned, he wrote a letter to his supporter, Thomas Patrick Moore, in which he declined an invitation to speak to his followers in Kentucky, calling it "improper" due to his candidacy.[8]

By the fall of 1826, the backers of President John Quincy Adams' re-election made Andrew Jackson's angry temperament a major issue in the upcoming presidential campaign. They enumerated the many public instances of his ferocity: the duels; the Benton gunfight; the firing squad deaths of militia deserters during the Creek campaign; the hanging of British citizens Arbuthnot and Ambrister in Florida, and other incidents all in order to buttress their claims that Jackson was emotionally unsuited for the White House. An episode from 1819 became widely circulated. When the Senate published a report that criticized the general's performance during the Seminole War, Jackson, then in Baltimore, rushed back to Washington, threatening to "cut the ears off" Senator John Eppes in revenge for his decisive anti–Jackson vote in the Senate. Supposedly, Commodore Stephen Decatur of the U.S. Navy, either by confrontation or persuasion, prevented Jackson from carrying out his threat.[9]

Since tradition forbade the candidate from responding personally to the relentless attacks upon his character, Jackson set up committees to thwart his political enemies. These groups of supporters were organized in Nashville (the most important), Washington, Philadelphia, Cincinnati, and elsewhere. Thus, the candidate hypocritically maintained his public stance that he did not seek and would not campaign for the office but would serve if only called upon by the people.[10]

The strategy was successful. In November 1828, Andrew Jackson was elected the seventh President of the United States, easily defeating incumbent President Adams. Jackson received 55 percent of the popular vote and an impressive 219 to 49 majority in the electoral college.[11]

Could He Have Succeeded Without Rachel?

Patricia Brady wrote it well. Understanding her husband's fury at having had victory snatched away in 1824, "her role was to sympathize, to listen, to bring him peace at home."[12] Her conjugal support likely was essential both in bolstering his ambition and in occasionally restraining his vehemence during his quest for the White House. Rachel's uxorial devotion even overcame her well documented reluctance[13] to travel outside Tennessee. However, she eventually embarked with her husband to New Orleans on the riverboat *Pocahontas* to celebrate the thirteenth anniversary of the battle that turned Jackson into a national celebrity. The Jacksons were away from their beloved home from December 27, 1827, until early February 1828.[14]

Rachel Donelson Jackson excelled in her role as the gracious hostess of The Hermitage. Jackson's home doubled as his political headquarters, especially since he had garbed himself with the insincere disguise of a non-interested political bystander. As a result, this "non-candidate" wore a straitjacket that both restricted his mobility and limited his campaign options.

The Hermitage witnessed a procession of visitors, some of whom were friendly, and many were political supporters. One significant visitor was the sixty-eight-year-old Marquis de Lafayette. The French hero of the American Revolution had embarked on a sentimental journey of the United States to commemorate the fiftieth anniversary of his role in the American War of Independence. Lafayette was greeted by Jackson upon the Frenchman's arrival in Nashville on the morning of May 4, 1825. Old Hickory presided over a public dinner in Lafayette's honor that night and hosted the eminent visitor for dinner at the Hermitage the following day.[15]

There, at his home, Jackson's political allies assembled to plan and plot his campaign. Some were intimate friends of long duration: John Overton, John McNairy, and William B. Lewis. Others, like Andrew Jackson Donelson, were recent admittants to the Jackson inner circle. Additionally, an aura of gaiety and youthful joy permeated the mansion, as a result of Rachel's large coterie of Donelson nephews, nieces, and their friends. In the center of activity was its graceful and gentle hostess,

Rachel. At home she assured both youthful frolic and successful political plotting.[16]

Mrs. Jackson's constant, fervent religious devotion may have eased, at least subliminally, her husband's emotional intensity during the 1820s. Either from a manifestation of deep devotion, or as an attempt to placate Rachel's unhappiness with his reemergence in partisan conflict, Andrew donated Hermitage land to build a Presbyterian church.[17] He and his neighbor, Edward Ward, a Presbyterian elder, contributed most of the money for the little brick building, which was completed in 1824.[18] The General's religious inclination seemed to be well-known since on May 30, 1825, the General Assembly of the United States Presbyterian Church meeting in Philadelphia voted to establish a theological seminary of the West. Jackson was named to its site selection committee. However, he was inactive in this role either because of health or politics.[19]

During these years Andrew was the beneficiary of his wife's ministrations towards his ill health. What care Rachel provided can only be assumed, but Andrew's ailments were both many and well documented in his correspondence. Previous chapters have recorded his bouts with smallpox, malaria, and near-constant dysentery. Treatments by his doctors resulted in mercury and lead poisoning, and previous conflicts with his enemies hobbled him with bullets in his left lung and left shoulder joint.

The candidate's voice was not muted regarding his state of health; his complaints were frequently and loudly expressed in letters to his supporters. It is mainly through these writings that this historian can comment on Jackson's illnesses doing his stealth campaign. Jackson twice became seriously ill, first during May 1825 upon his return from Washington. In letters to Richard Keith Call[20] and Samuel Swartwout, he complained of "fatigue" and a severe unnamed "affliction," possibly dysentery, that "confined me for many days." Both letters ascribed his physical collapse to entertaining General Lafayette on his visit to Tennessee. In the letter to Swartwout, he added, "riding on horseback which occasioned an inflammation in the rectum..."[21] which strongly suggests hemorrhoids.

The second episode occurred in late April and early May 1828 and was characterized in letters to John Coffee and James K. Polk as "a very sudden attack of the bowels"[22] and "seriously afflicted by a return of my old bowel complaint ... but am much debilitated."[23] These attacks were probably recurrences of his chronic dysentery.

Calomel ingestion, employed by contemporary physicians as a purgative, may have exaggerated the dysentery. The purgative likewise may have led to Jackson's loss of teeth. "I must be excused—having lost many of my teeth it is with great difficulty I can articulate."[24] However, the campaign was never far from his mind. In one letter he wrote, "I complain not, because I know, it would be grateful to my enemies...."[25] Later, in a letter to John Coffee regarding his maladies, Jackson wrote, "I trust providence will spare me until my enemies are prostrate."[26] Knowledge is scant regarding Rachel's specific medical care for Andrew during his medical crises. However, her emotional and loving presence, as well as her solid maintenance of their comfortable home, undoubtedly consoled him.

Any physical benefit from the treatments of those physicians who attended Jackson at The Hermitage is speculative. Dr. Samuel D. Hogg ministered to both Andrew and Rachel Jackson in their home. Hogg previously served as a surgeon under the general's command in the Creek and New Orleans campaigns. Subsequently, his civilian practice was centered in Lebanon and Nashville, Tennessee.[27] Jackson wrote in May 1819, "Nothing but the skill of Doctor Bronaugh & Hogg and their arduous attention saved me...."[28] Moreover, Dr. Hogg frequently treated Mrs. Jackson. In a December 1, 1821, letter to his close friend John Coffee, Andrew wrote, "...but I still hope Doctor Hogg will be able shortly to restore her [Rachel] to health."[29] Several years later he treated Rachel during her terminal illness.

The *Papers of Andrew Jackson* do not record Hogg's therapeutic approaches in any detail. However, a posthumous report of Hogg's treatments was published in the 1842 issue of *The Western Journal of Medicine and Surgery*.[30] From this report, it is possible to infer the treatments he imposed on the Jacksons. His armamentarium included frequent bleedings, repeated use of the cathartic calomel in large doses, emetics, tincture of opium (laudanum), and sinapisms (mustard plasters) applied to the abdomen. Rachel Jackson's chest of remedies and folk medicines has not survived, but an investigation of what other Southern ladies stocked in their medicine closets may be illustrative.

Jackson's Ambitions and Their Effects on His Wife's Reputation, Health and Life

Foreshadowed two thousand years ago by the Greek dramatist Euripides, the hubris of Andrew Jackson led to tragedy for his cherished wife. His political ambitions, his desire for the American presidency, resulted, perhaps inexorably, in catastrophe for Rachel. Her public character was in near-ruin, her physical well-being was severely weakened, and her death was hastened. She died at The Hermitage midway between his November 1828 election victory and his March 1829 triumphant inauguration in Washington. All that Rachel sadly had desired in life was to grow old comfortably in her home, close to her beloved husband, and surrounded by her loving family. It was not to be.

Defamation of the personal character of Mrs. Jackson by her husband's political detractors became a problem. In late 1823 during the early campaigning for the following year's national election, rumors surfaced regarding improprieties in the Jackson marriage that took place thirty years previously. The tales were widespread, occurring in Pennsylvania, Ohio, and the District of Columbia. The rumors alleged that Andrew Jackson had driven off Lewis Robards and lived with Rachel as husband and wife for several years before she and Lewis were legally divorced. The rumors contained a whiff of plausibility due to Old Hickory's public image. "Evoking Andrew's reputation for violence, gossips claimed that he had driven Rachel's husband away and then lived with her for several years before she was divorced."[31]

Since Jackson was judged to be an outsider, a very long-shot candidate in 1824, his many political enemies were unconcerned, at least initially, about his electoral chances. They threatened, but did not act, to place these allegations in print. Tennessee Senator John Henry Eaton, Jackson's eyes in the Washington corridors of power, became aware in late 1823 of the stirrings regarding the possible future use of this material. Through an unspoken agreement between these two men, Rachel was shielded from all knowledge of these rumors.[32] However, when Jackson became a more formidable candidate four years later, this threat was carried out. The anti–Jacksonians moved the issue from innuendo to explicit controversy during the 1828 presidential campaign.

The Jacksons' respite from scandal was short-lived. A January 1825 letter to Andrew from Virginia planter Charles Pendleton Tutt, a Jackson supporter, warned that the opposition intended to publicize Rachel Robards' divorce.[33] Characteristically, the response to Tutt's warning was both swift and very angry. Jackson exploded, "I never had a doubt of the honour of some of my political enemies, but that they would attempt to disturb the repose of an innocent female in her declining years is a species of wickedness that I did not suppose would be attempted."[34]

About this time, Charles Hammond, an ardent supporter of the sixth president of the United States, John Quincy Adams, Old Hickory's rival in both the 1824 and 1828 national elections, began to investigate the Jackson marriage. Hammond's investigation had two significant advantages: as the editor of the *Cincinnati Gazette*, he had access to his newspaper's resources; secondly, Cincinnati was only 125 miles away

VI—Rachel Jackson: Her Distress and Demise

from Harrodsburg, Kentucky, the location of the Rachel Donelson/Lewis Robards failed marriage. Hammond soon learned the facts about their marriage's dissolution, including the salacious but accurate information that the Robards' divorce was uncontested on the grounds of Rachel's adultery.[35]

The enterprising Hammond soon thereafter commenced the publication of *Truth's Advocate and Monthly Anti-Jackson Expositor*. When Jackson asserted that an investigation into a candidate's marriage and his wife's reputation was "a violation of all the charities and the decencies of life," the publisher had a rebuttal. Hammond responded that since a president would bring his wife to the White House, it was important to examine her worthiness for the position. He claimed that his duty compelled him to examine Mrs. Jackson's fitness to be First Lady. If she was unfit, then her husband's judgment and fitness to be president must be rejected.[36] Hammond continued his anti–Rachel and anti–Andrew campaign in monthly attacks. He only ceased his printed tirades when Jackson was elected president in November 1828.

No aspect of the campaign so deeply hurt and angered Andrew as the aspersions upon Rachel. Pro–Adams newspapers compared her to a "dirty black wench" and called Elizabeth, his mother, "a prostitute."[37] The scurrilous charges at first wounded, then incensed Jackson. Agonized, Jackson opened up to William B. Lewis about his mother in a December 26, 1826, letter:

> I am more anxious on this subject than perhaps I ought to be—but the Rascality of the attempt to blacken the character of an ancient & virtuous female who has thro life maintained a good reputation & has associated with the best circles of society in which she has been placed, and this for the basest purpose, by a coalition at the head of which I am sure Mr. Clay is—raises in my mind such feelings of indignation that I can scarcely control—but a day of retribution, as it respects Mr. Clay & his tool Colo. Hammonds, must arrive should I be spared.[38]

Jackson and his supporters responded at once to the slanders directed towards his wife. He correctly diagnosed they were instead aimed against him and his candidacy. Initially, the pro–Jackson newspapers in the state of Ohio shouted denials in print. *The Cincinnati Advertiser* bellowed that Hammond's claim was, "a BASE, WANTON AND MALIGNANT FALSEHOOD." Yet, the peculiarities of the Jackson marriage continued to stoke controversy both wide and deep. They led to an investigation by Jackson's Nashville Central Committee, his campaign brain trust. There was enough truth in the Jackson wedding narrative to make the Hammond story plausible. Moreover, the attacks were particularly damaging since Old Hickory's main campaign issue proclaimed his moral virtue versus his opponents' cesspool of civic corruption.

Consequently, a rebuttal to any specific errors within the Hammond story became imperative. Judge John Overton, a long-time friend, and more importantly, a very well-respected jurist, wrote this statement. It was widely distributed.[39]

Depositions were obtained from witnesses in several states who testified to the excellent character and disposition of Rachel and to her irrational and cruel treatment by Lewis Robards during their marriage.[40] One such disposition was a letter from Edward Butler of Cincinnati, who wrote,

> The character of my Dear Mrs. Jackson has ever been above the suspicion of friends and honest men, and if the baseness of desperate and unprincipled wretches make it necessary at this late period of her long, pious, and exemplary life, to vindicate the actions of its earliest period, and to blast, by contemporaneous evidence, their villainous assailants, let the painful, yet proud task, to be assigned ... to the Historian.[41]

Another prong of the Jackson counterattack was the interrogation of those thought to be behind the gossip. John Eaton was requested to interview Henry Clay, the Secretary of State and de facto Adams' campaign manager, about his connection with Charles Hammond and their involvement in the attacks against Rachel Jackson. Clay met with Eaton and denied any association on his part; astonishingly he also denied any participation on the part of Mr. Hammond.[42]

"No evidence links Clay to these attacks ... but that hardly pardoned his silence when they appeared.... Clay did not try to stop Hammond nor did he condemn his columns." Jackson never forgave Henry Clay for his presumptive involvement in Rachel's slander. Old Hickory's anger against the Kentucky politician smoldered; later his fiery temper was reignited when Margaret Eaton, one of the new president's favorites, was similarly maligned, possibly once again under Clay's direction.[43]

Still, the aspersions continued. On February 1, 1827, Thomas Dickens Arnold, a Knoxville lawyer running for Congress, published his letter to the *Freemen of the Counties etc.* Therein, Arnold labeled Jackson a "lump of naked deformity," and that, "He spent the prime of his life in gambling, in cock fighting, in horse-racing, and has all his life been a most bloody duelist." Arnold concluded, "...to cap all his frailties, he tore from a husband the wife of his bosom, to whom he had for some years united in the holy state of matrimony."[44]

The dimensions of the opposition's attack were both broad and deep. It even included two letters written by Dr. Francis May, General Jackson's erstwhile friend and physician, who treated him after the 1806 duel with Dickinson. Now, more than twenty years later, May accused Jackson of acting dishonorably in that duel; a second letter further charged the candidate with land fraud, together with his brother-in-law Robert Hays.[45]

Rachel knew of these attacks, probably as early as the middle of 1827.[46] Her reactions were expressed in a July letter to Elizabeth Warren:

> "Can say my soule Can be a testimony to the truth of that Gospel for who has been so cruelly tryed as I have my mind my trials have been severe—the Enemyes of the Genls have Dipt their arrows in wormwood & gall & sped them at me ... to think that thirty years had past in happy social friendship with society, knowing or thinking no ill to no one."[47]

Robert Remini summarized that in 1828, "More times than anyone ever realized Rachel broke down and cried hysterically over what was said about her."[48]

Old Hickory knew the motives behind his opponents' calumnies that continued to appear in hand bills, pamphlets and magazines.

> "Mrs. J is not spared, & my pious mother, nearly fifty yeas in the tomb ... has been dragged forth by Hammond & held to public scorn as a prostitute who intermaried with a negro, & my eldest brother sold as a Slav[sic] in Carolina ... but all my enemies expect is, to urge me to some rash action, this they cannot do until the action is over...."[49]

Jackson wisely avoided any rash action in response; public manifestations of his anger were kept hidden. But, in the privacy of letters to his friends, his vehemence was not controlled. In one letter he wrote, "...for the day of retribution & vengeance must come," and, in a further commitment to vengeance, he wrote close to the culmination of the 1828 campaign, "...still when Mrs. J. Character was so basely attacked, it was more than my mind could bear to hear it, and not redress it—I hope providence will spare me to that day, when I can freely act, when retributive Justice will await the actors in this vile procedure—."[50]

After Andrew Jackson won the presidential election over John Quincy Adams in 1828, John Eaton wrote to Rachel, "...my dear friend" in which he assured her that "the angry tempest has ceased to howl." He concluded that he looked forward to greeting her at the March inauguration ceremonies.[51]

Rachel's Health: Decline and Death

Rachel Donelson Jackson died on December 22, 1828, after thirty-five years of devoted wedlock to Andrew Jackson. Her death occurred less than two months after Jackson was elected the seventh president of the United States. She died in her beloved home after she had displayed the characteristic symptoms of a fatal heart attack (myocardial infraction in medical terminology). She perished not only as her husband's greatest and arguably most hard-working supporter, but also debatably as the most prominent victim of his overweening ambition.

Historian Robert Remini describes Rachel Jackson's appearance upon their 1821 return from Florida as "quite stout." A more colorful description related, "she was once a form of rotund and rubicund beauty, but now was now very plethoric and obese." To be blunt, Rachel was short and had become quite fat.

One doctor made the diagnosis of *phthisis* and prescribed smoking a pipe to relieve her symptoms. This diagnosis is likely erroneous, since it defines any disease causing a wasting away of part or all of the body, especially tuberculosis. Mrs. Jackson was corpulent, not cachectic. Tuberculosis was possible since "she spoke with short and wheezing breaths," but unlikely. More pertinent, Remini mentioned cardiac symptoms of heart palpitations and chest pains. He also suggested hypertension as a diagnosis.[52]

To his credit, Andrew acknowledged his wife's infirmity and was constantly solicitous for her physical well-being. When political aspirations and activity kept him away, his letters showed his concern when she was indisposed and elation when she was well.

"I rejoice to learn that your health is good & that your friends are attentive to you, & keep up your spirits."[53]

For her part, Rachel "kept him informed of every ache and pain she suffered, and especially how grieved she was over his absence." Andrew, from Washington, responded with soothing statements of regret, with added flourishes that "kind providence will soon relieve you from the pain." Assuming the role of health provider, he urged that she apply a "cooling wash" to treat her eye inflammation.[54]

The ambience of The Hermitage had a salutary effect upon her well-being. When the Jacksons departed from Washington in the spring of 1825, she was suffering from an unspecified illness. However, at home she soon regained her health. According to her husband, "Mrs. Jackson's health is perfectly restored, as soon as we got on the mountains [of Tennessee]."[55]

Jackson's letters disclosed a significant illness that sickened her in December 1825; it was severe enough that it prevented his visit to see his close friend John Coffee, who resided in Alabama. He wrote, "Mrs. J's indisposition prevents me and will prevent me this winter from visiting." This illness, not otherwise described, confined her for six weeks. In a March 1826 correspondence to the seemingly omnipresent Richard Keith Call, the candidate wrote, "her health is measurably restored altho her complexion remains somewhat sallow...." Rachel's treating physician was Dr. Samuel Hogg.[56]

Although no further disabling issues affected Mrs. Jackson until 1828, the status of her health concerned her physician. Dr. Miles Blythe McCorkle advised her to seek treatments at the Harrodsburg spa to improve her health. He also attended to the general medical care of The Hermitage, often in concert with Dr. Hogg.[57] In spite of her chronic problems with weight, breathing, and palpitations, Jackson's letters in early 1828 were optimistic, "We enjoy good health," "Mrs. J. is still good," and "Mrs. Jackson is well." She tolerated her 1828 trip with her husband, the hero of New Orleans, to commemorate the thirteenth anniversary of his victory.[58]

However, her health was not to last. One day Rachel took a long walk and found herself much exhausted by the exercise. Returning home, she exhibited cardiac symptoms of wheezing and panting. Her poor health and sagging spirits raised the question as to whether she should remain in Tennessee until after her husband's inauguration.[59]

A loyal and affectionate group constantly surrounded Rachel at The Hermitage. These friends undoubtedly kept some of the worst scandalous publications, especially those most graphic with their accusations, from her sight. Certainly Jackson shielded her from the most outrageous calumnies. However, her charitable instincts could not prevent the ill effects of anxiety and nervous strain. "Dr. Hogg, her physician watched her with increasing solicitude, and her pastor Rev. William Hume encouraged her forbearance and her Christian charity towards her persecutors."[60]

After the election results were known, the presumptive First Lady reconciled herself to leaving home. She poured out her thoughts to a very close friend: "I could have spent at the Hermitage the remnant of my days in peace & were it not that I should be unhappy by being so far from the General no consideration could induce me again to abandon this delightful spot."[61] She reluctantly traveled the twelve miles to the clothing shops of Nashville in order to select a wardrobe befitting her station as First Lady of the United States. Shopping wearied her, so she sought rest in the office of a friendly newspaper editor. There, she perused a magazine that contained some of the worst of the slanders against her. She wept and was found distraught and terror-stricken by her companions. Upon her return to The Hermitage, her husband, after studying her demeanor, inquired what was bothering her. She answered, and Jackson, "...now saw in her pitiful condition the human price of his bid for the presidency."[62]

Several days later, on December 17, Mrs. Jackson was struck with a stabbing pain in her chest that radiated down her left arm. Shortness of breath accompanied these symptoms of a massive heart attack. She was placed in bed, and all available physicians were summoned. Dr. Henry Lee Heiskell of Winchester, Virginia, who was just starting as a physician in the neighborhood, was the first to respond.[63] He was soon joined at the bedside by Dr. Hogg, the Jacksons' regular physician.

The following is from Dr. Heiskell's clinical notes. The initial examination of the patient on December 17 revealed, "a spasmodic affectation of the muscles of the chest and left shoulder, attended with an irregular action of the heart and great anxiety of countenance."

Rachel was treated according to the archaic standards of the early nineteenth century. She was bled a total of three times. Incredibly, the patient improved and was stable for several days. But, on the evening of December 22, Rachel cried out and died. At Andrew's urging, the attendant doctor made two further attempts to bleed the deceased, but both were fruitless. The patient was dead at sixty-one years of age.[64]

Dr. Heiskell submitted a bill for his professional services for Mrs. Jackson's terminal illness for $13.50. The young doctor's bill was professionally itemized. It listed the following charges: venesection ($1.50): pulverized mercury, probably calomel ($0.50); castor oil ($0.50); and uncomplicated house calls ($2.00 each visit). The invoice was paid in full by Andrew Jackson on January 16, 1829.[65]

Upon her death, the president-elect poured out his emotions in letters to friends.

> Mrs. J. was a few days past, suddenly and violently, attacked, with pain to her left shoulder & breast & such the contraction of the heart, that suffocation was apprehended before the necessary aid could be afforded. Dr. Hogg has relieved her.... The little Junto of calumniators here, have found their level; the verdict has been pronounced against them.[66]

A few days later he wrote,

> ...by the afflicting dispensation of Providence which has deprived me of the partner of my life. A loss so great, so sudden and unexpected, I need not say to you, can be compensated by no earthly gift. Could it be, it might be found in the reflection that she lived long enough to see the countless assault of our enemies disarmed by the voice of our beloved country.[67]

Rachel Jackson was buried in her garden near the entrance of The Hermitage. Her final site of rest had been determined previously by Rachel and Andrew. Her funeral was held on the afternoon of Christmas Eve, less than forty-eight hours after her demise. The throng of mourners was vast, numbering ten thousand according to one estimate. Sam Houston led the pallbearers. The deceased husband's grieving was visible at the gravesite, but he recovered when he entered his mansion.[68]

The president-elect's tribute to his beloved Rachel is written on her gravestone:

> Here lie the remains of Mrs. Rachel Jackson, wife of President Jackson, who died the 22d of December, 1828, aged 61. Her face was fair; her person pleasing, her temper amiable, her heart kind; she delighted in relieving the wants of her fellow-creatures, and cultivated that divine pleasure by the most liberal and unpretending methods; to the poor she was a benefactor; to the rich an example; to the wretched a comforter; to the prosperous an ornament: her piety went hand in hand with her benevolence, and she thanked her Creator for being permitted to do good. A being so gentle and so virtuous, slander might wound her but could not dishonor. Even death, when he tore her from the arms of her husband, could but transport her to the bosom of her God.[69]

The demise of Rachel, the most important woman in his life, exposed the new president to the influence of two very different ladies whose personalities, although dissimilar in most respects, were congruent in outspokenness, stubbornness, and in blunt opinion. Emily Tennessee Donelson, the wife of his personal secretary, succeeded the deceased wife to become the mistress of the White House. Margaret O'Neale Timberlake soon became Margaret (Peggy) Eaton, the wife of John Eaton, the president's first biographer, close personal and political friend, and the incoming Secretary of War. The social attacks upon her would be viewed by Jackson as distressingly similar to the attacks upon his now deceased wife.

Andrew Jackson previously knew both women well. Their lives would increasingly become entangled with his. Unfortunately, Mrs. Donelson and Mrs. Eaton loathed each other.

VII

Emily Tennessee Donelson
His Niece

> Emily, the youngest of thirteen was, "the spoiled darling of the family, petted by her father, indulged by her gentle mother, teased by her grownup bothers, and waited upon by her older sisters."
> —Burke, *Emily Donelson of Tennessee*, 39

> "During the Washington 1824–25 winter, she had frequented the balls of the Capital, including the brilliant ball at General Brown's Indian Queen Hotel…. By the time of her departure to Tennessee she knew either personally or by sight the nation's great that were assembled in Washington."
> —Burke, *Emily Donelson of Tennessee* I, 129–130

Emily Tennessee Donelson was the thirteenth and final child born to John Donelson and Mary Purnell Donelson. John Donelson was Rachel Jackson's older brother. In 1829, Emily became a Surrogate First Lady in her uncle Andrew Jackson's White House. Surrogates were those women, non-spouses of an incumbent president, who performed many, if not most, of the social, ceremonial, and household managerial functions of a First Lady when the president's wife was either deceased, disabled, or disinterested.

The indomitable Dolley Madison was the first surrogate, who occasionally acted as the social hostess for the widower Thomas Jefferson. The second was Eliza Hay, a very frequent White House substitute for her often-sickly mother, Elizabeth Monroe. Many commentators rated Eliza's performance in this role as less than successful.[1]

First Lady Louisa Adams described Eliza as, "full of agreeables and disagreeables, so accomplished and ill bred, so proud and so mean."[2]

VII—Emily Tennessee Donelson: His Niece

Emily Donelson was the third woman to serve as surrogate. She assumed the Executive Mansion's social and ceremonial responsibilities during most of another widower, Andrew Jackson's, two presidential terms (1829–1837). Many of the same commentators who disapproved of Eliza Hay's tenure extensively praised Emily's service for her uncle.

Emily Tennessee's first appearance in *The Papers of Andrew Jackson* is found in a January 18, 1824 letter to her future husband Andrew Jackson Donelson. He wrote in closing, "...present me affectionately to Miss. E...."[3]

As stated previously, she was the daughter of John Donelson and Mary Purnell and was their thirteenth and final child. Their oldest, Chesed, was born in 1780, twenty-seven years before Emily's birth. It was common for frontier families, notably members of the Donelson clan, to reproduce profusely for both economic and security reasons.

John Donelson usually was identified by his military rank of Captain (Capt.) to distinguish him from his father, Colonel John Donelson. The younger John was born in 1755 in Virginia, the sixth of eleven children of Colonel John and Rachel Stockley.[4]

In 1777, Captain John received his rank when he, together with Ensign Moses Hutchings, whose brother Thomas Hutchings was to become John's brother-in-law, commanded a Virginia militia company to combat "Indian outrages."[5]

Captain John was a surveyor like his father and his brothers, Stockley and William. On the Tennessee frontier, surveyors' positions yielded great rewards in an economy based on land speculation. Their profession furnished the brothers with both business opportunities and professional contacts, which helped to build the Donelson family land holdings. In addition, the energetic John became a Justice for the Davidson County Tennessee Court in 1789.[6]

Moreover, he owned a plantation, which was only two miles from The Hermitage. Thus, he would become a close friend of his neighbor and brother-in-law Andrew Jackson. The general frequently mentioned John and John's family in his letters: "present me to Capt. John Donelson & family"; "present me affectionately to Miss E., to my old friend Capt. J. D...."[7] Jackson, away as a senator in the nation's capital, wrote to his neighbor expressing gratitude, "to all my young female friends for their attention to Mrs. J...." Emily Tennessee, John's youngest daughter, undoubtedly was one of the "young female friends."[8]

Mary Purnell, the wife of Captain John and the exhausted mother of Emily, was a fifth generation descendent of the English settler Thomas Purnell and Elizabeth Dorman, the daughter of another settler. They, members of the Church of England, were residents of the Eastern shore of Maryland. Eventually the Purnells migrated to Pittsylvania County, Virginia, where they were introduced to the Donelsons. Over the decades, the Purnells' religious convictions evolved from Anglican to Presbyterian.[9] Mary Purnell was married to Captain John on August 17, 1779, at the age of 16. Their honeymoon was spent aboard the *Adventure* on its 985-mile river journey to settle the Cumberland Valley of Tennessee. Among her Donelson boat mates was twelve-year-old Rachel, who years later was to become her neighbor.[10]

John's wife Mary was also a good neighbor to the Jacksons. Andrew wrote to John Coffee, "I have had a hard time, but Mrs. J. Donelson Sent me over the other day a bottle of syrup (I know not the composition) that is checking the cough very much...." The Jacksons and the John Donelsons shared in the estate of Rachel and John's father Colonel John Donelson (1718–1786). As United States senator, Jackson was instrumental in securing for the Donelson family the rights to claim five thousand acres of public land in Alabama and Mississippi. Captain John Donelson had surveyed a tract of the inherited property.[11]

Mary Purnell Donelson was forty-four when Emily was born; she had borne children for the past twenty-seven years. Emily Tennessee appeared on June 1, 1807. She had wide brown eyes, silken hair of the hue made famous by Titian, and skin as soft as the petals of the wild rose around the house walls. The name Emily was a fancy of her mother, but Tennessee was probably the idea of Captain John, who loved the state. Aunt Rachel rode over from The Hermitage the same day to greet her new niece.[12]

Emily grew up in her father's large residence The Mansion, an ambling log house of two stories, commodious enough to accommodate his large Donelson family.

> It was one of the largest homes of its kind on the Cumberland." "The rooms were large with low beamed ceilings, big open fireplaces, over which there were high mantel pieces. An enclosed staircase in each room led to the room above. The upstairs rooms were not connected. There was a large rock chimney at each end of the house and a porch on each side.

The Mansion probably had been built in 1804 on land Captain John had inherited from his father. Two of Emily's sisters, Mary and Rachel, were married to John Coffee and William Eastin respectively at The Mansion in a double wedding in 1809.[13] Rachel Eastin became the mother of two daughters, Mary and yet another Rachel. Shortly after the birth of her second daughter, Rachel Eastin died, leaving the care of her children to her mother, Mary Purnell Donelson. Captain John understandably was concerned about his wife's ability to muster the physical stamina required to assume this responsibility. Mary rose to the occasion of a second motherhood; she died many years later at the age of eighty-five. This genealogic detour merits its placement here since the orphaned Mary Eastin, a mere three years younger than her aunt Emily, became Emily's closest friend and a filter between Emily and Uncle Jackson during their conflict years later.[14]

During her childhood, Emily was immersed in the hustle and bustle not only at The Mansion, but also at The Hermitage, only two miles distant. The Mansion was a normal, happy home in which to grow up into lovely womanhood. Emily, the youngest of thirteen was, "the spoiled darling of the family, petted by her father, indulged by her gentle mother, teased by her grownup brothers, and waited upon by her older sisters."[15]

Her formal education began at the little log schoolhouse on Lebanon Road near her home and ended at the Nashville Female Academy. The schoolhouse was erected in 1817 when Emily Donelson was ten. An itinerant missionary sporadically complemented Mr. McKnight, the resident teacher, to provide an education to the children on the American frontier. This schoolhouse may have witnessed the first flickering of a romance between this young student and her older cousin, Andrew Jackson Donelson. Emily entered the National Female Academy most likely in January 1820. At that time, the Academy contained about one hundred students, one of whom was her niece Mary Eastin. However, Emily's health, always fragile and a source of anxiety to her parents, was the reason for her withdrawal from The Academy. Her formal schooling lasted less than five years.[16]

Emily, while living afterwards at The Mansion, enjoyed much time with the amiable Aunt Jackson at the nearby Hermitage.[17] Frequent visits at her aunt's home soon evolved into a Tennessee plantation romance between sixteen-year old Emily and her twenty-four-year-old first cousin, Andrew Jackson Donelson. He, a ward and a young protégé of Andrew Jackson, often resided at The Hermitage. Their courtship, initially comfortable and unhurried, changed abruptly upon Andrew's receipt of an urgent request from Uncle Andrew. The letter read, "I had no person who I could reply to but you. Next fall I will have to bring you on with me [to Washington]; I have this winter at a great Loss for some confidential friend to aid me...."

The sweethearts faced a conundrum—to separate, at least temporarily, while Andrew fulfilled the elder Jackson's directive, or to marry almost immediately despite her youth and poor health. Emily feared that Captain John and mother Mary would not allow her to wed two months before her seventeenth birthday and so soon after her recovery from a winter-long sickness. Perhaps the unspoken support of Aunt

Rachel and Uncle Andrew persuaded Emily's parents to acquiesce to an early wedding.[18]

Captain John approved the trousseau shopping of his still girlish and immature daughter. Emily, with her sister Elizabeth Donelson McLemore as her companion, spent six hundred dollars in the elegant ladies' shops in Nashville. A second sister, Catherine Martin, was very supportive, praising Emily's letter-writing as "well written" and "well composed." Catherine hoped that Emily would grow into a fine woman; additionally, she penned, "I know her to be more than ordinarily smart."

September 16, the cousins' wedding day, began optimistically— beautiful early autumn weather; The Mansion, home of the bride, was well prepared for a joyous celebration. The early arriving Donelson guests were filled with happy anticipation. The buoyant atmosphere was disrupted by the news that young Rachel Jackson, the wife of William, the bride's brother, had died that morning. "Rachel Jackson, wife of William, is no more, she departed this life on the 16th ... the very day on which A & E Donelson were to be married ... what was to be done in this distressing circumstance was very perplexing. It was at length concluded to let the parson perform the ceremony & *it was done.*" The couple then was married by the Reverend William Hume.[19]

Two months after their September wedding, Emily with her husband set out for Washington in the company of the Jacksons. Upon their arrival, the seventeen-year-old bride become first an intimate of Aunt Rachel, and later a comfort, and occasionally an irritant, to Uncle Andrew. In an early impression, written in Washington regarding her relationship with the Jacksons, Emily wrote to her sister Elizabeth, "Uncle and Aunt ... treat me as their child."[20]

The Jackson party were guests at the Franklin House, whose proprietor was John Gadsby. Another guest was the sixty-eight-year-old Marquis de Lafayette, who charmed the impressionable Emily. An early visitor to the Jackson hotel suite was the twenty-five-year-old, gorgeous, and alluring Mrs. Margaret O'Neale Timberlake. The two women, according to Burke, developed an "instant antagonism between them."[21] Their female-to-female hostility later would have an encumbering effect upon Andrew Jackson's first two years as president.

Margaret, later to be labeled both by Washington society and future historians as the notorious Peggy Eaton, quickly formed a condescending opinion towards the "frail young thing, titian-haired (and) lovely." The sophisticated Margaret viewed the younger Emily, still a teenager, as "unused to the ways of the world, unsophisticated ... and totally unfitted for the social conditions of the Capital city." However, as biographer

VII—Emily Tennessee Donelson: His Niece

Pauline Burke noted, Margaret may have noticed the "lines of determination about Emily's mouth."[22]

Emily Tennessee's frailty and frequent illnesses were a constant concern. She was much beloved by her father, Captain John Donelson. Not only was she his youngest child, but she was frail, slight of stature, and frequently ill. John removed her from the Nashville Academy to protect her physical well-being; moreover, he was reluctant for her to marry because he feared for her survival. When his little Emily, not yet nineteen, went into labor with her first child on June 6, 1826, the ever stoic and steadfast father retreated into the woods to wait out the birth.[23]

Uncle Jackson also occasionally commented on his niece's well-being: "The ladies are all in good health & spirits—but Emily, who has a cold, which is common here..." However, in an acknowledgment of the young woman's resiliency, he continued, "...but will be able to visit the theater tomorrow evening if the weather will permit."[24] In another letter to John Coffee, which announced his return home from Washington, he elaborated, "We were detained on our return by the indisposition of Emily—she came home much mended, but I learn this morning, she is again confined ... being a complaint originating from a slight cold...."[25] Emily sickened in Cincinnati; Andrew Jackson continued on his homeward journey, leaving Rachel and Andrew Jackson Donelson to comfort the young woman. Captain John, forever fearful for his youngest child, dispatched a letter to his son Stockley: "I greatly fear for her. I was very unwilling for her to take the journey and perhaps we may never see her more; her life is in the hand of god [sic]...."[26]

Upon their return to Tennessee, the young Donelsons took possession of their new house, Springdale, generously provided by Uncle Jackson. Its three hundred eighteen and a quarter acres adjoined The Hermitage. The couple was able to enjoy a very comfortable lifestyle; Andrew also inherited land and enslaved people from his father and grandfather. In addition, Captain John had given his daughter land and enslaved people at the time of her marriage. The young bride was fortunate that Springdale was close to The Mansion. There she was instructed in the arts of domesticity by her extremely experienced mother. Under Mary Purnell's tutelage, Emily learned pickling, preserving, spinning, and weaving, competences she was expected to pass along to her enslaved household servants. The interval of summer 1825 to early winter 1828 was an idyllic time for the young Donelsons; these were the only years when they were able to enjoy a house of their own.[27]

In the main, Emily's unserious, lighthearted, possibly even frivolous ways continued. During the Washington 1824–5 winter, she frequented the balls of the capital, including the brilliant ball at General Brown's Indian Queen Hotel where General Jackson was the center of attraction. By the time of her departure to Tennessee, she knew either personally or by sight the nation's great that were assembled in Washington.[28] Later the young Donelsons entertained at their Springdale farm. On July 18, 1828, the couple hosted a large dinner party for her brother Stockley Donelson and his bride Phila Ann Lawrence, a friend of Emily's from the Nashville Academy.[29]

Until 1829, little Emily Tennessee's influence upon her towering uncle was slight, but it would change once she and her family set up residence in the presidential mansion. Hitherto she was viewed as a glittering ornament of Captain John's family, one who both entertained and comforted her Aunt Rachel, and one who elicited Uncle Andrew's concern and affection.

However, her greatest value to Jackson was her conjugal love for his favorite, and increasingly invaluable nephew, Andrew J. Donelson. Emily imparted to her Andrew affection, tranquility, and the ability to focus. Young Donelson, a West Point graduate and former military officer, had returned to Nashville to initiate a law practice. However, "Donelson allowed his law practice to languish as the majority of his time was consumed by Jackson's 1824 presidential candidacy." While Jackson served as a United States senator, the younger "Andrew assumed the functions of his private secretary—he tended to the senator's accounts, and, more significantly he retrieved letters and compiled evidence to refute the anticipated character attacks" by his uncle's political enemies.[30]

In the years leading up to the 1828 presidential election, Donelson continued his unofficial role as Jackson's private secretary, assisting him in answering correspondence and writing public statements. He also supported the general's political campaign by financially supporting Duff Green's pro–Jackson newspaper, *United States Telegraph*, and by taking depositions from witnesses who vouched for his uncle's character.[31]

VIII

Margaret Eaton
Wife of His Secretary of War

"On May 16, 1812, Margaret danced at the White House. The ebullient Dolley not only awarded her first prize in all five categories of dance but also placed a gold crown on her head."
—Phillips, *That Eaton Woman*, 11

"Mrs. Monroe, watching Margaret's unfeminine behavior from her adjacent abode, developed a strong disapproval of her young neighbor. Eventually when First Lady, she disinvited Margaret from entering the White House, even though, as the escort of United States Senator John Eaton, protocol allowed her attendance."
—Phillips, *That Eaton Woman*, 21

Margaret O'Neale Timberlake Eaton became the counterpoint to Emily Tennessee Donelson as they competed for social acceptance and presidential approbation during the first two years of Andrew Jackson's first term (1829–1831). Their struggle for President Jackson's endorsement, he being the uncle of one and the close friend of the other, was consequential to the success of his early presidency. Their personal combat was incorporated into the fierce political and social struggle that consumed the attention of Washington City for more than two years. Margaret and Emily certainly disliked, even despised, each other.

Although both ladies were mothers, first married while still in their late teens, and the beneficiaries of well-connected families, significant contrasts segregated them. Emily Donelson was spared a surname change on her wedding day. Margaret, her semi-antithesis, was an O'Neale at birth, a Timberlake upon her first marriage, and then an Eaton when as a widow she became the wife of Senator John Eaton of

Tennessee. Her third marriage in the far distant future would entail yet another change of her surname.

Emily owed her significance to her abundant Donelson family, the in-laws of the orphaned and childless Andrew Jackson. Her aunt was Rachel Donelson Jackson, who died mere months before her husband's presidential inauguration. Her father was Captain John Donelson, the prosperous neighbor and brother-in-law of Old Hickory. Undoubtedly, her most important attribute was her marriage to Andrew Jackson Donelson, the private secretary essential to their uncle, the seventh President of the United States.

Conversely, Margaret was the oldest daughter of William O'Neale, the popular and ever-affable owner of the most prominent inn and saloon in Washington. His establishment boarded the most important senators, representatives, and government officials, including in 1823, the newly appointed senator from Tennessee, Andrew Jackson. Margaret O'Neale, the saloonkeeper's daughter, had a responsibility to assure the ease and comfort of her father's guests. However, her strongest and most robust tie to Jackson was her long friendship with, and her subsequent marriage to, John Eaton, Andrew's intimate friend, fellow Tennessee senator, political agent, and first biographer.

Her Life Before the Jackson Presidency

Margaret insisted that *Margaret*, not *Peggy*, was her name, asserting in her autobiography, "I was never called Peggy in all my life."[1] The monumental *Papers of Andrew Jackson* project acceded to her wish, and identifies her as *Margaret* throughout its many volumes.[2] However, and contrary to her wishes, both her hostile contemporaries and most historians insisted on *Peggy*, since it connoted a less serious, superficial, a more social, and even flirtatious personage, which was more consistent with their biased views about Margaret.

Margaret, a congenital Washingtonian, was born December 3, 1799, in The Franklin House, her father's establishment in the embryonic nation's capital. Her father was William O'Neale, a New Jerseyan by birth and an Ulsterman by inheritance. O'Neale was gregarious, smart, entrepreneurial, and a lover of people, traits that led to business success, first as a manufacturer of stoves, and then for many years, as a hotel and saloon proprietor.

Her mother Rhoda, in addition to maintaining a wholesome home for her family, was stately, quiet, and pious.[3] Mrs. O'Neale was a devout Methodist who attended church regularly and expressed no interest in nonreligious subjects. Her religious convictions and other noble qualities were very appealing to Rachel Jackson, who was a boarder, and then an intimate, during the winter of 1824–1825.[4]

Margaret was the oldest of the six O'Neale children. Her sisters were Mary, who was five years younger, and Georgianna. William, Robert, and John, her brothers, were militarily inclined. The first two attended West Point Military Academy, and John O'Neale, "went to Mexico with Gen. Scott, contracted a fever there ... and died in my house while I was the wife of Maj. Eaton."[5]

She was described as "an exceptionally pretty little girl who grew more attractive each year. She had enormous dark eyes with thick lashes, and mass of dark brown hair with red highlights.... She was slender, with long legs, a tiny waist, and a high bust."[6]

When Congress moved the nation's capital to Washington, her clever father opened a hotel, soon to be named the Franklin House. O'Neale charged a reasonable $1.25 per day for a private room and board. In 1814, he opened his bar, which brought an expanded clientele. O'Neale called it a family hotel, and he invited his guests to join him and his family in its parlor after dinner. During the first decades of the nineteenth century, Washington was a frontier village with few amenities. Consequently, members of Congress and Cabinet members generally left their wives at home. Many resided at the Franklin House when Congress was in session. George Clinton, vice president to both Thomas Jefferson and James Madison, enjoyed a two-room suite at the O'Neale establishment. When he died in his room in 1812, the notoriety subsequently attached to the Franklin House only increased its following.[7]

Margaret was William's favorite; he delighted in her personality and her accomplishments, denied her nothing, and indulged her with gifts. She became a favorite of many of the hotel's guests as she danced around its quarters. One biographer wrote, "Peggy was a lively sprite, displaying, in very early childhood a strong will,"[8] and another described her as "A born coquette with the added virtue of innocence."[9] She was a natural flirt who was far more at ease with men than with women and one who always sought male companionship. Before she reached school age, she was adept at handling men.

For an adolescent American girl in the early 1800s, Margaret O'Neale was well educated. She was enrolled in Mrs. Hayward's school that was noted for its rigorous standards. Hayward's was a private institution established for the education of aristocratic children. The only girls admitted were the daughters of foreign diplomats. Margaret's entry was abetted through the intercession of her "uncles," politically prominent boarders at Franklin House. The school's curriculum included spelling, reading, writing, arithmetic, English grammar, bookkeeping, composition, belles lettres, history, geography, drawing, painting, and French as an elective which Margaret mastered. At ten she had learned all that Mrs. Hayward's school could teach her. Then her indulgent father enrolled his daughter in Mr. Generes' dancing academy. Unsurprisingly, she excelled and soon became the dance master's favorite.[10]

Her precocity was noticed by two First Ladies, the incumbent Dolley Madison, and the future, Elizabeth Monroe. Their opinions of the young Margaret were starkly contradictory, presaging perhaps the differing personal perceptions of her in future years. On May 16, 1812, Margaret danced at the White House. The ebullient Dolley not only awarded her first prize in all five categories of dance but also placed a gold crown on her head.[11] Future President James Monroe, James Madison's Secretary of State, was also the O'Neale's next door neighbor. His wife Elizabeth was serious, unsocial, and somewhat intolerant. Mrs. Monroe, watching Margaret's unfeminine behavior from her adjacent abode, developed a strong disapproval of her young neighbor. Eventually when First Lady, she disinvited Margaret from entering the White House, even though, as the escort of United States Senator John Eaton, protocol allowed her attendance.[12]

The nadir of American fortunes during the War of 1812 came in August 1814, when the British army burned the White House and most government buildings. Both the Madisons and the Monroes fled Washington, as did the O'Neale women and many of the city's residents.[13] Margaret, at fifteen, did not return to school, but worked at her father's establishment. She "thought herself a full-fledged woman. Daily association with adults ... matured her beyond the bounds of adolescence."[14] She enhanced her duties at her father's hotel by accommodating its boarders, playing the piano, and engaging the guests in spirited, agreeable, and reassuring conversations; eventually she operated its tavern. Consequently, she became the discreet confidante of many. The popularity of Franklin House guaranteed that every man of consequence in Washington was acquainted with Margaret, and she knew all of them by name. However, "No one stepped beyond the bounds of propriety."[15]

She impressed Kentucky Congressman William T. Barry, who wrote his wife, "a charming little girl ... who very frequently plays on the piano and entertains with agreeable songs."[16] Not unexpectedly, she attracted many suitors and even marriage proposals from distinguished men like Adjutant General of the Army Daniel Parker and United States Army Major Francis Belton.[17] Belton even challenged a rival suitor to a duel.[18]

Finally, during Indian summer when she was nearing sixteen, Margaret, in her guise as Peggy, decided on bold action rather than mere flirtation; she accepted a proposal of marriage from U.S. Army Captain Root. She later described the captain as being in his late twenties, tall, broad-shouldered, intelligent, dark-haired, and quick-witted. The impulsive romantic, correctly surmising that her parents would not agree to this marriage, plotted an elopement. However, her plans did not include the upsetting of a flowerpot as she descended a ladder toward her awaiting captain. William O'Neale, awakened by the noise, disrupted the elopement, expelled Root from the scene, and banished Margaret to New York City.

Margaret lodged at the home of Governor DeWitt Clinton, nephew of the deceased Vice President Clinton. Her activity remained under the owner's close scrutiny. The teenager was placed in the reportedly strict school of Madame Nau. However, Madame Nau may have been a covert romantic, since after the thwarted Captain Root was transferred to New York, she permitted the two lovers to meet at her school. However, Margaret's ardor for her beau cooled quickly; she begged her still indulgent father to rescue her and return her to their Washington home.[19]

During the following decade, three men would both appear in, and would significantly influence, this beautiful young woman's life. In order of appearance, they were John Timberlake, John Eaton, and Andrew Jackson.

John Bowie Timberlake entered upon Margaret's stage on June 1, 1816, and before midnight, the two were engaged.[20] Timberlake was extremely handsome, tall, dark-haired, and rugged in stature. He was a thirty-nine-year-old officer in the United States Navy and a purser by job occupation.[21] A Navy purser was a merchant who purchased a ship's goods prior to a long sea journey. The purser recouped his original expenditure and much more by selling his items to the ship's crew. Timberlake fought in the War of 1812 and was the purser aboard the USS *President* when it was captured by the English warship *Macedonia*. Commander Decatur, the American commander, ordered Timberlake's stores be thrown overboard; the British took the purser's books upon capture. These actions seriously damaged the Timberlake's livelihood. Eventually, the *Macedonia* was in turn captured by the USS *United States*, freeing Timberlake and the other American captives.

The wedding took place on July 18, 1816, at St. John's Presbyterian Church in Georgetown.[22] It was a splendid ceremony which was attended by four senators, eleven congressmen, an associate justice of Supreme Court, three Army generals, a Navy commodore, and many others. Margaret asserted in her autobiography that Dolley Madison, still First Lady, also attended.[23]

The Secretary of the Navy, a friend of William O'Neale and also an attendee, arranged a furlough for the bridegroom. O'Neale presented a house, adjacent to his hotel, as a wedding gift to the newlyweds. The Timberlake's firstborn, a son, appeared just thirteen months later. Unfortunately for the parents, the boy died six months after birth. Ashore, Timberlake deteriorated; he was a failure in business, became increasingly listless, and more and more turned into a drunkard.[24]

John Henry Eaton became a boarder at the Franklin House in 1818. Eaton was the newly appointed United States senator from Tennessee, and at age twenty-eight, its youngest. His importance was based on his very close friendship with fellow Tennessean General Jackson. However, in his own right, he was a scholar, an attorney, a biographer, a soldier, and a very wealthy Tennessee landowner. One of many important connections with the Jacksons was his marriage to the Jackson's ward, Myra Lewis, whose brother William B. Lewis was a perennial Jackson confidante.[25]

Eaton was altruistic, a virtue somewhat alien to the raw ambition and personal profiteering of many of his colleagues in Congress. However, he had an easy sociability that allowed him to get along with his congressional associates. An engaging conversationalist, worldly but not disrespectful to women, he became a favorite with both the O'Neales and the Timberlakes.[26]

He soon became a very close friend with both John and Margaret. Eaton's closeness to John Timberlake made him aware of the purser's many faults—indolence, procrastination, carelessness in the conduct of his business, and alcoholism. Both his wife Margaret and his close friend Eaton, "loved his spontaneity, succumbed to his unconscious, flexible, golden charm, and felt responsibility in regulating his life-work...." The senator, ten years the purser's junior and determined to rehabilitate Timberlake, volunteered to introduce a bill in the Senate to compensate him for his losses.[27]

Unfortunately, Eaton was unsuccessful in his first senatorial attempts to move a private bill of reimbursement. Dejected and listless, Timberlake once again took up the bottle for comfort. And once again Margaret was obligated to toil at O'Neale's hotel to pay for their room and board. Fortunately, biology intervened to brighten the Timberlakes' gloomy state. A healthy daughter, Virginia, was born in 1820.[28]

Andrew Jackson, the victorious general in the First Seminole War, resided at the Franklin House for nearly two months in 1819 while he battled Congressional censure resolutions for his arbitrary behavior in Florida during this war. Eventually the censure resolutions were defeated in both the Senate and the House of Representatives. The general declined O'Neale's offer of a hotel suite but acquiesced when the proprietor added a parlor at no additional cost. During his residence, Jackson spent a number of evenings relaxing with the O'Neale family, during which he became aware of their older daughter's quick wit, candor, and succinct opinions. To Margaret, he gave his greatest compliment: "Young lady, you remind me of my wife."[29]

Five years later, Old Hickory, then John Eaton's co-senator from Tennessee, would spend considerable time during the Congressional sessions of 1823–24 and 1824–25 as a guest of the O'Neales. During these Washington interludes, Jackson developed an increasingly favorable relationship with the then Mrs. Margaret Timberlake.[30]

Meanwhile, John Bowie Timberlake's fortunes continued uninspired, and his previously energetic behavior became listless. His relationship with his wife soured. He perceived that, "Between them there grew a barrier ... that she no longer respected him." Subsequently, Timberlake consulted Dr. Craven, the family physician, for answers; the patient's self-analysis concluded that he was sick of land and needed to return to sea.[31] His wife contemporaneously perceived Timberlake, who once had been an extravagant lover, now to be a dissolute husband, a wastrel more from weakness than wish. However, she remained faithful to him.[32] His wish became a reality through the efforts of his friend John Eaton with the Secretary of the Navy. As a result, Timberlake secured an excellent posting as the Purser of the *Shark*, one of the largest vessels of the U.S. Navy. He sailed in mid–1821.

Her husband's departure opened a gap in Margaret's social life which was filled conveniently by the return to the nation's capital of the newly re-elected Senator John Eaton. Eaton, then a long-time friend of Mrs. Timberlake, gentlemanly but naively and inappropriately, squired the beautiful Grass Widow Margaret all around town to balls and dinner parties and was her companion on private long walks around the capital city. "Best of all they liked their walks in the woods."[33]

Senator Eaton boldly escorted Mrs. Timberlake to President Monroe's White House ball held for members of the Senate. This action was beyond protocol for the easily offended First Lady Elizabeth Monroe. She promptly disinvited Margaret from all future White House events. The rejection of Peggy in the spring of 1821 was "based exclusively on moral grounds." A woman who appeared unfaithful to her husband was not welcome in polite company.[34]

Queena Pollack, a Margaret biographer, illustrated the situation. Margaret was indiscreet in her impetuosity. She sat on the porch after full dinners at the Franklin House where she talked with Eaton, even after the other guests had retired. "Peg, unfortunately, was an utterly natural person, free from conventionality and cant." She previously was admitted into good society, "but about the year 1821, Mrs. Monroe, the wife of the then President, sent her a message desiring her not to come to their drawing rooms." Congressman, later Governor, Wheeler avowed perversely, "Whilst I was in Congress, she was considered as a lady who would be willing to dispense her favors wherever she took a fancy."[35]

Andrew Jackson, newly appointed as a senator from Tennessee, returned in late 1823 to once again lodge at the O'Neale's.[36] The other Tennessee senator, John Eaton, remained an habitual O'Neale boarder. The genial hotelier provided a suite where Jackson would be served his dinners in private. John Eaton was regularly invited to dine with his fellow senator. Captain Richard K. Call, a former comrade-in-arms and presently a Florida delegate to the government, was another boarder who also ate most of his meals in the Jackson suite. A fourth attendee, first as a waitress at Jackson's request, was Margaret, the proprietor's daughter. "And it soon became habitual for her to join them after dinner for coffee" to participate in their conversations.[37]

However, Richard Call, far from both Florida and his fiancée, was intemperate and lecherous. He mistook Margaret's somewhat flirtatious congeniality for sexual availability. Abetted by tavern tales about her supposed lack of virtue, Call returned to O'Neale's from a nightly social in a lustful and possibly inebriated condition. There he found Mrs. Timberlake alone and he forced himself upon her. Much to his disappointment, his combative prey seized the fireplace tongs and beat her assailant repeatedly. Call was forced from the room.[38] A second biographer confirmed that Richard Call, "had apparently tried to take her in his arms, and urge her to more affectionate abandon. With his great strength, he had almost forced her to a settee near the fire, when she grasped the fire-shovel in one hand, the tongs in the other," and forced her attacker from the room.[39]

In tears Margaret quickly related the attempted seduction to Andrew Jackson. The chivalrous warrior, always protective of women in distress, immediately summoned Call to his suite to deliver a ferocious rebuke. The senator severely castigated his former subordinate and warned Call against any future misconduct. Subsequently, the foiled rapist avoided Margaret and moved to lodge at another Washington hotel. Unfortunately, he altered his mode of aggressive behavior towards her; instead of a physical attack, he spread verbal slanders. At his new hotel, he passed along his aspersions, labeling her as an "easy woman" to his tavern companions. In addition, the embarrassed and vengeful Call wrote to Jackson confidante and John Eaton's former brother-in-law, William B. Lewis, to condemn the Eaton-Margaret relationship.[40]

Andrew Jackson responded to Lewis's subsequent inquiry, saying

VIII—Margaret Eaton: Wife of His Secretary of War   99

that he, "had never seen or heard aught against the chastity of Mrs. Timberlake that was calculated to raise even a suspicion of her virtue in the mind of any who was not under the influence of deep prejudice or prone to jealousy."[41]

Jackson had repeatedly mentioned Margaret in his letters to Rachel: "She was lively, sweet, and much maligned, amiable, and free of the vices of which she is accused. Her wit relieved him when he suffered from 'gloom of the spirits.'"[42] The senator found Margaret enchanting, as he wrote in another letter, "We are in the family of Mr. O'Neale whose amiable pious wife and two daughters, one married and one single, take every pains in their power to make us comfortable and agreeable.... Mrs. Timberlake ... plays on the Piano delightfully, and every Sunday evening entertains her pious mother with sacred music...."[43] In July 1824, after Timberlake left for sea again, his wife presented him with a second daughter, Margaret, who was named after her mother. The pregnancy was difficult; Dr. Craven, the O'Neale family physician, put the expectant mother to bed for six weeks.[44]

Andrew Jackson returned to Washington with Rachel for the 1824–25 Congressional session. Bill O'Neale, after some financial difficulties, was once again the proprietor of a hotel, Gadsby's, which was the renamed Franklin House. The ever-gracious O'Neale provided the Jacksons with a suite. Rachel Jackson and Rhoda O'Neale became fast friends, deeply enjoying each other's company. Margaret won Mrs. Jackson's favor by behaving naturally in her presence. This sealed the young woman in Andrew Jackson's approbation. However, undisclosed to the senator was Margaret's written impression of Mrs. Jackson. It was not favorable; it described the guest as, "a large, portly woman with a sweet benevolent face, who always insisted on having prayers."[45]

While his wife continued to enjoy Washington, her spouse at sea, John Timberlake, had stumbled into a valuable posting as purser aboard the U.S. Navy heavy frigate, the *Constitution*. John Eaton, through his contacts, had secured this prize position in spite of the hapless purser's continued difficulties with the Navy over his sloppy account books.[46] Timberlake had continued his friendship with the senator; the two corresponded even while the one was at sea.[47]

Timberlake died in his bunk aboard the *Constitution* on the night of April 2, 1828. The ship had left Greece on its way to Spain and was anchored off Port Mahon in the Spanish Balearic Islands. Preceding his death, he wrote a sixteen-page letter to his wife that expressed his joy at their planned reunion in Europe; enclosed within was the passage money for Margaret and their two daughters for their travel.[48]

"The ship surgeon wrote in its official log that the cause of his death was 'pulmonary disease.'"⁴⁹ When the news of Timberlake's death reached Washington, rumors quickly abounded; gossip concluded that he died from drink, but more universally, that he committed suicide either by jumping overboard or slashing his throat, despondent over his wife's affair with Eaton.⁵⁰

The latter rumor was both base and false. A shipmate officer said that the deceased purser spoke frequently of his wife and children with the strongest terms of affection. Secondly, a pulmonary cause of death is supported by Margaret's recall that Timberlake was an asthmatic during their entire married life. Dr. Sims, a family physician, treated John's asthma at least once; Margaret even bled her husband during his asthmatic attack. Commodore Patterson of the U.S. Navy told Mrs. Timberlake that sometimes on the cruise, he saw the purser so tortured by an asthmatic attack that he grew black in the face. "Black as any negro I ever owned," was the Commodore's expression. Finally, the deceased's will bequeathed both his watch and his ring to his friend Eaton.⁵¹

Margaret mourned her husband; she went into seclusion.⁵² Eaton, still in the Senate, devoted all his time to Andrew Jackson's 1828 presidential campaign. Meanwhile, Washington continued to gossip about the presumed Timberlake-Eaton romance.⁵³

Andrew Jackson was overwhelmingly elected as America's seventh president in November 1828. Thereafter, Eaton and his lady needed to solve their personal dilemma. John Eaton, informed that he could expect a significant cabinet post in the new Jackson administration, became concerned not only for his own sake, but also for the liaison's effect upon Andrew Jackson's presidency. His worry over this latter contingency proved prescient.

Margaret at the time was very fond of Old Hickory and would become even fonder. Many years later she would write in her *Autobiography*, "I would rather Andrew Jackson had lived and died believing me as a vestal virgin, than to have heaped upon me all the wretched, vapid, sycophantic complements of the paid writers...."⁵⁴ She also confided, "Me he always treated like a little girl.... He thought me bright-witted. He was to me like a second father, and I never took advantage. I never sought his personal influence in my behalf."⁵⁵

Eaton appealed to the incoming president to resolve the lovers' dilemma. He wrote, "...another & delicate subject.... She who had in association with me, being censured by a gossiping world had been placed in a situation by the hand of Providence where it was in my power by interposing myself, to snatch her from the injustice which has been done her. Under such circumstances it was not possible to hesitate what was right & proper to be done."⁵⁶ To this delicate question, the

VIII—Margaret Eaton: Wife of His Secretary of War

President's resolute and direct response was, "If you love Margaret Timberlake, go and marry her at once and shut their mouths," and "Marry her and then you will be in a position to defend her."[57]

With his mentor's blessing, Eaton hastened back to Washington, and, in the presence of the O'Neales, proposed to Margaret. The marriage of Margaret O'Neale Timberlake and John Henry Eaton took place on January 1, 1829. The chaplain of the Senate officiated in his office, attended by William and Rhoda O'Neale and Margaret's two daughters. The bride was twenty-nine, the groom in his forties.

Jackson's fond attachment to Mrs. Eaton did not wane after he achieved the presidency. She even was able to gently chide the volatile general in front of many after Jackson asserted that he had never set foot on foreign soil. Margaret boldly corrected, "I guess you forgot that when you went to Florida, General." When Jackson became visibly embarrassed and his audience upset, she cleverly added, "It didn't stay foreign for very long after you got there."[58]

IX

Rachel, Emily and Margaret
The Eaton Affair

"...my heart is nearly broke. I try to summon up my usual fortitude but it is vain, the time, the sudden & afflictive shock, was as severe as unexpected...."
—January 7, 1829, letter AJ (Hermitage) to John Coffee, *Jackson Papers VII*, pp. 12–13

Mrs. Eaton posed "a bad temper and a meddlesome disposition," which "has been too much increased by her husband's elevation to make her society too disagreeable to be endured."
—Emily Donelson's impression of Margaret Eaton, 1829. Cheathem, Mark R.: *Old Hickory's Nephew: The Political and Personal Struggles of Andrew Jackson Donelson*, pp. 66–7

"The lady who presided there was never friendly to me. She was always jealous of what she supposed to be my influence over Gen. Jackson. Perhaps also she may have learned that my husband ... had no confidence in her husband, A.J. Donelson [sic].... I was always exceedingly careful about visiting the White House."
—Peggy Eaton referring to Emily Donelson: *The Autobiography of Peggy Eaton*, pp. 91–2

Andrew Jackson's political ambition was satisfied, at least temporarily, with his inauguration as the seventh president of the United States on March 4, 1829. However, his success as president, at least for the better part of the first of his two terms (1829–1833), was influenced, even complicated, by three women.

Rachel, his beloved wife, had passed away at the age of sixty-one years, barely three months earlier. She had been an intimate witness, an unwilling participant, and probably a victim, of the vicious presidential campaign of 1828. Her memory was almost a constant on the president's mind when he entered the White House. His awareness of Rachel's love, support, and virtue would provide the milieu within which he would judge the motives, actions, and behaviors of others.

Two other females, both young, determined, and outspoken, filled the void created by his wife's absence. There was to be no First Lady in the Jackson White House. Instead, there would be a surrogate to perform many of the non-conjugal responsibilities of a presidential wife. Emily Donelson, married to her cousin, the president's private secretary Andrew Jackson Donelson, became the social hostess and the principal female presence in the Executive Mansion.

Margaret (Peggy) Eaton, widowed but newly wedded to John Eaton, Andrew Jackson's incoming Secretary of War, fulfilled Old Hickory's chivalrous impulse to protect and even to champion a woman under unjustified attack. Just as he passionately defended Rachel's honor against vicious rumors, Jackson obsessively protected Margaret from charges of scandal. He viewed Mrs. Eaton as a reflection of his abused, now deceased, Rachel.

Unfortunately for the president, there was mutual disrespect and even antipathy between the two young women. The antagonism between Margaret Eaton and Emily Donelson became unrelenting and consequential. Their positions, one as the wife of a prominent Cabinet member who was an intimate friend, a significant political ally, and first biographer of Andrew Jackson, and the second by virtue of her role as mistress of his White House, inevitably drew public attention to their conflict and inevitably magnified its consequences.

A political scandal, known mainly as *The Eaton Affair*, and less frequently, as *The Petticoat Affair*, or *The Petticoat Malaria*, consumed Jackson's early presidency. Its effects upon Jackson were major: the dissolution of his Cabinet; the alienation and possibly the eventual resignation of his vice president; and the temporary banishment of both his presidential secretary and his social hostess, both close kin, from the White House.

If only Rachel had lived, Emily Donelson's role in the Executive Mansion would have been diminished significantly, Jackson's inherent anger and paranoia might have lessened significantly, and her generosity of spirit, religious temperament, and maturity of conduct likely would have healed or significantly muted the social ostracism of Margaret O'Neale Eaton, the daughter of a saloonkeeper.

Jackson in Mourning for Rachel Jackson

Andrew's profound grief over the loss of his wife was evident almost immediately in his correspondence even before his inauguration. Although his past absences from Rachel—military, political, or economic—were frequent, in his mind, she was ever present. For many decades she remained his emotional and psychological bulwark; undoubtedly, he had intended that she would continue by his side in the White House.

On January 7, 1829, he lamented to his close friend John Coffee: "...my heart is nearly broke. I try to summon up my usual fortitude but it is vain, the time, the sudden & afflictive shock, was as severe as unexpected...."[1] Later, a letter of lamentation from the White House was sent to the Marquis de Lafayette: "...melancholy pleasure in knowing that the dispensation of Providence which has thrown over my future days the mantle of sorrow, has engaged your sympathies."[2] A May 16, 1829, letter to the Sumner County, Tennessee, minister Hardy Murfree Cryer bemoaned, "...in the night I retire to my chambers.... It is then I feel the great weight of the late affliction of providence...."[3]

His sorrow lingered, which both deepened and compounded his loneliness. The void was allayed only partially by the presence of Andrew and Emily Donelson and the frequent White House visits of his cabinet friends, Secretary of War John Eaton and Secretary of State Martin Van Buren. A February 1830 letter to the wife of his military colleague, R.K. Call, plaintively evoked his persistent sorrow: "...she is gone. And alas, all my happiness here below—altho surrounded with company & labour, still I never cease to mourn her *loss*."[4] A subsequent letter of reply to Robert Minns Burton, a Tennessee lawyer and a Donelson connection, had this doleful response, "...occasioned tears to flow, which will never cease to flow, for departed worth...."[5]

The not yet twenty-two-year-old Emily Donelson came to Washington in 1829 as the wife of her Uncle Jackson's secretary, Andrew Jackson Donelson. Her husband was part of Jackson's Kitchen Cabinet, an unofficial group of advisers that consisted of his closest friends and political advisers.[6] The president charged his nephew with the maintenance of the Book of Applicants, those seeking government appointments. This was a major responsibility, since Jackson's supporters had every expectation of patronage as a reward for their past allegiance. The strategy was that success in securing a sinecure would strap subsequent support around Jackson's future policies. Moreover, the president required a capable scribe to attend to his mountainous paperwork and for him, "Donelson's writing skills were his biggest asset."[7]

Margaret (Peggy) Eaton, the new bride of Jackson intimate Secretary of War John Eaton, had become the president's friend, first meeting him in 1823.[8] Margaret's unsavory reputation, either by rumor or in fact, was the hub of the *Eaton Affair*, a political firestorm that inflamed the presidency for the subsequent two and a half years.[9] Andrew Jackson, imagining that Margaret's woes were a repetition of the defamations hurled against his beloved Rachel by his political enemies, became her foremost defender. He conflated Rachel's treatment with that of Margaret.[10]

The Emily-Margaret Brawl

To describe the feelings between the two women as just ordinary social incompatibility would be an understatement. "Disrespect," "scorn," and "hostile alienation" more aptly defined their antagonism. Their relationship became a subsidiary, yet a still significant thread, of the fabric that clothed the *Eaton Scandal*. Unfortunately, their feud seriously affected the ambience within the Jackson White House, disrupted its comfortable atmosphere, and, to some extent, disturbed the mind and personality of its principal occupant, Andrew Jackson. The antagonism between Emily Donelson and Margaret Timberlake Eaton accelerated the political firestorm that engulfed the early Jackson presidency. Their mutual animosity became a significant thread that weaved through the *Eaton Affair*. The *Affair* was protracted, lasting from March 1829 until September 1831.

Earlier, the just-married, seventeen-year-old Emily casually met the older, very sophisticated Margaret O' Neale Timberlake during the 1824–1825 Congressional session while Senator Andrew Jackson lodged at the boarding house operated by Margaret's father. According to Emily, she first met her future opponent in 1824, did not like Margaret, and developed a deep aversion to her.[11] For the young Donelsons, newlyweds, the grueling twenty-eight-day horseback and coach journey to the nation's capital from Nashville substituted for a traditional honeymoon.[12] This was the background when Emily Donelson met Margaret Timberlake for the first time, as the latter rushed to welcome Andrew and Rachel Jackson. Their introduction apparently was less than successful. According to her biographer's description of the meeting, Emily saw "a glamorous beauty, eight years her senior, the mother of three [sic] children whose husband ... was absent at sea—his wife a woman of twenty-five who had been used to the rather free atmosphere of a tavern all her life." Margaret saw in Emily "a frail young thing—titian haired and lovely ... but unused to the ways of the world, unsophisticated, and totally unfit, in her opinion, for the complicated social conditions of the Capital city. There was instant antagonism between them."[13]

In early 1829, soon after the Donelsons arrived in the nation's capital city, Margaret Eaton dutifully called upon them in the White House. Emily, perhaps reluctantly, returned the call "to please Uncle." The socially savvy Mrs. Eaton publicized this visit and suggested that she and Emily were best friends. Unfortunately for Margaret, this was a major faux pas, at least for the young Mrs. Donelson. Emily became disgusted over this attempt to ingratiate herself, and "could not think of visiting her again." She concluded, probably presumptuously, that Mrs. Eaton posed "a bad temper and a meddlesome disposition" which "has been too much increased by her husband's elevation to make her society too disagreeable to be endured."[14]

In early 1829, Margaret was twenty-nine. An acquaintance, attempting to be objective, wrote this description to his absent wife: "Her small, active form, well-rounded and voluptuous, trailed an odor of toilet water, which men were apt to admire more than women. Her apple complexion was still perfect; her large dark eyes, never still, could communicate much ... the generous mouth would yield to immoderate laughter exhibiting the prettiest teeth in Washington."[15]

Emily accentuated her social distance during the March 1829 Inaugural Ball. Twelve hundred guests were present at Caruso's Assembly Rooms, the Ball's venue, to celebrate the new president. The Donelsons were among the guests. They attended along with Vice President and Mrs. Calhoun, Secretary of the Treasury and Mrs. Ingham, and Margaret and John Eaton. Emily and most cabinet women snubbed Mrs. Eaton by ignoring her at every function on Inauguration Day. Her prior reputation together with her modest family background definitely contributed to her social ostracism. Emily, immature and possibly a social climber, completely accepted the Washington socialites' aversion to Mrs. Eaton. To them it was unthinkable that a former a barmaid in her father's establishments should gain an entree into the capital's prominent social set.[16]

John Eaton responded to his wife's mistreatment in an April letter to Emily. His words, thought by him to be conciliatory, were interpreted by both Emily and Andrew as condescending. Eaton wrote Emily that, "she was young and uninformed of the ways of the malice of her new friends," referring to Mrs. Calhoun, Mrs. Ingham, and the Washington socialite clique in general. He counseled the young woman not to follow the lead of Margaret's detractors. Eaton's subsequent follow-up letter was patronizing, if not intimidating; therein he intimated threateningly that Emily might suffer the same fate as her aunt Rachel if she

IX—Rachel, Emily and Margaret: The Eaton Affair

continued on her present course. To this, the two Donelsons issued a strong reply. Subsequently, all communication between the two couples was suspended for several weeks.[17]

The Navy frigate, *Potomac*, was the next scene in the Emily–Margaret drama. President Jackson brought on board a large contingent of friends for what he expected to be a pleasant and refreshing July sail on the Potomac River to Fort Monroe near Norfolk, Virginia. On board, Emily, seven months pregnant with the Donelson's second child, fainted in the heat. Mrs. Eaton was nearby; in a friendly manner she quickly offered aid to the stricken woman in the form of her fan and cologne bottle. Emily's hostility refused any assistance from Margaret. Mrs. Eaton became understandably bitter by this embarrassing rejection. She viewed Mrs. Donelson's behavior as a significant insult, delivered in public, that plainly illustrated that the president's niece harbored "a disposition not to be intimate with her." Margaret, a short time later while still aboard the *Potomac*, confronted Andrew Donelson. In a brief conversation, she not too subtlety threatened to have the Donelsons removed from the White House in a forced return to Tennessee. This interchange convinced Andrew Donelson that Margaret was deliberately estranging the Donelsons from their uncle Andrew Jackson.[18]

Margaret's *Autobiography* recounted her reception at the White House when she visited the president: "The lady who presided there was never friendly to me. She was always jealous of what she supposed to be my influence over Gen. Jackson. Perhaps also she may have learned that my husband ... had no confidence in her husband, A.J. Donaldson [sic].... I was always exceedingly careful about visiting the White House."[19]

Secretary of State Martin Van Buren, for several reasons (one of which was likely political self-aggrandizement), was drawn into the turmoil by becoming a staunch supporter of both of the Eatons. Van Buren had the distinct advantage of being a widower and not subject to a wife's influence. Emily had criticized Margaret in his presence as disagreeable, meddlesome, and bad-tempered. Van Buren disagreed, opining, "Even if Mrs. Eaton was disagreeable, Emily should not continue to decline her society to the extent she had, considering her role as Jackson's hostess. Similarly, she should not be controlled in her course by other unduly influenced people." In spring 1830, Van Buren tried again to influence the stubborn behavior of the young woman. He visited the White House Hostess and once again encouraged Emily to reconcile with Margaret Eaton. The obstinate young woman again refused the advice of the older man.[20]

President Jackson sought to manage the problem, which continued to be both a distraction to his official responsibilities and an interference to his desired solace and comfort at the White House. In June 1830, he invited Margaret Eaton to join him for dinner at the Executive Mansion. She audaciously, possibly foolishly, declined the invitation, writing, "I could not expect to be happy at your house for this would be to expect a different course of treatment from part of your family, different ever yet it has been my good fortune to meet. You meet on such occasions to enjoy ourselves, but there would be none to me.... I ask to say to you that whatever may be the cause of the unkind treatment I have recd from those under your roof...."[21]

Donelson, as Jackson's private secretary, screened the president's correspondence. Upon perusing Mrs. Eaton's letter, he sought to justify the actions of his wife and himself in order to protect their standing with their uncle. Donelson angrily appended this footnote to the confidential letter: "All is imaginary or worse ... letter abundant evidence of the indelicacy which distinguishes her character, and is disgraceful to her husband." He was furious that Mrs. Eaton had not come to him "*as the head of my family.*" Donelson charged that Margaret had "approached the President with childish importunities ... to pour upon him the poison...." The secretary's pride was immensely offended by Margaret's presumed attack upon his role as leader of his family and home: "In the patriarchal South of Donelson's day, criticism of the male head of a household, especially by a woman, challenged established authority."[22]

The inevitable rupture between Uncle Andrew and his Donelson family occurred the following year during July and August of 1830 in Nashville. Jackson, the Donelsons, and the Eatons travelled to Tennessee for the summer vacation. Boldly, but unwisely, the Donelsons declined to reside at The Hermitage as expected by the president. Instead they stayed with Emily's mother at a nearby plantation in order to avoid the detested Secretary of War and his spouse. The senior Andrew, both affronted and angry, banished his White House Hostess from a return to the Executive Mansion. Emily "would only be allowed to resume her former position as hostess if she was willing to assume that dignified course that ought to have been at first adopted of extending the same comity and attentions to all the heads of Departments and their families."[23]

The Assaults on Mrs. Eaton and Her Defense by the President: Andrew Jackson Considers Margaret as a New Rachel

The *Eaton Affair* was more than a private scuffle between two indignant families. Jackson's troubles with the women in his orbit began

IX—Rachel, Emily and Margaret: The Eaton Affair

shortly after his arrival in Washington in February 1829. He had been there for only a few days when the entire Tennessee congressional delegation called on him. They urged against the appointment of John Eaton to the Cabinet because of his marriage to Margaret Timberlake, a woman of bad reputation. The incoming president emphatically rejected their request by stating that the matter was closed. It was impossible that the honorable Eaton, also a Mason, would ever marry an unworthy woman.[24] Subsequently Jackson complained to close friend John Coffee, "...great exertions have been made by Clay's friends to raise a clamour about my taking Major Eaton into my cabinet, and some of my friends from Tennessee weak enough to be duped by the artifice were made instruments, the object was to intimidate me, from the selection, & thereby destroy Major Eaton ... and Major Eaton will become one of the most popular men in the Departments, to be a great comfort to me...."[25]

Washington society was abuzz with gossipy innuendoes about the former Mrs. Timberlake's virtue, or rather her lack thereof. Her alleged moral transgressions included extramarital assignations with John Eaton and others, hotel trysts with Eaton in New York City boarding houses, and an out-of-wedlock miscarriage.

A few days after his meeting with the Tennessee congressmen, the president received a letter from a friend, the Reverend Ezra Stiles Ely, sent from Philadelphia. It listed a series of unsubstantiated rumors about Margaret Eaton. Ely wrote, "When I left this city I knew nothing of Mrs. Eaton; but some vague reports.... I did not believe anything could be substantiated against her." However, referring to salacious rumors that were current in the nation's capital, the Presbyterian minister urged, "...it would be requiring too much that all the wives of your officers should be above suspicion."

Ezra Ely's correspondence aroused both the president's sense of honor and his grief by raising the ghost of Rachel Jackson. Ely attributed his motive for writing, "...for this reason, *the name of your departed and truly pious wife is stained through Mrs. Eaton.*" This writer claimed that in 1824–5, Rachel Jackson did not return the call of Mrs. Timberlake while in Washington. The gossipy preacher alleged that Mrs. Jackson had feared to place her seal of approval on Margaret.[26] Thereby, Ely inadvertently conflated Margaret's character and ill-treatment with that of the sainted Rachel. The president's characteristic fury and stubborn determination had been aroused. He would vindicate Margaret! He would defeat his enemies!

Always quick to be offended, Jackson immediately identified a political dimension to this controversy. At first Old Hickory singled out his current and chronic political nemesis, Henry Clay of Kentucky, as the instigator of the personal attacks. Henry Clay was the outgoing Secretary of State whose wily backstage maneuvering probably denied Jackson the presidency in 1824. The president wrote to John Coffee, "Much pains were taken to prevent me from Taking Mr. Eaton into the Cabinet, his wife was assailed secretly, in the most shameful manner, & every plan that Clay and his minions, could invent to deter me...."[27] He continued by fulminating to Ely, "...I sincerely regret you did not personally name this subject to me before you left Washington, as I could in that event, have apprised you of the great exertion made by Clay ... to destroy the character of Mrs. Eaton by the foulest and basest means...."[28] Jackson continued to blame Henry Clay in a May letter to Coffee: "There never was a more insidious attempt to intimidate me & to destroy a man, than there was to destroy Eaton. & with him myself."[29]

His exertions to salvage Margaret's reputation accelerated. To the Reverend Ely, he submitted solicited attestations to her character from former boarders at the O'Neale hotel and from his campaign supporters in Baltimore, Pennsylvania, and Ohio. Furthermore, he wrote that Ely was "... badly advised.... Mrs. Jackson to the last moment of her life believed Mrs. Eaton to be an innocent and much injured woman so far as it relates to the tale about her and Mr. Eaton.... She believed it a base slander."[30]

Jackson next determined to expose the fiction that Purser Timberlake was distraught and suicidal over his wife's liaison with Senator Eaton. Instead, Mrs. Eaton's first husband, when alive, possessed a positive view of her second. In rebuttal, Jackson informed Tennessean John McLemore that Margaret's husband previously had given his friend John Eaton power of attorney over the Timberlake estate. Under lawyer Eaton's careful management, Mrs. Timberlake was saved $25,000.[31] In the same correspondence, Jackson wrote, "I did not come here to make a cabinet for the Ladies of this place ... but for myself."[32]

Moreover, he corrected his former military subordinate R.K. Call regarding any supposed hostility between Eaton and Timberlake. Instead, "The purchase of the Tobaco [sic] pouch & Turkish pipe but two weeks before his death & sent to me 'Through his friend Major Eaton' was conclusive in my mind, that until that period no information could have reached him [Timberlake] that could have lessened his confidence in Major Eaton." In further rebuttal the president enclosed two letters from shipmates of the purser who could not recall any opprobrium by Timberlake towards John Eaton.[33]

Richard Call had been unmasked as one of the principal slanderers of Mrs. Eaton's reputation. Despite this, he continued his slurs in letters to his former commander.[34] Finally Jackson, exhausted by the deceitful

IX—Rachel, Emily and Margaret: The Eaton Affair

and ignoble man, confronted his former subordinate with a warning regarding his 1824 assault upon the then Mrs. Timberlake: "...would place you, in the discussion before the public, should one take place, in a very unpleasant situation...." His bitter anger was underlined by his implying that Call was guilty of one of Jackson's most despised sins, disloyalty, stating,

> ...you cannot regret more than I do that you assisted in giving currency to any reports about Major Eaton and his wife at the time you did. That the hired slanderers of Mr. Clay should have attempted to destroy Major Eaton and through him to reach me ... but when my own personal & confidential friends should have aided in such an unhallowed work by lending their countenance to such unfounded falsehoods.... I must confess that I was both astonished and mortified."[35]

Meanwhile, the Reverend Ely was convinced that Margaret Eaton had been falsely attacked. He offered to assist in her exoneration by visiting New York City to disprove the tales of her illicit boarding house trysts with John Eaton. Ely shortly ascertained to his satisfaction that these reports were untrue.[36]

President Jackson continually personalized the attacks on Margaret Eaton. He interpreted the *Eaton Affair* as both a personal and a political assault upon him. In his view, Margaret Eaton's character was targeted in order to discredit the Secretary of War, the president's close ally, and to drive Eaton from his cabinet. Not his self-esteem, not his honor, not his belligerence, could permit this. Moreover, the memory of his beloved Rachel, ever present in the background, encouraged his intensified efforts. The result was that he harnessed his prodigious energy to exonerate Mrs. Eaton and confront her detractors.

Jackson previously solicited letters in support of Margaret's character. Responses from Samuel Fisher Bradford, Peter Brady, James Inslee Anderson, John Ellsworth Hyde, and a long-time acquaintance of the accused only identified "as a pious matron of the Washington Methodist Church," all attested to her innocence. Bradford, at Jackson's urging, likewise personally investigated the rumors of the Eatons' clandestine assignations in New York City, and found them to be false. Instead, Mrs. Timberlake visited the city in the company of John Timberlake, her husband, and William O'Neale, her father.[37]

Margaret Eaton, accustomed to defending herself from slander and criticism in general, upon knowledge of his accusatory letter rushed to Philadelphia to confront the Reverend Ely. A six-hour contentious interview ensued. The offended women charged, "You have turned aside from your high calling to clap this slander on my back." The minister, challenged by the woman's boldness, defensively divulged that the Reverend John Nicholson Campbell was the source of Ely's written accusations.

Ironically, Campbell was the Presbyterian Minister who presided over the Washington Church that both the President and Margaret Eaton attended.[38]

Subsequently, both Eatons confronted Campbell at the reverend's Washington home. They were furious, but the minister was defensive and adamant in maintaining his assertions, especially the tale that Margaret suffered a miscarriage in 1821 when Timberlake, then her spouse was away at sea. Overcome with anger and frustration, Margaret slipped and nearly fainted. Fortunately, she quickly recovered in time to restrain her enraged husband from striking the minister. Thereafter, exhausted, she took to her bed. That evening the president visited the Eatons. When apprised of their confrontation with Campbell, Jackson remarked in typical fashion, "Major, how could you keep your hands off the scoundrel?"[39]

Soon afterwards, the president participated in several meetings with John Campbell. The last was a showdown that included the president, the president's secretary, the Reverends Ely and Campbell, and the entire Cabinet, except Secretary of War Eaton. On this occasion, Jackson, with the assistance of Navy personnel records, refuted Campbell's allegation that Margaret became pregnant while Timberlake was overseas. The dates, the pregnancy, and the allegations of so-called witnesses, all components of Campbell's tale, were disproved completely.[40] Shortly afterwards, an enraged John Eaton wrote the Reverend Campbell to demand that Campbell either prove or retract his story on Mrs. Timberlake Eaton's miscarriage. The minister refused to speak except in a court of law, where he would appear, "with perfect confidence of the results." The Secretary of War rejected this reply; he scorned the idea of settling a personal wrong with a lawsuit and demanded satisfaction. He castigated Campbell as both a liar and a coward.[41] Campbell later reneged on his promise to the president to maintain silence in the Eaton Affair. He blamed John Eaton for his retraction and promised in no way to correct or change his prior allegations of wrong-doing. Campbell escaped Eaton's challenge to a duel by invoking his exemption as a minister.[42]

Andrew Jackson took on Margaret's enemies, first Ely, who became convinced that Mrs. Eaton was a victim and remained a friend of the president. The second was Campbell, against whom he remained unyielding in his hostility, commenting in letters to Samuel Swartwout and John Christian McLemore. To McLemore he wrote, "the horror and disgust for a Clergyman who professes to be the ambassador of Christ ... secret slanderer of his neighbor...."[43] The president's disgust with Campbell did not wane. He wrote Ely, "His conduct has done the Presbyterian

IX—Rachel, Emily and Margaret: The Eaton Affair

Society much injury, as well as the cause of religion generally." Additionally, the president quit attending Campbell's Second Presbyterian Church in Washington.[44]

Henry Clay of Kentucky was a long-time political opponent of Andrew Jackson.[45] Moreover, the Kentuckian was once known to disparage Mrs. Timberlake Eaton's virtue, both past and present. "Age cannot wither nor time stale her infinite virtue," he was quoted saying sarcastically at a Washington party.[46] As Secretary of State, the Kentuckian was a major Adams' strategist in his 1828 reelection campaign against the Tennessee general. It was claimed that in this role, Henry Clay was behind the initiative to defame Rachel. Jackson contended the allegation was true; Clay strongly averred that the charge was false. In this contentious milieu, the president delighted in Clay's political setbacks, writing in 1830 to W.B. Lewis, a close political and personal ally, "The news from Kentucky of the late election is quite grateful. Clay has lost a majority in the State Legislature."[47] Clay refused to withdraw from the political area; the inveterate campaigner challenged the incumbent Jackson in the 1832 presidential campaign. Old Hickory, the victor in the contest, had his final revenge.

During the first months of 1829, Clay's machinations were savaged in correspondence with Coffee, Ely, John McLemore, and the disloyal Richard Keith Call. The president's initial analysis of the *Eaton Affair* continued to be that it was principally a political maneuver to intimidate Secretary of War Eaton, force him to resign his Cabinet post, and thereby damage the president. Jackson wrote, "The hired slanderers of Mr. Clay should have attempted to destroy Major Eaton and through him to reach me...." The principal target of the attacks upon Margaret were, Jackson thought initially, was not her personal reputation, but rather the success of his presidency: "I have not the least doubt but that every secret rumor is circulated by the minions of Mr. Clay for the purpose of injuring Mrs. Eaton and through her Mr. Eaton...."[48]

Henry Clay's position as the principal political antagonist in the mind of Andrew Jackson was vacated by the beginning of 1830. His Vice President, John C. Calhoun, would unconditionally fill this spot. At first the president only referenced his vice president by allusion: "...the base hypocrisy of this *great secret agent*..." "the combination & conspiracy to injure & prostrate Major Eaton—and injure me—I see the *great Magicians* [sic] hand in all of this."[49] These and numerous other literary fulminations illustrated Jackson's narcissism and self absorption; he obsessively believed that the rumors against Margaret were really directed against her husband, but more importantly, against him.

The *Eaton Affair* was one of several matters that alienated the president from his vice president. Jackson discovered in 1830 that many years earlier, Calhoun, while serving in the Monroe cabinet as Secretary of War, had strongly condemned General Jackson's actions during the Seminole War. For years Calhoun deceitfully suggested that he had supported Jackson and not disavowed him in this matter. For Jackson, personal disloyalty added upon falsehood could never be forgiven. In addition, major differences of opinion in important national matters progressively separated the two: state's rights, the indissolubility of the Union, and the tariff, among other issues. John Calhoun's philosophy of government asserted the primacy of the state over that of the United States federal government. As a result, he was a prominent advocate of South Carolina's movement to nullify the new United States tariff.[50] The effect was that Calhoun's political stock waned. He realized that his immediate, even his eventual, prospects for the presidency were in ruins. He was appointed as senator from his home state, and then resigned as vice president three months before the expiration of his term.[51]

Mrs. Eaton's detractors were legion: the Society Ladies of Washington; the Donelsons, Andrew J and Emily who were members of his family; and three cabinet secretaries, Navy Secretary John Branch, Treasury Secretary Samuel Ingham, and Attorney General John Macpherson Berrien. The Washington Ladies were dismissed; Emily Donelson was banished from the White House for a year, and her husband's close allegiance with Uncle Jackson was weakened; the three cabinet members were fired.[52]

Floride Calhoun was the thirty-seven-year-old wife of Vice President John C. Calhoun. As such, she would be the highest-ranking woman in the incoming administration of Andrew Jackson, a widower. She, like her husband, was an aristocratic South Carolinian who abided by the traditional gender roles of Southern society. "She was to exemplify submissiveness, piety, purity, and domesticity ... to be the repository of goodness, thereby ensuring the survival of a moral society.... Her job was to stay out of the world, but at the same time ensure that the world remained properly moral in the face of all the assaults against it."[53]

The Eatons paid the appropriate courtesy call at the Calhouns' Washington residence before Jackson's inauguration. Floride received them politely. However, she decided after discussion with her husband not to repay their visit. She deliberately snubbed Margaret, basing her resolution on the Society Ladies' banishment of the woman from their social acceptance. According to Mrs. Calhoun, Margaret did not fulfill the role of a proper woman in Washington society.[54]

Floride signaled her rejection at the incoming President's Inaugural

IX—Rachel, Emily and Margaret: The Eaton Affair

Ball by publicly avoiding any contact with the wife of the incoming Secretary of War. Thereby she served as an exemplar for those society women who disapproved of Mrs. Eaton. Included in her circle were Mrs. Ingham and Emily Donelson. "She was left alone and kept at a respectful distance from these virtuous and distinguished women with the ... exception of a seat at the supper table ... notwithstanding her proximity, she was not spoken to by them."[55] Mrs. Calhoun soon departed for her South Carolina estate, in reality a classic Southern plantation. Some viewed this as a convenient way of shunning the "scarlet woman." However, in previous years she had seldom accompanied her husband to the nation's capital. She shunned the seat of government during the rest of Jackson's presidency.

President Jackson in 1829 was obsessed with finding a solution to the *Petticoat Affair*. Old Hickory, both hypersensitive and self centered, inevitably interpreted the Eatons' travails as attacks upon himself and upon the success of his presidency. An inescapable question arises: Was his presidency damaged? The most satisfactory answer is:

> Probably Not!
> A principal reason was that the new Congress was out of town during most of 1829. The Twenty-first Congress of the United States was selected in November 1828 at the same time that the seventh United States president was elected. It met in special session from March 4–17, 1829, to approve the Jackson cabinet. It then adjourned until December 7, 1829. At the time it was customary for Congress to avoid the capital's unpleasant and malarial summers, only to recommence the nation's business in a more comfortable Washington in December.[56]

However, during the lengthy legislative hiatus, the executive branch of the United States government continued to function. Its cabinet officers were in place and at work. Jackson was busy with innumerable requests for jobs in his government, to which he wrote this salty response, "I have been crowded with thousands of applications for office, and if I had a tit, for every applicant to suck the Treasury pap, all would go away well satisfied."[57] He also confronted fraud in the Navy department and had his eyes on the country's foreign relations, especially with the governments of Mexico and France.[58] Regarding domestic affairs, Treasury Secretary Samuel Ingham initiated important discussions about a new policy towards the Bank of the United States.[59]

In December 1829 the Congress convened, the Washington social season restarted, and the Eaton frenzy rekindled. The president was forced to confront anew the Ladies of Washington, the members of his Cabinet (and indirectly their wives), and, with the most difficulty, his own kin, Emily and Andrew Jackson Donelson.

X

Emily and Margaret
The Eaton Affair Denouement

"John C. Calhoun is at the bottom of this."
—Peggy Eaton, *The Autobiography
of Peggy Eaton*, 88–9

"I believe no lady has been more basely slandered or cruelly persecuted than Mrs. Eaton."
—Andrew Jackson to Susan Wheeler Decatur,
January 2, 1830, *The Papers
of Andrew Jackson VIII*, 5

According to tradition, the Capital's social season was contemporaneous with the Congressional session, both commencing in December of each calendar year. December 1829 witnessed the customary Washington convening of senators, congressmen, senior government officials, the foreign diplomatic corps, and those Americans who wished to do business with the United States government. The season of dinners, balls, and all forms of socializing launched for another year.

It was up to Andrew Jackson as the president to preside at the first official dinner of his cabinet. He delayed its scheduling until November 26, 1829, in the hope that during the summer hiatus, the social rancor of the previous spring had receded. He was disappointed. All members of his cabinet and all representatives of the foreign service with their wives attended the affair. John and Floride Calhoun, both still in South Carolina, were absent. Unfortunately, Margaret was again shunned by the usual suspects. She was humiliated.[1]

Subsequently, Vice President Calhoun declined the opportunity to officiate at the second formal cabinet dinner of the social year; Floride Calhoun, his wife, remained in South Carolina. Therefore, the Calhouns were spared the obligation of entertaining, and thereby socially

X—Emily and Margaret: The Eaton Affair Denouement

accepting, Mrs. Eaton. Martin van Buren, as Secretary of State, was the next senior government official in line. Although a widower, the former governor of New York eagerly accepted the responsibility to host the second official dinner of the season. His reasons may have been as much political as social.

At this early stage of the Jacksonian presidency, the astute Martin Van Buren realized that he would earn the president's gratitude by openly supporting the societal acceptance of Margaret Eaton. As the dinner's host, the Secretary of State was both attentive and gracious to Margaret. Van Buren had already concluded that his rival for political advancement, at least where Jackson was concerned, was Vice President Calhoun. Therefore, his support for the Eatons would serve only to ingratiate the Secretary of State with the president.

The maneuverings of these two seasoned politicians over the reputation and social acceptance of Margaret O'Neale Eaton, a tavern-owner's daughter, certainly affected the careers of both. *The Eaton Malaria* was a significant, but far from the only, factor for the New Yorker's ascent at the expense of the South Carolinian. Van Buren's allegiance was easy, uncomplicated for the widower, and agreeable since he was fond of both Eatons. It proved to be great leverage with Andrew Jackson. The vice president of the United States, realizing that his national ascendancy was thwarted, resigned his post early to become known most familiarly as the secessionist senator from South Carolina. His rival Van Buren, re-earning the epithet "The Little Magician," succeeded Calhoun as vice president, and later Jackson as president.

Floride Calhoun was a Southern aristocrat who shared a plantation with her husband. She had married John Calhoun at age eighteen or nineteen and bore him ten children. John Calhoun was twenty-eight when he wed Floride. The bride and groom were second cousins, and just as in Tennessee, cousin marriages in South Carolina were common at the time.[2]

Floride Calhoun was an infrequent visitor to Washington during her husband's vice presidency (1824–1832). However, she attended Jackson's inauguration and became the catalyst for Washington society's ostracism of Margaret Eaton: "When she refused to socialize with Peggy Eaton or return her calls, the other cabinet wives followed suit. Floride's action put Calhoun in an awkward position but he honored her decision because he knew that nothing anyone did or said would shake her resolve."[3]

Andrew Jackson, initially a political ally of his vice president, gradually distanced himself, first over the *Eaton Affair*, subsequently over a personal matter, and later due to significant policy disagreements. The personal matter was Jackson's surprise that Calhoun, a decade earlier, had been both disloyal and deceitful towards him. In late 1829, the president was startled to learn that John C. Calhoun, then Secretary of War in the Monroe cabinet, had condemned, rather than supported, as presumed, Old Hickory's conduct during the first Seminole War in Florida. Politically, their positions on states' rights, the tariff, and state nullification of federal law clashed, widening their estrangement. The final alienation occurred in 1832 when Calhoun petulantly cast the deciding vote that killed his rival Van Buren's nomination for the ambassadorship to England.[4]

Very early in the Jackson presidency, the Eatons perceptively concluded that, "John C. Calhoun is at the bottom of this." John Eaton subsequently advised Margaret that the *Eaton Affair* was a political matter and that she should prepare herself to become a target during the ensuing political battle.[5]

The 1829–1830 Washington social season continued without any lessening of the ferocious female friction. Mrs. Eaton remained ostracized not only by the ladies of the capital, but more importantly, by the wives of three cabinet members, and most significantly, by Emily Donelson, who not only was Jackson's niece but also served as his official hostess. The behavior of the anti–Mrs. Eaton cabal alienated Jackson and additionally consumed his time, attention, and energy. Meanwhile, he continued his efforts, both substantial and continuous, to resolve the situation, which was both annoying and acrimonious.

Martin Van Buren, increasingly accommodating and supportive of the president, had his own plans to rehabilitate the standing of Margaret. He organized two dinners at his home; for the first he cleverly invited Martha Jefferson Randolph, the widowed daughter of President Thomas Jefferson, to be the guest of honor. Van Buren's ploy was ineffective since every cabinet member including John Eaton accepted the invitation for himself but excused the female members of his family.[6] Margaret did attend the secretary's second dinner, but once again her enemies chose not to attend. Underlying social tension likely contributed to a confrontation on the dance floor between Mrs. Eaton and socialite Mrs. Macomb after both ladies inadvertently bumped into each other. Fiery words created a scene which the diplomatic Secretary of State managed to resolve.[7]

Van Buren continued to try. His diplomatic allies Sir Charles Vaughan, minister to England, and Baron Paul de Krudener, minister to Russia, gave balls to which they explicitly invited Margaret. She appeared, but once again her female nemeses did not. An incident marred the tranquility of Baron de Krudener's festive celebration.

X—Emily and Margaret: The Eaton Affair Denouement 119

Madame Constantia Huygens, the wife of Dutch minister Chevalier Bangeman Huygens, refused to sit next to Margaret at the dinner table; almost immediately the Huygens undiplomatically retired. Madame Huygens exacerbated the conflict by announcing that the minister and she would give a party to which the Eatons would most definitely not be invited.[8]

The president was informed of Madame Huygens' public intent to ostracize Mrs. Eaton. Jackson was furious; he viewed Huygens' behavior as a personal attack upon him; it was an egregious diplomatic breach that required that the minister be recalled by the Dutch government. He asked his Secretary of State to proceed with the Dutch government. The three members of the Calhoun cabinet clique, Berrien, Branch, and Ingham, soon intensified the cabinet's discord; all three hosted events to which Margaret was not invited, thereby cementing her social alienation.[9]

His cabinet's disharmony with its rumor- and gossip-driven disunity exasperated Andrew Jackson. Inherently a man of action and never one to passively watch events take their course, Old Hickory decided to confront the three cabinet members at the center of the controversy. Accordingly, he dispatched Kentucky Congressman Colonel Richard M. Johnson to meet with Attorney General Berrien and Secretaries Branch and Ingham. Johnson, a friend to all three, conveyed the president's dismay over the cabinet's lack of harmony, and importantly for Jackson, his distress that their three families refused to have any social discourse with Margaret Eaton. However, the three were reluctant to impose these social demands upon their wives and daughters. Their hesitancy was somewhat suspect, since their explanations showed uncharacteristic wifely deference in an era of male dominance.[10]

Jackson, ever persistent, followed up with individual meetings on January 29 and 30, 1830. His explicit demands for a more amenable social behavior by the three intransigent families is unclear from the historical record. The three recalcitrants claimed that they indignantly repelled the president's ultimatum and agreed to remain in the cabinet only after their president retracted his demand.[11] Jackson transcribed his recollections of these meetings in a Memorandum, softening somewhat his injunction but also disparaging their behavior: "I do not claim the right to interfere in any matter in the domestic relations or personal intercourse of any member of my Cabinet nor have I in any manner attempted it. But from information, and my own observation.... I am fully impressed with the belief that you and your families have ... taken measures to induce others to avoid intercourse with Mrs. Eaton and sought to exclude her from society and degrade (John Eaton)."[12] This partial compromise permitted the Jackson cabinet to adhere for another year.

The president in this Memorandum and in subsequent letters to Susan Decatur, the wife of the deceased Navy hero, and to Robert Minns Burton, Rachel's nephew-in-law, stressed three themes. The first was the innocence of Mrs. Eaton: " I believe no lady has been more basely slandered or cruelly persecuted than Mrs. Eaton."[13] Secondly, Jackson concluded that John, not Margaret, Eaton was the intended target of the *Eaton Affair*: "...the secrete [sic] & wicked combination to destroy E for political effect, by which, it was to injure me for having taken Major Eaton into my Cabinet...."[14] Finally, the president charged that he was the ultimate target of the political imbroglio: "...upon the fullest and most dispassionate view and consideration of this subject to regard this course in any other light than a wanton disregard of my feelings & a reproach of my official conduct."[15]

A Dysfunctional Cabinet

The abscess that was the social stigma of Mrs. Eaton continued to fester, absorbing Jackson's behavior and attention for another year, until lanced by the resignations of his entire cabinet. The departures of Secretaries Van Buren and Eaton encouraged the president to request the resignations of Secretaries Branch and Ingham and Attorney General Berrien. Jackson's public explanation for his dramatic and unprecedented action was the restoration of harmony to his administration. However, the Navy Secretary's letter to the *U.S. Telegraph* was far more accurate: the cabinet dissolution was caused by "those who attempted to use the power and influence of the Government to compel society to admit her innocence." However, the influence of Margaret (Peggy) O'Neale Timberlake Eaton over the president of the United States continued.[16]

President Jackson had selected his cabinet on the based on political geography rather than merit. Jackson biographer Robert Remini called the cabinet uniformly second-rate with the single exception of Martin Van Buren. It surely ranked among the worst cabinets in the nineteenth century.[17] Secretary of State Van Buren was a New Yorker; Treasury Secretary Ingham was from Pennsylvania; the Secretary of War was a native Tennessean; Southerners Attorney General Berrien hailed from Georgia and Navy Secretary Branch from North Carolina. Postmaster General William Barry was a Kentuckian.

Attorney General John Berrien, previously a U.S. senator from

X—Emily and Margaret: The Eaton Affair Denouement 121

Georgia, initially enjoyed cordial relations with the president. Indeed, in a July 31, 1829, letter, Jackson expressed confidence in Mr. Berrien's rectitude.[18] During the following two years, the active attorney general issued many unchallenged opinions on Army court martials, Army pay and emoluments, pardons, diplomatic immunity, maritime jurisdiction, and Indian removal. An important legal message to Jackson concerned recess appointments to the federal government and bore no trace of discord.[19]

The president's June 15, 1831, letter of dismissal to Berrien stated that there was no dissatisfaction with the attorney general's performance of his duties. Rather it was a necessary action to restore unity to his cabinet. Jackson explained, "...the harmony in feeling so necessary to an efficient administration had failed in a considerable degree...."[20] However, Berrien did not go quietly into the night; he publicly criticized Jackson for his year-earlier insistence that the families of cabinet members socialize with Mrs. Eaton and thereby ease her acceptance into Washington society. The president contended that he had not made such a demand.[21]

Berrien's public criticisms evoked, not unexpectedly, near-histrionic and extremely angry fulminations from President Jackson. In correspondence with Martin Van Buren, Willie Blount, John Coffee, and even to his erstwhile friend R.K. Call, he savaged Berrien as a person. To Van Buren, he wrote, "I had a hope that Berrien would have retired like a Gentleman—but I fear he is a stranger to what constitutes one, as much as he is to truth."[22] To Willie Blount, a Jackson political ally and a former Tennessee governor, he proclaimed, "the attempt of these Judas's (to destroy me) has failed."[23] Jackson repeated this epithet to John Coffee, branding Berrien, Branch and Ingham "the three Judases." and charged Berrien with deceit: "They came into my Cabinet by the recommendation of Eaton.... Berrien says he came into it, from assurances from his friends that Eaton would soon be forced out of it—and Branch has the unblushing affrontery [sic] to say, that he told me the appointment of Major Eaton would give my enemies an opportunity to assail me."[24]

Ironically, even long-time associate Richard K. Call supported John Eaton and castigated Berrien as corrupt, "whose character for truth and chivalry is equally tarnished."[25] This was the same Richard K. Call who previously, but unsuccessfully, sexually assaulted Margaret Timberlake. Furthermore, this was the same man who had spread salacious rumors about Margaret Eaton at the onset of the Jackson administration.

John Eaton reacted to any perceived insults towards his wife in the same manner as his mentor previously, by challenging the offender to a duel. Two years previously the secretary of war leveled similar demands for satisfaction to both the Reverend Campbell and General Towson; both challenges were refused for different reasons. On July 25, 1831, the then ex–secretary of war challenged Berrien to a duel, charging him with the "countenance and sanction to base slanders" about Eaton's "domestic relations."[26] Four days later, Berrien declined an immediate acceptance. On September 13, in his "Candid Appeal to the American Public," the tempestuous Eaton accused the ex–attorney general of cowardice.[27] Berrien publicly responded by way of a letter to the *National Intelligencer*, within which he caricatured the aggrieved's demands and threats as "idle bravado" and "a palpable evasion of the combat."[28] Thus, Mrs. Eaton's character was not forcibly upheld, but her notoriety continued its pall over the administration of her stoutest defender, Andrew Jackson.

Secretary of Navy John Branch

John Branch was selected by the president to serve as his secretary of Navy. He was an old friend and agreed with many of Jackson's political views, especially his stern criticism of the banks. His knowledge of naval matters is nowhere recorded, but his inexperience was not considered to be disqualifying. Branch's long immersion in the politics of North Carolina added to his attractiveness; in Jackson's eyes, this selection would shore up his Southern support.[29]

Branch's prolonged government service to his native state included three terms as speaker of the North Carolina Senate, three times its governor, a member of the United States House of Representatives and its senator. Branch just had been elected to a second Senate term when he was appointed Navy secretary.[30]

During 1829, the secretary was in frequent communication with the White House regarding Navy business. The subjects included the disposition of warships, promotions, removals of personnel, and even the status of Navy chaplains.[31] The Navy secretary during his tenure endeavored to maintain friendly relations with Andrew Jackson. He blithely rationalized his family's social exclusion of Margaret Eaton; he explained that upon his family's arrival in Washington, they recognized that Mrs. Eaton was shunned by its society, "and did not deem it their duty or right to endeavor to control or counteract the decision of the Ladies of Washington, nor did they consider themselves at liberty to inquire whether these decisions were correct or otherwise."[32]

Branch cheerfully accepted the president's suggestion that he meet John Eaton to resolve the two cabinet members' social disagreements.

X—Emily and Margaret: The Eaton Affair Denouement

However, in response, the Navy secretary insisted that the disharmony which Jackson seemed to think existed "has not originated in any conduct of mine."[33] Subsequently, as aforementioned, Jackson met individually with Branch, Ingham, and Berrien, his three intransigent officials, to avert an immediate cabinet rupture. His action was successful, and any public intimation of conflict was delayed for more than a year. However, what was actually resolved between the two at the time has "remained in dispute."[34]

The immediate aftereffect of Branch's letter of resignation was cordial. Old Hickory's acceptance letter praised the secretary's "integrity and zeal." Writing to Donelson, Jackson professed the "fullest confidence" in Branch's friendship.[35] The departed secretary later alleged that upon relieving him of his position, the president offered him a foreign diplomatic post or the territorial governorship of Florida. Branch declined both; ironically, years later he accepted President John Tyler's appointment to become Florida's territorial governor. He assumed its governorship when Florida achieved statehood in 1845. Eaton nemesis Branch succeeded as territorial governor the seemingly ubiquitous Jackson colleague and erstwhile Margaret Eaton accuser, Richard K. Call.[36]

The initial cordiality suddenly and completely evaporated when Branch slipped away from the capital the day before news of his hostile anti–Jackson letter to a North Carolina paper reached Washington. The president's volcanic furor immediately erupted. In letters, he characterized Branch as weak and depraved, "dishonorable to the extreme," and "one of the three Judases." A final insult was the North Carolinian's contention that he had warned Jackson not to appoint John Eaton to the cabinet. The president's angry rebuttal in a letter to Coffee exclaimed, "...and Branch has the unblushing affrontery to say this. If Mr. Branch had even intimated such a thing to me, I would at once have told him, as Major Eaton was necessary to me, I would from his fears dispenced with Mr. Branch's services in my Cabinet...."[37]

Treasury Secretary Samuel Delucenna Ingham

The state of Pennsylvania was critical to Old Hickory's successful 1828 campaign for the presidency. Jackson, in appreciation, consulted with the Pennsylvania congressional delegation for a suitable choice for his cabinet; they recommend Ingham, a prominent legislator from the state. Consequently, Ingham was nominated to become the new president's secretary of the treasury. Incidentally and prophetically Vice President Calhoun supported this selection.[38] Ingham thereupon became the third member of the Judases that poisoned the waters of the Jackson's cabinet.

The Secretary was described as being "Of medium height, of broad shoulders and strong. His forehead was broad and high, his eyes rather small, light blue and keen in expression. His manner was grave and dignified."[39]

The *Papers of Andrew Jackson* volumes VII and VIII (1829 and 1830) indicate that this cabinet member was both industrious and diligent. Numerous messages between the two in 1829 discussed appointments, clerkships, customs administration and reforms, land revenues, the national debt, and the management of government funds.[40] During 1830, there were no fewer than forty-one official messages between them.[41]

The president received an unsolicited warning about Ingham's loyalty from Pennsylvanian Henry Petrikin in April 1830: "But your sincere friends—are surprised that you retain in your cabinet a man who is plotting, not only your destruction, but against the peace and welfare of the best interests of the country. Ingham came into your support at a late hour, and only when they found that a vast majority of people were against their favorite, Calhoun."[42]

The secretary's professional relationship with his chief remained cordial and cooperative during the early presidential term. However, Petrikin's earlier caution regarding Ingham was accurate. The secretary of the treasury's communication with Eaton, his cabinet colleague, was cold and unharmonious while his behavior towards the secretary's wife remained frigid and mean-spirited.

On April 18, 1831, Jackson met with Ingham, and uncharacteristically chose indirection rather than confrontation to attempting to dismiss the treasury secretary. Initially, Ingham confessed befuddlement regarding the president's intention, but the following day, he understood and submitted his resignation letter. On April 20, 1831, Andrew Jackson accepted the resignation. The president, perhaps insincerely, commended Ingham's "testimony and zeal with which you (Ingham) have managed the fiscal concerns of the nation," while also justifying his motivation that Eaton and Van Buren would be harmfully blamed for the cabinet's disharmony if the others remained.[43] At the president's request, Ingham remained at his post until late June, mainly to conclude a study that compared the weights and measurements standards employed at the various United States Customs Houses.[44]

The pretense of cordiality and goodwill was shattered after Ingham was mentioned in a *US Telegraph* exposé that alleged the cabinet's breakup was because of Margaret Eaton. John Eaton again immediately,

X—Emily and Margaret: The Eaton Affair Denouement

and in true Jacksonian fashion precipitously, confronted Ingham in writing, setting off a series of events as unusual as they were bizarre. The ex-treasury secretary responded, also in writing, with a sequence of progressively contemptuous and vicious commentaries. To Eaton's initial letter, he sneered, "It is too absurd to merit an answer.... You must be a little deranged, to imagine that any blustering of yours could disavow what all the inhabitants of this city know, and perhaps half the people of the United States." There was no way for John Eaton to tolerate this slur upon his wife's character other than a challenge to a duel in order to preserve both his and Margaret's honor.[45]

Ingham dismissed the challenge by writing two days later on June 20, 1831, "I am not to be intimidated by threat, or provoked by abuse, to any act consistent with the pity and contempt which your condition and conduct inspire." To which Eaton immediately responded, "It proves to me that you are quite brave enough to do a mean action, but too great a coward to repair it. Your contempt I heed not; your pity I despise."[46]

The reciprocal anger and scorn inevitably evolved towards a physical confrontation, that approached, but did not reach, a fatal dénouement. Since Ingham would not accept a written challenge, Eaton furiously sought him out to deliver it in person while the ex-secretary made a last visit to the Treasury Building to retrieve his personal belongings. Ingham desperately avoided Eaton's vengeance and escaped to Philadelphia, unscathed, before he was wounded or worse.[47] After his flight he complained to Jackson that John Eaton and five others, all heavily armed, had paraded in front of the Treasury Building and outside his lodgings for hours in a threatening manner. Ingham feared an assassination attempt. He accused the president, as the chief magistrate of the District, of a failure to protect its residents, especially him.[48]

In response to Samuel Ingham's literary harangues from Philadelphia, Andrew Jackson in Washington delegated his response to Nicholas Trist. Trist wrote, "...your charges ... do not appear to be founded in fact; and that he (Jackson) cannot but ascribe them to a reliance on false statements or vague surmises, or to the workings of an over-excited imagination."[49]

Subsequently, the president's Vesuvian anger over Ingham erupted, and the lava flow of his hostility quickly entombed any residual positive relationship with this subordinate.

During the summer of 1831, Jackson fulminated against the ex-treasury secretary in letters, denigrating Ingham as a tool of the unfaithful Calhoun. To Andrew Jackson Donelson, he wrote, "I did not know that my Cabinet, like J.C. Calhoun was smiling in my face & secretly endeavoring to destroy...." To Benjamin Howard, he corresponded, "The whole career of Mr. Ingham ... since my election convinces me that they only supported me for the purpose of prostrating Adams and Clay ... paving the way to the gratification of Mr. Calhoun's restless ambition." He continued this theme in an August letter to Hardy Murfree Cryer, writing, "So you see, that the Secrete attempts by Calhoun, thro' his tools, Ingham, Branch & Berrien, with all their notes & note Books, has done me no injury."[50]

Jackson-Donelson Family Disfunction

Andrew Jackson's Scots-Irish pride impelled him to chide Andrew Jackson Donelson, his rebellious nephew, for the Donelsons' resistance to their uncle's wishes regarding Mrs. Eaton. Referencing the "Judas" Berrien, the president admonished, "How much I expostulated with you and your family. ... The trio knew well I would not permit Eaton to be drove out of my Cabinet ... they cannot injure me. I have not long to live, & wearied with treachery."[51]

Emily Donelson refused to accede to her uncle's and, as the social hostess of the White House, her president's insistence on comity with Margaret Eaton. Stronger-willed and more determined than her husband-cousin, Emily convinced Andrew Jackson Donelson to accompany her in the social rejection of the "immoral" Mrs. Eaton. For the president, the intransigence of the Donelsons, treasured members of both his official and his intimate personal family, was a beyond-painful experience, far more unsettling than the disloyalty of his vice president and the Judases, Berrien, Branch, and Ingham. The proud president, whose spirit felt love, suffered rejection, and expressed anger more than most, interpreted the Donelsons' behavior as an unbelievable insult both against his presidency and against him as the patriarch of his White House family.

Jackson banished Emily to Tennessee, depriving him both of his White House social hostess and of a beloved female presence in his Washington home. His fatherly friendship and supportive official working relationship with his presidential secretary became frayed to the extent that the president considered a replacement for his nephew. Whether Andrew Jackson Donelson's disappointing political career post–Jackson withered due to Andrew Jackson's residual resentment remains a relevant proposition.

"As president and a patron, Jackson had every reason to expect Donelson's acquiescence and deference to his wishes; that Donelson behaved otherwise was, in Jackson's mind, a violation of everything he

X—Emily and Margaret: The Eaton Affair Denouement 127

had taught him about life. Because of his nephew's supposed betrayal of him during the affair, Jackson never fully trusted Donelson again." Cheathem, Donelson's biographer, summarized the consequence of young Andrew's rejection of Margaret, "[He] emerged from the Eaton affair a wounded son whose confidence in himself and his uncle was never the same."[52]

Why did this formerly acquiescent nephew damage his future prospects in exchange for transient, apparently ephemeral reasons? The primary reason was his love for his headstrong and determined wife. Emily controlled her husband's actions in the *Eaton Affair*. Other reasons for his loyalty to the forces arrayed against the Eatons were both political and personal. He became suspicious of the president's new political intimate, Martin Van Buren. Previously he felt threatened by John Eaton's and William B. Lewis' influence with Jackson. The two threatened his assessment that he was a very significant confidante of his uncle. A final explanation was that his brother, future Confederate General Daniel Smith Donelson, married Margaret Branch, the daughter of Jackson nemesis, ex–Navy Secretary John Branch.[53] Donelson infuriated his uncle when he took an out of the way route home to Nashville when he visited Branch in North Carolina in September 1831.[54]

Andrew Jackson and the Donelsons returned to Tennessee on July 6, 1830, for the first time since they had departed for Washington in January 1829.[55] The Donelsons surprised the president by electing to board at Emily's widowed mother's home, rather than to stay, as expected, at The Hermitage. Their discomfiture with their uncle over Margaret was dissuasive; they remained adamant in their decision to shun the Eatons, who were expected guests at the Jackson mansion.

The two months spent in Tennessee were hardly the pleasant summer respite sought by the harried Old Hickory. He sulked around his treasured territory as he brooded with hurt and anger. He became so alienated from the Donelsons that he started to consider a replacement for Andrew as secretary to the president. With reference to his alienated niece and nephew, in a letter to Lewis, he further appraised this option. Therein he floated his thoughts about the matter of a successor, "...but strange as it may appear, some of our friends have acted most strangely ... it may so happen that I shall return to the city in company with my son alone—on this event I shall want a Secretary who can write & compose well—one who can from a brief do justice to any subject—will you make enquiry where such a young Gentleman can be had, without making it positively known that he is wanted to be my Secretary."[56] Two weeks later in a letter to John Eaton, he confirmed his intention to fire Donelson: "Our enemies calculate much upon injuring me, by raising the cry, that I had forced A.J. Donelson from me, & compelled him to retire, because he would not yield to my views, which they call improper, I mean to shew [sic] that I only claimed to rule my Household, that it should extend justice & common politeness to all & no more, & thus put my enemies in the wrong, and if my friends desert me that is theirs and not my fault."[57]

The president seemingly approached Nicholas Trist, a clerk in the State Department, to serve as his private secretary. Jackson sent a $300.00 check to Trist, which the clerk endorsed, "On my acceptance his offer of the post of his private Secretary, he told me that I should not suffer in a pecuniary point of view—having reference to the highest salary attached to a clerkship." Trist was Jackson's secretary during much of the turbulent 1831, and occasionally later. In 1833 Andrew Jackson appointed him to be the American Consul in Havana.[58]

At the same time, the president confirmed to Lewis that Emily was banished to Tennessee, and at least temporarily, she was to relinquish her White House duties. "I shall have no female family in the city this the ensuing winter."[59] Emily accepted her uncle's eviction from Washington with good grace despite the inevitable lonely separations from Andrew. Months later, she resolutely resisted her husband's offered resignation as President Jackson's secretary in a long letter, begging him not to desert their uncle. Emily cooled Andrew's impetuousness by claiming that she would stay at home and gladly tolerate her loneliness if it would improve Uncle Andrew's spirits.[60]

The president hoped that the capital's *Eaton Malaria* would abate if Margaret also remained in Tennessee to care for her widowed mother-in-law. Before returning to Washington, he wrote Lewis, "If Mrs. E would consent to remain untill midwinter here, she would obtain a complete triumph everywhere, & the enemies, *here*, of Major Eaton completely put down." John Eaton agreed with this idea, but the headstrong Margaret refused to submit to her president's request and her husband's acquiescence. She accompanied Secretary Eaton back to Washington. Unbowed upon her return, she held a large dinner party that greatly impressed a visiting court magistrate from Missouri.[61]

Jackson lamented Emily's absence from the White House during the 1830–1831 winter. He bemoaned to his great-niece Mary Ann Eastin who remained with Emily in Tennessee, "Major Donelson has informed you that the House appears lonesome, and on his account it would give me great pleasure that you & Emily with the sweet little ones were here." Thereby the proud president projected his personal pain and longing upon the shoulders of Andrew Donelson. Mary Ann Eastin was Emily Donelson's niece and both her companion and friend in the White House.[62]

X—Emily and Margaret: The Eaton Affair Denouement

Donelson did return to the White House to reclaim his role as his uncle's private and presidential secretary. Their relationship for some time was fragile at best, embittered most often, and vitriolic at its worst. Throughout the following twelve months, although saddened, Jackson's predominant personality traits of obstinacy and anger forbade any final reconciliation with his niece and nephew.

Donelson attempted to justify his and Emily's behavior in writing:

> It is impossible that a delicate female, introduced to a new social circle as was Mrs. Donelson in the winter of 1829, should not be governed in some degree by the views of character which she found prevailing in it. An insensibility to such an influence would imply the absence of a moral sentiment which I would be unwilling to ascribe to any virtuous woman ... we commenced an intercourse with the family of Majr Eaton ... and yet a short time after your inauguration a letter is addressed to Mrs. D by Mr. Eaton in which he descends to the insinuation that she has placed herself under the guardianship of slanderers. This denunciation is applied to a very responsible family in this place, one member of which was an old and very esteemed friend and correspondent of our lamented aunt.[63]

The virtue-signaling of the Donelsons, when added to Secretary Donelson's awkward referencing of the sainted Rachel, "our lamented aunt," infuriated the president. In Jackson's mind this was insolent disloyalty towards him, the benefactor who had long conferred great material generosity and valuable social beneficence to both of them. He had sponsored their wedding and had bestowed generous presents at their marriage. He viewed them as ingrates, and disrespectful to him as paterfamilias, as patron, and as president. He was appalled by their blindness towards any appreciation that the slanders directed against Margaret were meant to wound Secretary Eaton, her husband, and, as a consequence, to destroy the Jackson presidency.

Possibly, Emily's behavior might be explained as other than disloyalty. She attended the Nashville Female Academy, a training ground to prepare for upper class womanhood. Therefore, it was not so surprising that she looked to her social peers for signals about whom to accept and whom to reject socially than her uncle. She became especially friendly with Mrs. Ingham, who had a portrait made of Emily.[64]

The reciprocal rancor reduced all communication between Andrew Jackson and Andrew Jackson Donelson to letters. From October 25 to October 31, two essential officials of the U.S. government, close kinsman and residents of the same house, could interact only by passing written correspondence back and forth through intermediaries.[65]

Such immature foolishness could not continue; the U.S. executive needed to function, and the social ambience of the Executive Mansion required at least a minimum of comity and peace. Still President Jackson continued to castigate, to self-pity, and to mourn. He admonished his nephew for his foolish alliances and wrote, "I have said before my Dr Andrew, whenever your own inclination leads, & you determine, you are welcome to withdraw...."[66] On the first day of 1831, after the annual White House celebration, Jackson self-indulgently wrote, "The crowd having retired, and having lost 20 ounces of blood, for I am not well." In another letter he wrote, "My health is not very good. I have been afflicted with headache for the last two or three days."[67] Rachel's memory remained in his thoughts; his profound sorrow was expressed in messages to his family, even two years after her death, "...it brought fresh to my recollection ... a bereavement which has left for me no prospect of happiness this side of the grave...."[68]

The dissolution of the first Jackson cabinet in April 1831 began the resolution of The Eaton Imbroglio, although General Berrien and Secretary Ingham tarried in their government posts until June.[69] Several plans for Emily Donelson's homecoming to the White House were nullified before the Donelson family's ultimate arrival on September 5, 1831. John and Margaret Eaton departed Washington for Tennessee two weeks later on September 19. The comings and goings of these two divas brought to a conclusion thirty months of one of the most disorderly and fractious episodes of an American presidency.[70]

One of the delays for Emily's return was a July report that her name was celebrated together with Mrs. Calhoun and Mrs. Ingham as ones who had opposed the Eatons. Jackson once again fulminated to Andrew Donelson, "...but when you see the manner in which my bitter and insidious enemies, once professing has arrayed you and your family against me...."[71]

Margaret was very unhappy after the cabinet resignations; she suspected that Van Buren had engineered the entire scenario for his self aggrandizement. She believed that she had been vanquished, rather than exonerated, by the political maneuvering. In this morose mood, Margaret was rude to the president and to Van Buren when they, in a celebratory frame of mind, spontaneously visited Mrs. Eaton. She kept them waiting for fifteen minutes. They expected cheerfulness and informality, but instead they experienced formality and coolness.[72]

XI

Emily Donelson
Presiding Lady Again

Emily Donelson: "...was strikingly beautiful, tall, slender and a most dazzling complexion, having bright red cheeks with very regular features ... dark brown eyes and a most graceful carriage. All who remember her agree that she did the honors of the White House perfectly and was really one of the prettiest women that have occupied the position ... she had the reputation of having used the best taste in dress."
—*Our Early Presidents: Their Wives and Children.* Harriet Taylor Upton, 373, as quoted in Pauline Burke, *Emily Donelson of Tennessee* Volume 2, 59

Emily with her gift of familial sociability brought him only pleasure, "as he sat by the fireside surrounded by members of his family. Mary McLemore soothed his nerves with her exquisite playing on harp and piano; Mary Coffee brought laughter from him as she gave her impressions of the giants of the nation fighting their verbal battles on the floor of the Senate and House; Emily Donelson ordered him around for the sake of his health, and her babies delighted him with their antics."
—Pauline Burke, *Emily Donelson of Tennessee* Volume II, 32

On September 5, 1831, Emily Donelson arrived at the Executive Mansion to resume her duties as presiding lady of the White House. Her journey from mid-Tennessee had been long and arduous. When her stagecoach rolled up the outside carriageway, the president was in his study writing a letter to Martin Van Buren. Jackson immediately laid down his pen and hurried to greet the arrivals.

Emily immediately discovered that the Executive Mansion was socially austere with its living quarters occupied only by the president, his close political aide Major Lewis, the president's young ward, Andrew Jackson Hutchings, and the painter, Ralph Earl.[1] Her traveling party, consisting of herself, Andrew Jackson Donelson, their two children Andrew Jackson Donelson, Jr., and Mary Rachel, and Emily's two nieces, Mary Eastin and Mary McLemore, quickly enlivened the quiet building.[2]

Emily Donelson remained close to her uncle for nearly five years, until early June 1836, when her declining health compelled her to relinquish her White House responsibilities and to return to her home in Tennessee.[3] She accompanied Jackson on his vacation trips to the Rip Raps, an artificial island at the entrance to Hampton Roads, Virginia, and on his 1832 and 1834 summer respites in Nashville.[4] During his eight year presidency, Old Hickory summered at the Rip Raps or The Hermitage in alternating years.

Emily's separations from the president during these years were few. She did not accompany her uncle on his spring 1833 political trip to New England and the mid-Atlantic states. Additionally, there were two brief excursions to benefit her nieces. On September 18, 1831, the Donelsons traveled to Philadelphia to deposit their niece Mary McLemore at boarding school. They enjoyed sightseeing in New York City for five days during their return journey.[5] The second excursion was to Castle Hill, Virginia, in July 1834, so that a second niece, Elizabeth Martin, could visit with her fiancé Lewis Randolph for several days.[6]

Emily Donelson's second stint as White House Hostess witnessed a presidential campaign, the successful re-election of her uncle, his bouts of chronic ill health punctuated by several medical emergencies, intense political battles over the National Bank, Indian removal, and with John Calhoun over tariffs and nullification. Despite two more successful pregnancies, a relentless illness and eventual death from tuberculosis, young Emily Tennessee Donelson was indomitable and significantly influenced her uncle-president.

Her sway extended to both public and private matters. To the public, Mrs. Donelson was the White House Hostess. In private, she enhanced the ambience within the president's home with her increasing brood of children. Emily provided a warm and joyful environment for a troubled chief executive, and she assisted as best she could in monitoring her uncle's health and in assuaging his physical complaints. Finally, she morally supported her husband, Jackson's secretary, as he fulfilled the president's unceasing demands.

White House Hostess

Emily, restored as Andrew Jackson social First Lady, was as successful as she had been before her banishment. She "...was strikingly beautiful, tall, slender and a most dazzling complexion, having bright red cheeks with very regular features ... dark brown eyes and a most graceful carriage. All who remember her agree that she did the honors of the White House perfectly and was really one of the prettiest women that have occupied the position ... she had the reputation of having used the best taste in dress."[7]

Mary Purnell Donelson, Emily's mother, raised her daughter to entertain large numbers of guests. Mary and John Donelson, Rachel Jackson's brother, raised thirteen children; Emily Tennessee was their youngest child. The Mansion, their estate, bordered the grounds of The Hermitage, where Emily and her siblings spent many youthful days under the vigilant eye of Rachel Jackson. Undoubtedly, both Mother Mary and Aunt Rachel passed many of their social and matronal skills onto the young woman.[8]

Upon moving into the White House, Emily Donelson reportedly commented that she wanted to make it "a model American home." While serving as Surrogate First Lady, despite her youth, she proved to be very effective. Contemporary observers concluded, "She was a very agreeable woman." As the chatelaine of the White House, another commented, "With quiet dignity she assumed charge."[9]

In the early Jackson White House, the dinners were unremarkable, to say the least. In an 1829 letter to his wife, David Campbell described a weekly dinner, "as plain a one and as badly cooked as you ever sat down to ... but, the wine was good." However, after Jackson fired steward Antoine Guista, a holdover as Steward from the Adams administration, and hired Joseph Boulanger as chef, the dinner fare improved markedly. Concurrently, Emily, the social First Lady, became more and more comfortable with her surroundings. As a result, the elegance and sophistication of the White House dinner parties were enhanced, as favorably illustrated by an acute connoisseur.

John B. Montgomery, a Pennsylvania attorney, described an "informal" dinner at the White House that he attended in February 1834. Eleven guests were present in addition to the president and the Donelson family. "The table was very splendidly laid and illuminated.... The first course was soup in the French style; then beef bouille, next wild turkey boned and dressed with brains; after that fish; then chicken cold and dressed white, interlaided with slices of tongue and garnish with dressed salad; then canvas back ducks and celery; afterwards partridges with sweet breads an lat pheasant [sic] and old Virginia ham." This "informal" dinner included a variety of desserts and the courses were accompanied by an array of wines. Montgomery sat near Mrs. Donelson, "a very agreeable woman, so that the evening passed very pleasantly."[10]

The actual management of the White House (1829–1833) fell to Steward Antoine Michel Guista and his wife. Guista efficiently managed a staff of twenty-four. He also kept the books, did the marketing, and supervised the other servants. Previously Guista was the steward to John Quincy Adams, whom he preferred to Andrew Jackson. He exhibited his favoritism by supplying the ex-president's home with food from the White House kitchen. Unhappiness over this practice was a possible reason for Guista's resignation in May 1833. He was succeeded as White House Steward by Joseph Boulanger. By 1833, the paid staff had been reduced in number; their responsibilities were filled by enslaved people.[11]

Housekeeping at the President's House never seemed a source of worry to Jackson during his administration, perhaps because Emily Donelson relieved him of much of the responsibility. Arbiter in politics, he deferred all matters of etiquette to her, and when she would appeal to him to settle any knotty social point, he would reply, "You know best my dear. Do as you please."[12]

During his first White House levee, held on January 10, 1830, the president together, with his White House Hostess and Mary Eastin, his grandniece, stood while shaking hands with his guests for five hours. One guest lauded Emily and Mary's conduct with great praise: "They affected no superiority, show no pride.... Their honour sat so easy on them that they seemed not to know it.... This perfect good breeding had been taught them from their earliest infancy both by precept and example by their Aunt the good and amiable and ever to be lamented Mrs. Jackson."[13]

Mrs. Donelson's banishment from the Executive Mansion left it without a presiding Lady for a year, from the middle of 1830 to middle of 1831. Her absence was noticed at a levee: "...there was something wanting, and the ladies appeared without a pivot to move on." Moreover, something was missing, "...the want of a presiding lady.... The presence of ladies will prevent intrusions, to which I perceive that you are exceedingly liable."[14]

The President's Caregiver

Andrew Jackson's physical well-being was dire in the womanless White House during most of 1831. The self-indulgent president complained to that effect in his many letters to family and friends during that year. Immediately after the 1831 New Year's levee, he wrote, "The crowd having retired. and having lost 20 ounces of blood, for I am not well."[15] In his correspondence, he lamented his frequent headaches which were both lasting and severe. The significant bullet-related pain in his left arm remained a frequent grievance. Jackson took medicines for his headaches, but their identity is unknown.[16]

Andrew Jackson's letters of distress evoked suggested remedies from his correspondents. William Gray sent a pot of his ointment. It was later analyzed to be a mixture of linseed oil, lead soap, lead acetate turpentine, and wax. It is unrecorded whether the president discovered its effectiveness or even applied it. Martin Van Buren advised rest and a trip to the curative waters of Virginia Springs. Hartwell Carver recommended liverwort to treat Old Hickory's bleeding from the lungs.[17]

The lonely president took his biannual vacation at the Rip Raps, unescorted this year by the young families who usually accompanied him. His guest there was his venerable friend, Judge John Overton. Excruciating headaches accosted him, which he attributed to "the repainting of my dwelling," and consequently, his expected respite was less than completely fulfilled.[18] Returning to the White House, he chronicled his ill health in letters (July–August 1831) bemoaning, "I caught cold, & am troubled with a cough, but it is subsiding."; "I am not very well."; "I labor under a severe headache."[19]

In late September, Old Hickory "was confined to (his) bed with a severe illness," which shackled him to his bed for several days. He characterized this "indisposition" as "an attack of the prevailing fever of this place." Most likely Jackson suffered a typical attack of malaria whose major symptom was several days of a high fever that predictably would subside, leaving the patient temporarily weak with the happy assurance of a rapid return to full health. Malaria was endemic in Washington ("this place") for many years after its establishment as the nation's capital city before its swamps were drained and mosquito control became effective.[20]

The fear of disease was an important motive for both the legislative and executive branches of government to escape the city during the miasmic summer months. President James K. Polk and First Lady Sarah Polk remained in the White House during all the summers of his tenure; both caught malaria. Sarah was sick with the infection in May, and again in September–October 1847, and the president in September 1847, and again in June 1848.[21] Several of Jackson's biographers speculated that he may have contracted malaria earlier during his military campaigns in Florida.

On September 18, less than two weeks after her victorious restoration as White House Hostess, Emily and her family traveled to Philadelphia and New York City. Her journey was interrupted by news of Uncle Jackson's illness: "But hearing of uncle's illness hurried on home, we found him convalescent tho looking debilitated."[22] Subsequent November testimony from the president attested to a remarkable and complete recovery from his bout with malaria. Recuperated, he wrote that, "(I) feel more from affliction than I have for the past ten years."[23] These salutes to his physical well-being coincided with Emily's resumption of her position in the White House. Was this coincidental or consequential?

The exact nature of Emily's restorative ministrations to her ailing uncle remain undocumented. Her administration of tender loving care is a given. Moreover, this Donelson niece was certainly well-schooled in the application of layman's health care, both by her mother Mary Purnell and possibly by her aunt Rachel Jackson. Moreover, the necessity of taking care of a husband and young children certainly honed her care-giving skills. Assuredly the ambience of the White House with the presence of young women and charming children was further salutary to Jackson's emotional and psychological well-being. The presence of any member of Washington's medical establishment during this episode is not recorded. A medical historian recently demonstrated that Jackson was promiscuous rather than celibate towards physicians during his lifetime. Quinine, the effective antimalarial medication, was available at the time, either in compound form or as Jesuit bark. The administration of the bark and by whom is also unrecorded.[24]

Health problems were unmentioned during Andrew Jackson's successful 1832 campaign for reelection to a second term. Biographer Marquis James graphically illustrated his subject's upbeat mood: "The eve of the battles, whose littered fields were to exhibit President Jackson's greatest contributions to the American saga, saw Old Hickory in the finest fighting trim since he had taken the oath three years before. His step was springier, his eye brighter. Something of the old banter reanimated his social conversation, making it, indeed, difficult to remember the heart-crushed old man of 1829...."[25]

The arrival of new children enhanced the atmosphere. Emily and Andrew Donelson's third child and second son was born on May 18, 1832. John Samuel was christened in the White House with President Jackson serving a godfather.[26] In the spring of 1833, Andrew Jr., and Sarah Yorke Jackson arrived from Tennessee with their first child and initial Jackson grandchild. This Rachel Donelson, born in Tennessee in November 1832, would become the old man's most treasured present from his son and daughter-in-law.

The fifth year of the Jacksonian regime commenced with his triumphant inauguration in March 1833. A month-long political trip to the mid-Atlantic and New England states followed. It was designed to be celebratory but was instead eventful. Its onset was inauspicious. While on a preliminary side trip by steamer to Fredericksburg, Virginia, the president was assaulted by Robert R. Randolph, a discharged Navy lieutenant. Randolph "thrust his fist violently into Jackson's face as if to pull his nose." Although aging, Jackson's Scots-Irish inheritance of ferocity responded. Seated, he rose, kicked a table away, shouting, "I want no man to stand between me and my assailants, and none to take revenge on my account." Randolph was arrested, but the president refused to give evidence, recalling his mother's admonition, "I have to this old age complied with my mother's advice to indict no man for assault or sue him for slander." Randolph's attack was the first physical assault upon an American president. It would not be Jackson's last.[27]

The primitive, often harmful, therapies of the practicing physicians of the era did not dissuade Old Hickory from soliciting a doctor's attention. Bleeding, cupping, calomel, and sugar of lead baths did not discourage him from consulting physicians, which occurred on two occasions during this trip. Philadelphia jubilantly welcomed President Jackson in June 1833. After his arrival, the president promptly sought out the medical opinion of the renowned physician Dr. Philip Synge Physick. The consultation was sought because of the constant pain in his side and the prostrating lung hemorrhages. Charles Dickinson's bullet resided in Jackson's left lung and produced episodic lung hemorrhage with the coughing up of blood (hemoptysis), chills, sweating, and extreme weakness. His only effective remedy was repose. Dr. Physick, in contrast with most of his professional peers, did not bleed his patient; instead, he encouraged Jackson to keep up the good fight. The patient explained, "I have seen Dr. Physick who encourages me, and says my heart is not affected in any way, and the pain in the side can be removed by cupping."[28]

Philip Synge Physick, renowned as the "Father of American Surgery," had trained in London under the famed anatomist John Hunter, and subsequently received his medical degree from the University of Edinburgh. He served on the medical faculty of the University of Pennsylvania for many years; at the time of Jackson's examination, the doctor was its Emeritus Professor of Anatomy and Surgery. Jackson esteemed Physick's skill; subsequently in 1835, the president expressed his gratitude for the doctor's examination of his granddaughter Rachel, who is "perfectly recovered" and to the "(doctor's) skill and kind attention."[29]

The president continued on his journey to Boston, where his

reception was also triumphant. However, on his fourth day there, he was confined to his bed in the Tremont House with a severe cold and a recurrence of bleeding from his left lung. Josiah Quincy, the president's Massachusetts guide, summoned the Quincy family physician John Warren. This doctor bled the president. When there was no symptomatic relief, Warren bled the president again.[30] The treatment was ineffective since a few days later, while lingering in Salem, Massachusetts, Jackson felt weaker and suffered a recurrent hemorrhage during the night.[31]

John Warren was far more than the Quincy's family physician. A graduate of the University of Edinburgh, he succeeded his father as the Harvard Medical School's Professor of Anatomy and Surgery. He founded the Massachusetts General Hospital, introduced ether anesthesia, and was a leader in the establishment of both *The New England Journal of Medicine* and the American Medical Association.[32]

Andrew Jackson, exhausted and very ill, returned from his New England trip on July 4, 1833. Emily Donelson and Sarah Yorke Jackson "did all within their power to minister to his needs." "For forty eight hours the doctors gave little hope, but they reckoned from experience with other patients," and not with Andrew Jackson.[33] The extent of Emily's and Sarah's doing "all within their power to minister to his needs" is speculative. Basic nursing care certainly was administered, but whether "home medicines" from the White House medicine chest were dispensed is unclear.

Three respected Washington physicians, acknowledged "Pillars of the Profession," are linked to Jackson's medical care during his White House tenure. Doctors Henry Huntt, Thomas Sim, and James Crowdhill Hall had active Washington practices, and they treated all American presidents from James Monroe to Abraham Lincoln. James Hall has the dubious distinction of serving at the deathbed of three presidents: Harrison, Taylor, and Lincoln. President Jackson escaped this physician's lethal embrace when he departed Washington for The Hermitage.[34]

Henry Huntt, although without a medical degree, was identified as the Jackson family physician during his 1829–1837 tenure. He was a proponent of the use of sugar of lead, but Jackson, after surviving a near fatal lung hemorrhage in 1836, was relieved that the attack ceased, "without the aid of that potent, but pernicious remedy to the stomach, sugar of lead." However, this doctor was likewise a proponent of heroic bleeding of his patients, including Andrew Jackson.[35]

Thomas Sim was a graduate of the University of Pennsylvania School of Medicine. He was Jackson's physician during his 1823–5 Senate term, but no authentication can be found for any care during Jackson's presidency. His competence was suspect by some, but the then

XI—Emily Donelson: Presiding Lady Again

senator affirmed his confidence in his usual hyperbolic style: "Dr. Sim is my friend ... an old and valued friend. His professional reputation, his standing as a physican, his feelings as a man, as a friend, are all at stake in this matter.... He shall cure me, or he shall kill me...." The previously referenced Dr. James Hall was a graduate of the Jefferson Medical College in Philadelphia; between 1832 and 1835, he billed the president for various surgical procedures, including a hydrocele repair.[36]

President Jackson was wont to refer ailing friends and family members to the care of doctors whose experience he trusted. He dispatched Dr. Hogg, his "good friend" from The Hermitage to the Alabama home of his ailing friend John Coffee. When in the spring of 1835, Rachel, his beloved grandchild, became ill, the president sent the child to Dr. Physick of Philadelphia for treatment. Rachel was cured, and the president's gratitude to the physician was effusive, "I owe you a debt of gratitude that I am sure I can never repay, but will always be remembered with the most grateful and lively recollection."[37]

Weak in body and precarious in health, the president departed for a hoped-for respite at The Rip Raps. He was assisted onto the boat while leaning on the arms of Andrew Donelson and Andrew Jackson Junior. His anticipation of a salubrious stay on the sand of the beach with food and drink supplied by the Hygeia Hotel was enhanced by the accompaniment of not only Emily and her three children, Jackson, Mary Rachel, and John Samuel, but also Sarah Yorke Jackson and little Rachel, her infant daughter, a nurse and two servants. He may have suffered a relapse there, and his feet and ankles became badly swollen. Fortunately, Jackson was in good spirits at the conclusion of his twenty-five-day vacation.[38]

The president's physical well-being was without significant incident until January 30, 1835. He had just attended the funeral of Mississippi United States Representative Warren Davis that was held in the U.S. Capitol. "As the elderly and frail Jackson, leaning heavily on the arm of Treasury Secretary Levi Woodbury, walked from the rotunda, Richard Lawrence ... drawing a pistol from beneath his cloak, took aim from a distance of no more than eight feet and pulled the trigger...." The pistol misfired. Lawrence removed a second pistol from his pocket and fired again with the same result. "The President himself, enraged by the event, struggled to get at him with his cane, shouting, 'Let me alone! Let me alone. I know where this came from....'" Richard Lawrence was an unemployed house painter and a certifiable paranoid schizophrenic. His behavior was driven by a delusion that he was King Richard III and that Jackson was standing in the way of Lawrence receiving money owed to him. Even prosecutor Francis Scott Key agreed that Lawrence was not guilty by reason of insanity. He remained in a mental institution for the rest of his life. Andrew Jackson thereby escaped unscathed from a second assault.[39]

Unfortunately, 1835 did not witness any improvement in Jackson's health. To the contrary, it deteriorated. He was in constant pain, and his headaches became excruciating. Painful, cramping constipation (costiveness) became an additional affliction: "My bowels are become quite torpid and I have become weary of taking mine so frequently. I postponed it too long, having passed over three days without a passage." He self-treated the constipation with the cathartic Dr. Rush's Thunderbolt. This concoction was a compound of calomel, jalap, and gamboge (a cathartic from Cambodia).[40]

In mid 1836, Emily Donelson's delicate health collapsed, which forced her to leave her uncle in order to attempt a convalescence in the Donelsons' Tennessee home. Andrew, her husband, was confronted with an unwinnable choice: to comfort his wife in Nashville or to loyally assist the president in the White House. He strove to compromise by attempting both.

On November 19, 1836, as he worked in his study composing his final message to Congress, "the President was seized with coughing. Blood gushed from his mouth." Dr. Huntt was summoned and, over two days, drained his veins of sixty ounces (1.7 liters) of blood. The hemoptysis and the therapeutic drainage of one-third of his total blood volume left the patient nearly lifeless and semi-comatose. Andrew wrote Emily, "Uncle was very sick," which prevented his departure to attend to his dying wife. Forty-eight hours later, Jackson was sitting up, attributing his remarkable recovery to divine will: "A kind Providence, who holds our existence here in the hollow of his hand." Only then was Donelson able to speed to his dying wife's bed. He arrived in Tennessee too late.[41]

Conservator of White House Comfort and Happiness

Jackson biographers uniformly praise Emily's fulfillment of her responsibilities as the official mistress of the White House and "First Lady of the Land": "Her tact and charm of manner did much to make the Jackson Administration stand out as a brilliant one."

"Close to Jackson, she and Andrew were able to cheer him most of the time, greeting his guests and presenting a gracious face to the outside world." Undoubtedly, the warmth and grace that Emily exhibited in her official capacity transferred seamlessly to her behavior within the privacy of the Executive Mansion.[42]

President Jackson viewed himself as the father of his White House family, a presumption that previously caused problems over the Eaton Affair. But now, under the skillful management and fecundity of Emily, with her gift of familial sociability, his self-appointed patriarchy brought him only pleasure, "as he sat by the fireside surrounded by members of his family. Mary McLemore soothed his nerves with her exquisite playing on harp and piano; Mary Coffee brought laughter from him as she gave her impressions of the giants of the nation fighting their verbal battles on the floor of the Senate and House; Emily Donelson ordered him around for the sake of his health, and her babies delighted him with their antics."[43]

The Donelsons produced four children; Emily gave birth to three in the White House, a record. Their third child, John Samuel, was born on May 18, 1831. He was the only child of Andrew Jackson Donelson to be present at the funeral of Andrew Jackson. Later, John Samuel Donelson died, fighting for Tennessee, at the Civil War battle of Chickamauga. Rachel Jackson Donelson, Emily's fourth child entered the world on April 19, 1834.[44] Future president James K. Polk was Rachel's godfather.[45] Soon, the White House nursery received additional occupants, the children of Andrew Jackson, Jr., and Sarah Yorke Jackson: Rachel, followed by Andrew Jackson.

Emily's extensive kinship and vitality attracted young women of similar age to spend extended visits as White House guests. Among them were nieces Mary Ann Eastin, Mary McLemore, Mary Coffee, and Elizabeth Martin. Their presence sparkled with vivacity and excitement. Shortly after her restoration, Emily, although initially disappointed wrote, "The city has been extremely dull since we have been here. Uncle seems quite happy and everything is moving harmoniously...."[46]

Mary Coffee was Emily's niece. Mary's correspondence with her Alabama family is a source that illustrated the social whirl within the Executive Mansion. She wrote her sister of "everlasting parties" and further elaborated upon the active socializing by herself, cousin Mary McLemore, and aunt Emily. Moreover, she confided to her mother a description of disputes between Emily and niece Mary McLemore. She wrote that Mary McLemore would do nothing that Aunt Emily asked her to do, concluding, "Cousin M was always of a tyrannical disposition." Fortunately, Emily sternly assured that Uncle Jackson was kept unaware of this.[47]

The presence of marriageable Donelson family members and other young women about the White House encouraged the president to partake in one of his favorite pastimes—matchmaking. Mary Ann Eastin fell in love with a naval officer nearly twice her age and had set a wedding date for Valentine's Day, 1832. Lucius J. Polk, a cousin of James K. Polk, previously had fallen in love with Mary Ann when he met her at The Hermitage. Polk, energized by the news of her engagement, took the next stage to the nation's capital, persuaded her to break her previous commitment to marry, and wed the young woman in the East Room of the White House on April 10, 1832. Andrew Jackson gave the bride away at the wedding ceremony. Less than a year later, the Polks named their first-born Sarah Rachel.[48]

During his 1832 stay at his Tennessee home, Emma Yorke Farquhar, a cousin of Sarah Yorke Jackson, married Thomas Jefferson Donelson, the twin brother of Andrew Jackson Junior, Jr. The senior Jackson also may have given away the bride. On November 29, 1832, the White House was the scene of the wedding of Mary Ann Lewis, the daughter of the president's confidante W.B. Lewis.[49]

Andrew Jackson's penchant for matchmaking continued as Mary Coffee, the daughter of the president's beloved John Coffee, became engaged to her cousin Andrew Jackson Hutchings. Affectionately called "Little Hutchings," he had been raised from infancy by Andrew and Rachel and was possibly adopted by them. Finally, the aforementioned Mary McLemore became engaged to "the much loved Dr Hogg's assistant, Dr. James Wallace, a graduate of Transylvania School of Medicine."[50]

The hostess of the White House did not falter in her mission to spread joy and happiness within its walls. She, with Sarah Yorke Jackson's assistance, organized an elaborate party on Christmas Day 1835 with games, presents, and treats. His grandchildren, great-nieces and nephews were joined in the merriment by numbers of their young friends. The president attended to his great amusement and pleasure.[51]

Emily Donelson: Illness and Death

Emily Donelson, returning to the White House after the Eaton malaria had been cured, dutifully fulfilled her consequential and weighty responsibilities to her uncle Andrew. Previously, this young woman's health always was considered to be delicate; for this reason, her parents were both troubled and even fearful, both over their barely seventeen-year-old daughter's marriage to her cousin Andrew and over their lengthy honeymoon journey to Washington.[52]

XI—Emily Donelson: Presiding Lady Again

Tuberculosis, the White Plague of the nineteenth century, probably infected the frail and vulnerable Emily at an early age. The disease was chronic, its symptoms were cyclical, and its prognosis during the pre-antibiotic era was frequently fatal.[53]

Prior to Jackson's first inauguration, Emily wrote to her sister, "My health was so bad, I was scarcely able to keep out of bed one half of my time." In January 1831, during her banishment from the White House and separated from her husband, she lost weight and reportedly looked like a specter.[54]

Although Emily wrote in August 1832, "My health has been very delicate.... I had an attack of chills and fever," she was fairly strong until summer 1834. That summer, Jackson and the Donelson family made their biannual trip to their Tennessee homes.

Emily resided with her mother at The Mansion while making trips to inspect the progress of construction at the Donelsons' new house. Due to declining health, she did not return this time to Washington with her uncle and husband. Downplaying her illness, she sent reassuring letters to Andrew Donelson, although tuberculosis began to take hold and was relentless. Unaware of the severity of the disease, her husband urged her to return to Washington. She complied and left Tennessee in November.[55]

In July 1835, the president made his alternate year trip to the Rip Raps for the final time. Emily's family and Junior's family accompanied Jackson. However, her husband, still her uncle's secretary, remained in the White House to complete official business. Emily became very ill at the Rip Raps. Jackson sent frequent bulletins of her condition to Andrew Donelson, writing, "our dear Emily requests me to say she is better."[56]

Emily's health in Washington (1835–1836) continued to deteriorate, and her physical strength continued to weaken. As a consequence, she and her three youngest children left Washington prematurely in early June 1836. Andrew, weighted with the twin responsibilities of finalizing the president's secretarial requests and monitoring his uncle's fragile health, remained at the White House with Jack, their oldest child. During the Donelsons' month-long separation, Andrew expressed his concern and tenderness in frequent letters to his wife. He wrote, "I trust that Providence is equally kind to you and our dear children," and, "Accept, my dear Emily, the constant prayers of an affectionate and devoted husband for your health and happiness." When her husband finally arrived in Tennessee in late July, he was shocked to find Emily gravely ill.[57]

In September, Emily had a massive pulmonary hemorrhage, a sign that a tubercular demise was impending. She apparently had suffered prior, but less severe, bouts of hemoptysis. Her husband and the entire Donelson family became terrified. Andrew remained home with Emily and their four children.[58]

The president was chagrined when he traveled alone to the White House. He wrote a tender letter to his nephew, "...with painful sensations read the melancholy information of her continued ill health and fore bodings of the result of her disease. I trust in the mercy of a kind superintending providence that he will restore her to health and bless her dear little children with her kind superintending care they so much need." When his wife exhibited some improvement. Donelson's emotions were conflicted. He had a major responsibility to remain in Tennessee by his severely ill wife's bedside. Conversely, he was drawn to the White House where the president was ill and in dire need of Donelson's aid. He decided to fulfill his duties in Washington. Family members were greatly distressed by the necessity of Donelson's leaving his wife at this crucial period.[59]

Upon his arrival in Washington, the presidential secretary strove mightily and resolutely to balance his love for his dying wife with his love for his president. When Andrew Jackson's lung hemorrhage recurred, the president wrote a strange letter to the moribund Emily that not only detailed his own pulmonary bleeding but also estimated the amount (60 ounces) of Dr. Huntt's near catastrophic blood letting. Whether his intention was empathetic, or an example of his petulant complaining remains unknown.[60]

Andrew Donelson tried to manage his wife's medical care from a long distance. In Washington he consulted Dr. Huntt, who had been Emily' physician there. The doctor prescribed the usual treatment of the day. When his wife ran a high fever, plasters were ordered placed between her shoulders and a "medicated skin" was recommended.

His letter to Emily on October 23, 1836, further detailed Dr. Huntt's recommendations: "Few drops of elixir vitriol to be added to the cherry tree bitters you are taking." "You require blisters alternatively on the breast and between the shoulders." Additional advice included a light fruit diet and the avoidance of animal food. Finally, he encouraged his wife to ride when the weather is good. Emily responded, "Dr. Sales has just been here." He measured her pulse rate, first at 120, then at 112 beats per minute. She attempted to reassure her distant husband by downplaying her shortness of breath as "little" and her cough as "diminished," adding, "My appetite is very good."[61] A rapid heart rate (tachycardia) (normal is 72/minute), shortness of breath (dyspnea), and cough are symptoms of pulmonary tuberculosis deterioration.

Donelson was alternatively relieved and demoralized by contradictory medical reports from Nashville. His determination to complete his clerical work was frantic. When he received dire news from his wife's sickbed, he immediately returned in a frenetic gallop to reach his wife before she died. His travel was in vain; Emily died on December 19, 1836, age 29, two days before his arrival. The indomitable young woman was buried by the side of her father and sister three days later.[62]

The Washington Globe published a laudatory obituary on January 4, 1837, from which the following is abridged:

> With melancholy feeling we record the death of Mrs. Donelson, the beautiful and amiable wife of Andrew Jackson Donelson, late Private secretary to the President of the United States. This most estimable lady went to Tennessee during the summer.... For the most part, since the beginning of this Administration, Mrs. Donelson has presided at the President's mansion, and all who have visited it know with what amenity of manners, with what engaging and unpretending kindness she welcomed the guests to its hospitalities....[63]

Andrew Jackson Donelson

Three of the women who influenced Andrew Jackson were married to men who were emotionally close to Old Hickory: John Eaton, Andrew Jackson Donelson, and Andrew Jackson Junior. Only one outlived his wife. Donelson survived Emily for many years. The author has made the decision to include brief synopses of the three's post-Jackson lives for comprehension.

Emily's death cloaked her husband with grief. His loving and much-loved partner, his wife of twelve years, and the caring mother of their four young children, was gone. In addition, his capitulation, out of loyalty, to his president's demand that Andrew return to the White House instead of remaining by his dying wife' bedside at Poplar Grove, filled him with guilt, remorse, and self-blame. Andrew Jackson perceived his nephew's depression and expressed regret that he had delayed Donelson's return to Tennessee for too long. However, the self-absorbed Jackson made the unseemly demand that Donelson, still in mourning, travel back to the White House to "arrange his personal affairs for the trip back to The Hermitage."[64]

The now ex-president advised Donelson as a salve to his unhappiness, "to seek out a discret [sic] Lady for a partner and Marry. This alone can make you happy at home." Within eighteen months of his uncle's advice, on November 10, 1841, Donelson married his cousin, twenty-six-year-old Elizabeth Anderson Martin Randolph. His bride was the daughter of Catherine Donelson, Emily's older sister. She had often stayed with her aunt Emily in the White House previously. Additionally, Elizabeth Martin Randolph was a principal care giver to Aunt Emily during her fatal illness. Elizabeth's first husband was Meriwether Lewis Randolph, a grandson of Thomas Jefferson. Randolph perished in 1837, a mere two-and-one-half years after their wedding.[65]

Their second marriage was a congenial one and lasted for thirty years. Elizabeth supported her husband through his travails, his political disappointments, and his financial problems, both chronic and severe. The couple produced eight children; their last child, yet another Andrew Jackson, was born after Donelson passed the age of sixty.[66]

Although blessed with the comfort of a successful second marriage, the nephew of Andrew Jackson endured both financial and political setbacks during the balance of his life. He was constantly in debt, and his political decisions often were contingent upon his quest for solvency. As he approached old age, he was forced to sell Tulip Grove, formerly Poplar Grove, the home that he and Emily had built together.[67]

Among Donelson's creditors were Martin Van Buren and John Eaton. Andrew owed the former president a substantial amount, a sum that continued to grow and was never repaid. He was also indebted to his old foe John Eaton. In 1847, Eaton reminded Donelson of a $541 unpaid bill from 1841. Donelson ignored the request, leaving the courts to render a judgment against him.[68]

His political career after the White House was both frustrating and unsatisfying. He was given hope of a position in both the Van Buren and Polk cabinets; neither was realized. However, less substantial appointments came his way. He was most successful as chargé d'affaires to the Republic of Texas. His activities may have been pivotal to the annexation of Texas into the United States. Less successful were his tenure as Minister to Prussia and as owner and editor of the *Washington Union* newspaper.[69]

In the 1850s, Donelson, angry and disappointed after years of frustration with the Democratic Party, switched his party affiliation to the Know Nothing party. He swiftly moved up in its organization. In 1856, Millard Fillmore was its candidate for president and Andrew Jackson Donelson its candidate for vice president. The party came in third place in the 1856 election.[70]

Cheathem's conclusion in his biography of Andrew Jackson Donelson incisively summarized his subject's career:

> It appears that Donelson understood, but found it difficult to accept, what Jackson had come to realize during the Eaton Affair: he (Donelson) did not have a firm understanding of the political world. Before the Eaton affair, Donelson was

XI—Emily Donelson: Presiding Lady Again

confident, self-assured, and focused. He knew his uncle's expectations and lived up to them as best as he could. After the Eaton affair, Donelson was insecure, self-doubting, and unsure about how to prove himself to Jackson.

He spent his later life in an attempt to prove to, "...himself and others that Jackson had anointed him as his political successor." He failed.[71]

XII

Margaret Eaton
Trials and Triumphs After the White House

"I am at the peaceful and hospitable Hermitage; would to heaven you were with us, for I believe you would be more happy ... you will see how devoted I have been in my attachment towards you ... better able to tell who are your real friends."
—John and Margaret Eaton's Hermitage, joint letter to Andrew Jackson Washington, April 16, 1832

"Madam, I will never rise and stand before any human being but Andrew Jackson."
—Peggy Eaton when urged to stand at the approach of the Queen of Spain's carriage. *The Autobiography of Peggy Eaton*, 187

"Andrew Jackson as a man? He wasn't a man, he was a ... God!"
—Margaret's response to a Tennessee reporter when in her seventies. Queena Pollack, *Peggy Eaton: Democracy's Mistress*, 272

The resignation of John Eaton as Secretary of War preceded the Eatons' departure several months later to Tennessee. Their departure eased the controversial Margaret away from the capital's social and political turmoil and ended the acrimony over The Eaton Affair. Her future returns to Washington would be socially tranquil, politically quiescent, but more often than not, personally distressing and disquieting. Years later she died in Washington, the city of her birth eighty years earlier.

XII—Margaret Eaton: After the White House

Andrew Jackson remained an important figure in Margaret's life until his death in 1845. The Eatons temporarily alienated the ex-president over a political matter, but their mutual personal affection fortunately effected a tearful reconciliation at The Hermitage before Jackson's demise.

Mrs. Eaton remained connected to the retired president through the important sinecures her husband received through Andrew Jackson's influence. Margaret was a social triumph during several of her husband's assignments away from Washington. Then the Eatons retired from public life. A placid period followed, marked by John's successful law practice, Margaret's daughters' maturation and marriage, and the happy introduction of grandchildren.

Andrew Jackson Donelson was near-euphoric at the news of his adversary John Eaton's resignation from the Jackson cabinet. He celebrated Eaton's impending departure for Tennessee, where Donelson nastily predicted, "He will scarcely play a part of such consequence in the future political operations of our party." He forecasted with undisguised glee that all sincere friends of Andrew Jackson "must pity Eaton's situation at the same time they deprecate the injury which the Administration has sustained on his account."[1]

However, to the undoubted disappointment of Donelson, President Jackson entrusted more significant official assignments to Eaton than to his nephew. Almost immediately after his resignation, Eaton was dispatched with John Coffee to negotiate the removal of the Chickasaw and Choctaw tribes from the southern states to west of the Mississippi River. Afterwards Jackson appointed his friend Eaton first to the Territorial Governorship of Florida, and subsequently to the Ambassadorship of the Kingdom of Spain.[2]

Donelson's chronic indebtedness involved him with Eaton at least twice. In 1841, he incurred a debt to the ex–Secretary of War. He owed Eaton $541 for some unknown reason and procrastinated in producing any payment. In the late 1840s, the lender requested payment in a letter; the nephew ignored the request and left the matter to the courts. In 1853, in an astonishing move, Donelson hired Eaton as his attorney to address his many other creditors.[3]

There is no record that their two wives either met or corresponded after Emily returned to the White House in 1831. However, during the summer of 1836, their paths crossed on the Ohio River in an ironic metaphor. Margaret's boat was carrying her on her journey from Florida to Washington. The *Sandusky*, travelling in the opposite direction, was taking the extremely ill Emily home to Tennessee and her death.[4]

Five months after his cabinet resignation, John Eaton composed and published a fifty-five-page pamphlet to refute the public accusations of his opponents within the Jackson cabinet. *A Candid Appeal to the American Public in Reply to Messrs Ingham, Branch and Berrien in the Dissolution of the Late Cabinet* was written by the former Secretary of War, "with extreme reluctance," to combat, "He who drags before the public its helpless inmates and subjects them to rude assaults, deserves to be considered worse than a barbarian." Therein he accused his former cabinet colleague of shunning "an honorable accountability." He also charged Branch, Berrien, and Ingham of dishonesty, treachery, and conspiracy. Eaton was compelled to clear his public reputation.

In *A Candid Appeal to the American People*, the author concluded that the whole affair was an attempt to force him out of the Cabinet, and thereby to limit Andrew Jackson to a single presidential term. He blamed Vice President Calhoun as the beneficiary of the political plot.[5] The extent, if any, of Margaret's contribution to the *Appeal* is unknown.[6] After its publication, the Eatons retired to their Franklin, Tennessee, home. They read Calhoun's rebuttal but wisely and uncharacteristically decided not to reply.[7]

The Eatons' return travel to Tennessee was not as tranquil as anticipated. Instead, it was interrupted by Margaret's illness: "Major Eaton was detained in Baltimore until yesterday by the severe illness of Mrs. Eaton."[8] Biographer Queena Pollack, in her characteristic ornamental prose, suggested that the cause of Margaret's illness was psychological, even emotional. Mrs. Eaton had collapsed in Baltimore: "Peg was ill, very ill.... For two weeks she tossed in troubled delirium." In mid-autumn she finally was well enough to move on to the Eaton home in Tennessee.[9]

Arriving at the home of John's mother in Franklin, Tennessee, the Eatons welcomed both its comfort and relief after their escape from the pandemonium of Washington. After a short interval, the famous couple was fêted by neighbors, friends, and local politicians as returning celebrities. The women of Tennessee socially accepted Margaret, some initially out of curiosity, but most out of friendship and even admiration. Andrew Jackson Donelson's predictive schadenfreude was not realized.[10]

In April 1832, the Eatons wrote a joint letter to the president from The Hermitage. John reassured Jackson on the state of the plantation; Margaret consoled him with sweet memories of the departed Rachel: "The first thing I did (upon arrival) was to visit the Tomb of your departed wife." She tenderly continued, "I am at the peaceful and hospitable Hermitage; would to heaven you were with us, for I believe you would be more happy ... you will see how devoted I have been in my attachment towards you ... better able to tell who are *your real friends*."[11]

However, Margaret was unhappy. Eaton wrote to the president that she "was in bad health, and has been so, since her arrival in this State."[12] The medical nature of her illness is speculative; it may have been a sense of defeat that her enemies had won the battle. The Donelsons were ensconced in the White House while she resided in near-oblivion in the middle of Tennessee.[13]

Both Eatons journeyed to Baltimore for the 1832 Democratic presidential nominating convention. They attended out of loyalty to view the re-nomination of their patron Andrew Jackson and the nomination of their friend Martin Van Buren as candidates for president and vice president respectively. The convention atmosphere rejuvenated their then dormant interests in politics: "Peg felt not prostration but prowess ... scenting competitive aggrandizement ... that Eaton could not withstand the lure of politics any less than she." John Eaton, with restored political enthusiasm, then entered the 1832 race for United States Senator from Tennessee. He lost.[14]

Both Eatons were dispirited by his election defeat. They returned to the nation's capital city, but neither Margaret's mood nor her health recovered: "Peggy, still inert by illness, was dispirited." Eaton was frankly worried. She seemed to have no will to live. "My wife is so low and declining every day. I dread to anticipate but fear greatly the result." Washington at this time was experiencing another of its periodic cholera outbreaks. Pollack hinted without evidence that a cholera infection was the reason for Mrs. Eaton's physical decline. The 1832 cholera pandemic reached many parts of the United States, principally along its eastern seaboard. New York City was hard hit. Archival evidence demonstrated that the 1832 cholera pandemic reached Baltimore on August 4, 1832, and Washington on August 8, 1832.[15]

Margaret's dire state was illustrated further in a December 2, 1832, letter from Jacksonian insider W.B. Lewis to Old Hickory's Nashville friend, John Overton:

> She has been quite ill since we returned to the city. She looks very badly indeed.... I was shocked by her pale sickly and emaciated appearance. I was then fearful she would never be well again, and every time I see her I am more and more confirmed in that opinion.... [Eaton] believing as I no doubt he does that she has fallen a victim to the cool and relentless persecutions of monsters in the shape of Human Beings.[16]

President Andrew Jackson did not abandon his loyal friends John and Margaret Eaton. Her autobiography claimed that Jackson offered the governorship of the Michigan Territory to the ex-secretary. Eaton declined the appointment because his ailing wife's health required a warmer climate.[17] The president responded by offering his friend the post of the third governor of the Florida Territory, succeeding Andrew Jackson and William Pope Duval. John persuaded an initially reluctant Margaret that even a single winter in the sunshine would be beneficial to her health.[18]

Jackson officially nominated Eaton to a three-year term as Florida governor on March 28, 1834. The Eatons did not arrive at Tallahassee, the territorial capital, until December 11, 1834; the delay was in order to escape the humid heat of this subtropical city.[19]

A review of the list of Florida's early governors is replete with irony and paradox. Andrew Jackson was its first territorial governor. After a decade, John Eaton became its third territorial governor. His successor as governor was Margaret's defamer of long standing, Richard K. Call. Later, when the territory achieved statehood, its governor was another enemy of the Eatons, the deposed Secretary of the Navy, John Branch. Call had become a man of substance in Tallahassee and a significant landowner. Eaton and Call never set aside their disdain for one another, but Margaret and Call's wife, Mary, got along well. Furthermore, the Calls' daughter was stunned when she first observed a recrudescent Mrs. Eaton, describing her as "...beautiful and fascinating without. Of good height and graceful form, a wealth of brown hair encircling a face of bright complexion, made variable in its expression by an ever-sparkling deep and clear blue eye, with mouth and chin of finished beauty together with a vivacious and affable manner."[20]

The governor's wife soon tired of Tallahassee, an unimpressive and "grotesque" place whose population was a mere fifteen hundred people. Instead, she spent most of her time in Pensacola, more populous and historical city, whose inhabitants were often bathed with pleasant Gulf of Mexico breezes. Mrs. Eaton remained herself: "Margaret Eaton continued to flout society's norms and maintained her reputation for unorthodoxy." She swam in a nearby lake with her attractive daughters; they tanned themselves without embarrassment. At the racetrack she bet like a man, where her flamboyant bonnet was decorated with ostrich plumes.[21] Her health and beauty had responded to the southern sunshine.

Margaret, later in life, fondly recalled her experience as First Lady of Territorial Florida: "We resided in Florida two years. They were beautiful years to me. My neighbors were pleasant, I had no ugly passages in my history, and I was away from my husband's political persecutors."[22]

John Eaton was a dutiful executive, but his tenure was unexceptional. While in the state capital, he spent much of his time signing

XII—Margaret Eaton: After the White House

divorce decrees; he did little to solve the increasing menace from the Seminole Indians. It was only at Andrew Jackson's urging that Eaton reluctantly returned to Florida for a second year.[23] Margaret and John Eaton were rescued from their Southern miasmic outpost on March 16, 1836, by another presidential appointment. John quickly wound up his gubernatorial affairs to depart Florida on April 19, 1836.[24]

President Andrew Jackson continued to favor the ever-loyal Eaton, his friend, and Margaret, both a friend and vulnerable protectee. He nominated his colleague of long standing to the prestigious post of Minister to the Kingdom of Spain. Perhaps the aging gallant hoped that Mrs. Eaton's personality and style would glitter on the stage of the most elaborate court in Europe. The Senate routinely confirmed the appointment, either from boredom over the scandals five years previously or from a desire to ease the infamous Pompadour's departure from the country. Van Buren was amused "at the spectacle of a senate, more or less the same as that during the Eaton Imbroglio, endorsing Eaton's appointment without murmur. Mrs. Eaton was not good enough to associate with Washington's women … but she was evidently representative of American womanhood to be sent to the most formal court of Europe."[25]

The couple sailed to Europe aboard the *Independent*. While aboard John Eaton's wife assumed her former, but unforgotten, guise as Peggy, sparkling, fun-loving, and inherently flirtatious. A fellow passenger wrote to Jackson that Margaret and her daughters, seventeen-year-old Mary Virginia and eleven-year-old Margaret Rosa, proved to be "the life of the cabin, rendering many an hour that would have been tedious, cheerful and sprightly." Richard Rush, the quoted passenger, was traveling to England under Jackson's order to obtain materials then in the English Court of Chancery. Margaret recalled, "He was a gentleman, a scholar, and a statesman; and he added very much to the pleasure of the voyage. He was devotedly kind to me as if I had been his sister."[26]

Turbulence and instability were the harrowing characteristics of Spanish society during the 1830s due to a conflict over the succession to the royal throne. King Ferdinand VII, convinced by his wife, Maria Cristina de Borbón, decreed that his successor upon his demise would be their six-year-old daughter Isabella. Queen Maria Cristina was to rule as Regent with absolute power until her daughter achieved maturity. However, Don Carlos, Ferdinand's brother, determined that he was the rightful successor and commenced a civil war (the Carlist Rebellion) to seize the throne.[27]

Margaret Eaton's first contact with Spanish royalty occurred shortly after her arrival in Madrid. The Queen's entourage passed her on the street; all her subjects were supposed to stand out of deference.

Margaret strenuously objected when asked to rise, exclaiming, "Madam, I will never rise and stand before any human being but Andrew Jackson."[28]

The Spanish Queen became very fond of the minister from America and constantly gained on Mrs. Eaton's "affections by her sweet amiability." The minister's wife happily recounted years later, "Through those years we received every attention. Our relations with the court and the representatives of other countries were exceedingly pleasant ... the Queen at all our entertainments had showed us marked attention."[29]

Some accounts of Margaret's three-and-one-half years in Madrid suggested a very warm, even intimate relationship with Queen Cristina, "sisters under the skin," according to Pollack. Both were bold, spirited and subjected to, but usually unfazed by, public disapproval. Both women had been criticized for extramarital affairs, either imagined or real. Cristina, while still married to the king, took on a lover who was a courtier in the royal court. After Ferdinand's death, she married Munoz, her paramour and bore him two handsome children.[30]

The minister's wife was happy in Madrid and enjoyed the double triumph of political and social influence: "There, thank God, I was beyond the reach of venom...." Margaret was informed that whenever her name came up in conversation, she was commended and not scorned as in the past. She mused, "I should have liked to have spent my life in Madrid."[31]

In contrast, her husband may have become bored with his post, one so distant from Washington and Tennessee. He implied as much in his infrequent letters to Washington. Andrew Jackson warned John Eaton before his departure to Spain about the unacceptable silence of American diplomats abroad with the American capital. In response Eaton promised to write, but he did not. A disappointed Jackson advised President Van Buren that if he were still president, he would fire Eaton. Moreover, the State Department was convinced that Eaton appeared to favor Spanish over American interests.[32]

President Van Buren recalled John Eaton from Spain, which ended the minister's four year representation. The diplomatic mission in Madrid, that of representation by a minister, was downgraded to that requiring only a chargé d'affaires. Business with Spain was judged insufficient to demand loftier representation.[33] The initial reaction of both Eatons at news of the minister's recall was one of relief. Then anger set in. John was upset not only by its suddenness but also by its disrespect, "especially in view of the fidelity of his friendship with Mr. Van Buren." For her part, Margaret was mad, chagrined, and humiliated.[34]

Shortly after his return to the nation's capital, the deposed diplomat rushed to an interview with President Van Buren. Van Buren smoothly attempted to allay Eaton's anger by expressing his friendship. He also blandly reminded Eaton of his desire, communicated in letters more than once, to return to America. The president considered his recall to be a simple attempt to abide by Eaton's wishes.

The Eatons returned to the United States just as the 1840 presidential campaign was raging. The contestants were Democrat Martin Van Buren, who was striving for re-election, and Whig General William Henry Harrison. Until then John Eaton always had been a loyal Jacksonian Democrat: "Whether it was Eaton's hidden resentment at recall, his desire to swell the winning tide so that he could swing back into office, or simply a matter of personal animosity ... he came out openly for Harrison as against Van Buren."[35] Harrison won easily; he captured 53 percent of the popular vote and carried nineteen states to Van Buren's mere seven.[36]

Andrew Jackson was infuriated by Eaton's disloyalty: "He comes out against all the political principles he ever professed and against those on which he was supported and elected senator." Not having emptied his well of ire, he fulminated against two close associates of many years, one of whom was John Eaton: "Once they were aroused by the designs of aristocrats and apostates to raise 'a monied king to rule.'" He referring to Eaton as "an ulogiser [sic] of Harrison." The second apostate was perennial protégé R.K. Call. Call, as Florida governor, previously was criticized by Andrew Jackson for his failures in the Second Seminole War. The long-term ally was deeply hurt by his mentor's disapproval; this might be the reason for his desertion to the Whigs.[37]

While on the campaign trail for Van Buren, Jackson accidentally ran into Eaton, who was an active advocate for Harrison. Both men behaved properly during the encounter and nothing embarrassing or untoward happened.[38] Although Eaton continued to politically support the Whigs, Jackson at first was generous towards his acolyte, and "charitably hoped that Eaton might have been favoring a fighting man, instead of a practiced politician, merely as a principle of democracy." However, Andrew Jackson was slowly dying, and he was embittered that his bosom friend and filial disciple should have switched fully to the enemy. He turned around toward the wall his former protégé's portrait that hung at The Hermitage. The two men did not reconcile until a year before Jackson's death in 1845.[39]

Shortly after Margaret's younger daughter, also named Margaret, married Lt. John B. Randolph of Annapolis and Virginia, the Eatons left the East Coast for Tennessee. While there, John decided to sort his old papers. He pulled those related to Andrew Jackson's political life and wrote his old mentor with an offer to send them to The Hermitage. At the same time, he requested that the ex-president return any papers related to Margaret's virtue. Jackson replied, forgave Eaton, and invited both to dinner. They traveled to The Hermitage where Peggy "perked up again. With all the wealth of her magnetism and drollery she mimicked contemporary Whig leaders, life in Spain, his old enemies and his old friends with an enchanting contagion until Jackson took them back into his heart, with two-fold thankfulness that he'd done so before death."

In June 1845, a slave ran to the home of W.B. Lewis with a message that Jackson was dying and wanted Lewis and Eaton to come at once. When Sam Houston, the president of Texas and another old companion of Jackson, rushed to his bedside, it was Peggy who opened The Hermitage door to him. She told him he had come too late.[40]

This story may be apocryphal since there is no corroboration by Remini, Meacham, or even in Margaret's autobiography. However, affirmation that John and Margaret did visit the dying Jackson although prior to his demise appears in Phillips' *That Eaton Woman*. In June 1845, when the Eatons arrived in Tennessee for the summer, they "learned that Old Hickory was dying. They made a hurried journey to his bedside, and saw him briefly before he passed away."[41]

A second surrogate son, Andrew Jackson Donelson, was absent at Jackson's death. He was away on a diplomatic mission in Texas. However, he was represented at the Jackson home by his second wife, Elizabeth, and their son, John. The dying man beckoned John to move close to him, kissed the young man, blessed him, and gave the young man parting advice.[42]

After their Spanish interlude, the Eatons returned to Washington. They and Margaret's two daughters moved to a house on I Street, which was once a part of the O'Neale-managed Franklin Hotel complex. Margaret's widowed mother, Rhoda O'Neale, lived close to, but mostly with, the Eatons. Rhoda, still glamorous and insightful as she aged, maintained an active role in their lives and remained a source of advice and comfort to her daughter until death. The Eatons spent their winter months in the nation's capital and their summer months in Franklin, Tennessee, John's hometown.[43]

For almost two decades, Margaret and John lived tranquilly, and occasionally triumphantly, in Washington. The former, once a much-condemned source of *The Eaton Malaria*, was warmly welcomed by their previous friends: "The storms that had been raised for political reasons, so far as we were personally concerned, had lulled." The one-time Peggy Eaton became an accepted member of Washington society. She hosted well-attended social events at her home. Moreover, the Eatons were frequent guests at the White House during the administration (1845–1849) of James K. Polk. Additionally, they were friends of the Tyler administration (1841–1845), likely due to Eaton's political support. One of President Tyler's sons spent "one half of his evenings with her Ladyship."[44]

After mid–1841, Margaret's health improved. She no longer was afflicted by "the debilitating illnesses that earlier had crippled her." Marszalek later speculated that Mrs. Eaton suffered from tuberculosis when he wrote that her granddaughter, "Emily, 17, developed consumption, the disease Margaret once suffered herself." Mrs. Eaton, a native Washingtonian, sought to assist those residents who were poor and marginalized. She worked among the capital's unfortunates. Thereby, she earned the title "Alma Mater." One co-worker commented upon Margaret's appearance, "I have never seen anyone so beautiful."[45]

John Eaton lived a comfortable life in Washington until his death in 1856. He loved and was loved by his wife, he helped raise and marry off two stepdaughters, and for a few years, enjoyed playing with his grandchildren. He successfully practiced law in Washington and was elected president of the Washington Bar Association. Eaton argued cases before the United States Supreme Court; he victoriously defended his old nemesis, Andrew Jackson Donelson, against the U.S. Treasury; he even won a judgment of $12,000 against former political ally Amos Kendall's actions as attorney general.[46]

Eaton did not discard all his former political associations. He remained friendly with Jackson protégé James K. Polk, who succeeded John Tyler as president in 1845. Polk had been a strong supporter of Andrew Jackson, both as Speaker of the House of Representatives and as Tennessee governor. The Eatons were often invited to dinner at the Polk White House. This president also sought out Eaton's professional advice: "When Polk wanted to sell some property in Tennessee, the matter was handled for him by Eaton, who was then known for the rest of Polk's term, until March 1849, as the 'president's lawyer.'"[47]

However, another former ally, William B. Lewis, was less generous. Lewis, a fellow member of the Jackson kitchen cabinet, thought that the ex-minister was mentally ill: "I have thought ever since he returned from Spain that he would kill himself drinking or perhaps blow his brains out." Lewis was wrong. John Eaton read, drank, and lived a comfortable life until his death in 1856.[48]

During the late 1840s and extending into the 1850s, Margaret's life often centered on her two daughters. After much effort, she was able to obtain a half Navy pension for the support of Virginia and Margaret as the children of the deceased naval purser John Timberlake. Virginia, "Ginger," the oldest, was beautiful, ebullient, and, like her mother, flirtatious. As a result, she was very popular with young men in Spain and in Washington. Her most flamboyant suitor in the nation's capital was Philip Scott Key, the son of the composer of "The Star-Spangled Banner." Instead, Ginger married the Duc A. de Sampayo, the Secretary of the French delegation to the United States, in May 1843. Shortly after, the couple sailed to Paris to live and had one child. Virginia never returned to America, and Margaret never again saw her daughter nor met this grandchild.[49]

Margaret Rosa, the younger Timberlake daughter, was a far less flamboyant woman. She married well into the illustrious Randolph family of Virginia on March 24, 1845, in Washington. Navy Lieutenant John C. Randolph was at sea for much of his marriage to young Margaret. However, his shore leaves were productive: grandchildren John Chapman, John H. Eaton, Mary, and Emily enriched the Eaton's lives. Unfortunately, Lieutenant Randolph contracted dysentery on an Asian cruise, although he managed to return to Washington before he expired. His loving and fertile wife died from cholera eight months later on March 24, 1855.[50]

John Eaton died on November 17, 1856, at the age of sixty-six. He had aged well, but "his heart gave out." He left his widow seventy thousand dollars, three hundred books, and two hundred casks of wine. His estate corroborated that he had lived well and enjoyed both reading and drinking. Margaret, then almost fifty-seven, had been married to her second husband for more than twenty-six years.[51]

Therefore, in her late middle age, Mrs. Eaton became the guardian of her four grandchildren. She focused her energies and care upon them. In these tasks, she fortunately was aided by her still vibrant and intelligent mother, Rhoda O'Neale, whose counsel she often sought: "My mother lived with me from the time of my return from Spain until her death which occurred long after my husband's." She also wrote, "I did try according to the measure of my strength and income to labor amongst the poor."

The grandchildren were well educated. Moreover, their grandmother, perhaps recalling that she danced before First Lady Dolley Madison, enrolled them in dancing school. Unfortunately for Margaret, they fell under the charm of the dance master, Italian Antonio Buchignani. The handsome, but very poor, Buchignani beguiled his students, who in turn wheedled their grandmother into letting the dance master live with them.[52]

On June 7, 1859, the wealthy, fifty-nine-year-old widow married the nineteen-year-old Italian. Rhoda approved, along with the grandchildren. However, there were consequences. Once again, Margaret, as the newly wed Mrs. Buchignani, became a pariah in Washington Society. Mr. Buchignani took a position as assistant librarian of the House of Representatives.[53]

The marriage was surprisingly tranquil and loving until Buchignani's treachery and thievery became manifest. In 1865, the police informed Margaret that her husband had pawned a silver setting of hers worth seven hundred dollars. She covered up her husband's theft. Subsequently, more household thievery occurred. Furthermore, the swindling dance master persuaded his wife to move to New York City and invest twenty thousand dollars into his business (which failed). He finally convinced his wife to sign over her remaining estate of seventy-three thousand dollars to him. In retrospect, the naïveté of Margaret, whose past personality and intelligence were anything but, is astonishing.[54]

Buchignani's treachery reached its nadir when he seduced his wife's youngest granddaughter, seventeen-year-old Emily, ran off to Europe with her, fathered a child, and squandered all of Margaret's money. When he slithered back to New York City, Margaret demanded a warrant for his arrest and divorced the wretch in 1869. Margaret resumed her married name of Eaton.[55] Mrs. Eaton and her grandson John returned to the District in 1873. John helped to support his grandmother and remained loyal to her all his life. He "worked for the War Department ... rising to become an Undersecretary in the 20th century."[56]

During her seniority, living in her beloved Washington, Margaret was sought out for frequent interviews by the press and others. One interviewer was enchanted by the aged lady: "She was now old ... when at all excited, her beautiful fiery eyes gleam and sparkle with original fire.... She (still) held that powerful influence over men that requires a master mind no less than a lovely face."[57] A reporter from Franklin, Tennessee, asked the aged Mrs. Eaton what she thought of Andrew Jackson as a man. Her admiration and loyalty for her old friend and supporter remained unabated after almost thirty years. She replied, "Andrew Jackson as a man? He wasn't a man, he was a ... God!"[58]

The widow, both poor and aged, could not afford to pay for medical care during the last two years of her life. Toward the end, her characteristic *joie de vivre* emerged: "I am not afraid to die, but this is such a wonderful world to leave." Margaret (Peggy) O'Neale Timberlake Eaton passed away on November 9, 1879. She is buried next to John Eaton, daughter Margaret, and son-in-law John Randolph in Oak Hill Cemetery, District of Columbia.[59]

XIII

Sarah Yorke Jackson
His "Daughter"

"She is quite pretty, has black hair and eyes and is about an inch lower than myself—she is quite agreeable and we are all very much pleased with her, and Uncle seems very much pleased."
—Emily Donelson's assessment of Sarah Yorke Jackson, and her uncle's delight with her. Galloway, *Andrew Jackson Junior, Son of a President*, 36

Sarah "...arrived at the White House on November 26, 1834. She immediately began to take on the role as co-hostess of the White House along with the President's niece Emily Donelson."
—"Sarah Yorke Jackson," *World Heritage Encyclopedia*

"This gift and bequest is made for my great affection to her as a memento of her uniform attention to me and kindness on all occasions, and particularly when worn down with sickness, pain and debility. She has been more than a daughter to me, and I hope she never will be disturbed in the enjoyment of this gift and bequest by any one."
—Andrew Jackson's will and appendix, June 7, 1843, Galloway, *Andrew Jackson Junior, Son of a President*, 64.

Andrew Jackson, during his second presidential term and later as a retiree at his beloved Hermitage, once again depended upon a capable woman. Sarah Yorke became a Jackson when she married his adopted son, Andrew Jackson Junior. The president had long contemplated the desirability of his son's marriage to an amiable and responsible partner. He had written to a friend, "It is the only hope by which I look to a continuation of my name."[1]

In 1809 the childless Rachel and Andrew Jackson adopted at birth one of the twin sons of her brother Severn Donelson and his wife Elizabeth. Thereafter the adoptee was always known as Andrew Jackson Junior. However, the expectations of the heroic father were never fully met by the adopted son. Biographer Linda Galloway forlornly assessed Junior's future life as, "a sad and almost useless one; he never acquired fame except through the name he bore.... He was remembered as a man of fair ability, a kind husband, a good neighbor, a confiding friend, a man of upright principles, excellent character and Christian life; and if at times he was a too trusting and confiding friend, that is not to be a detriment to his character."[2]

Andrew Jackson, from the day of adoption, treated the boy "with devotion, educated him, and bestowed ... all the affection a father would bestow on an only son."[3] Old Hickory also paid for Andrew's attendance at Davidson Academy in Nashville; this institution later became Cumberland College.[4]

The senior Andrew began to assign Andrew Junior various responsibilities when he reached the age of sixteen. One assignment was that of being a conscientious and gracious host to many of his father's political followers. Junior lived well, wore excellent clothes, and was served by a personal valet. He was college educated.[5]

When twenty, young Andrew accompanied the president-elect on his pre-inauguration journey to Washington. There he became a society favorite, being both handsome, polished, and endowed with social ease. After a brief stay in the nation's capital, Junior returned to The Hermitage to assume the important responsibility of management of his father's plantation.[6]

Back in Tennessee, young Andrew quickly developed a romantic interest in a "Miss Flora" who lived nearby at Hunter's Hill. "Miss Flora" was the nineteen-year-old Mary Florida Dickson, the youngest daughter of the late Nashville physician and congressman William Dickson, and subsequently the ward of Jackson's neighbor Edward Ward.[7] The romance, perhaps just an infatuation, enmeshed Junior for three months during the summer of 1829. The president, an inveterate matchmaker, profusely advised his son with five letters regarding both courtship behavior and useful tactics to satisfactorily conclude his relationship with "Miss Flora."

The senior Jackson wrote the following on July 26, 1829: "You can judge of the anxiety I have that you should marry a lady that will make you happy which would add to mine ... that no good can flow from long courtship ... and should her reply be adverse to your wishes, you ought not to be offended, but continue to treat her as a friend...."[8]

His letters on August 20 and September 21 expressed a father's love and concern. The father accurately predicted the unhappy conclusion of the youngsters' relationship. More importantly, Jackson attempted to protect his son from any future mistakes of the heart, writing, "Remember my son, that you are now the one solace of my mind, & prospects of my happiness here below, & were you to make an unhappy choice it would bring me to the grave in sorrow." "I expected the result you name with Flora—she is a fine girl—I am happy you are clear of your little engagement with Flora—and all I have to request is, that you will engage in no other without first obtaining my advice...."[9] Apparently Andrew Jackson Junior was never the primary object of Flora's romantic desire since she married Henry Baldwin, Jr., the following year.[10]

While in Washington City in 1830, Junior's romantic eye focused upon Miss Mary Smith. His infatuation overruled the prudence previously prescribed by his father, since he followed Miss Smith to her Virginia home. There the young man's ardor apparently violated the then accepted rules of courtship; he was summarily banished from the Smith residence. After he returned to the White House, the president quickly sent Junior back to Virginia with a letter of apology to her father. The letter made this appeal:

> I am fearful that he has committed an error.... He has made known to me ... the attachment he has formed for your amiable daughter, which he informs me has been expressed to her and if not reciprocated, has at least won her favorable opinion. He has erred in attempting to address your daughter without first making known to you and your lady his honorable intentions, and obtaining your approbation; but he has been admonished of this impropriety, and he now waits upon you to confess it.

Both the appeal and the suitor were rejected. Junior, perhaps humiliated, did not return to the White House but instead traveled to The Hermitage.[11]

At the Jacksons' Tennessee plantation, the young man settled down both to immerse himself in the estate management of The Hermitage and to conduct various pieces of business for his father. Andrew Junior visited the White House in 1831; he returned to Nashville by way of a circuitous route that included Philadelphia. The detour to Philadelphia proved to be both fortuitous and fortunate. A chance street encounter in the company of a Captain McCaluley led to a conversation with the captain's friends, a "beautiful young woman" and an elderly lady. The serendipitous meeting became the occasion for the proverbial "love at first sight" between Andrew Jackson Junior and Sarah Yorke, the "beautiful young woman." An ardent courtship followed; when Junior returned to the White House in Fall 1831, he busied himself writing letters to his new love.[12]

Andrew proposed marriage; Sarah accepted without hesitation. The president was informed around the middle of October 1831 when his namesake divulged his plans by showing his father one of Sarah's letters. Andrew Jackson, with a mixture of relief and hope, acquiesced to his son's engagement.[13] He wrote to his son on October 27, "Since my heavy and irreparable bereavement in the loss of My Dr. & ever to be lamented wife ... you will please communicate to her, that you have my full, and free, consent that you be united in the holy bonds of matrimony—that I shall receive her as a daughter."[14]

Meanwhile the president engaged in some astute background checking of his prospective daughter. The results of his investigation were detailed in letters to John Coffee and Andrew Jackson Hutchings. He revealed that Andrew was "to be married ... to a young lady who my friend Henry Toland says of respectable connections, accomplished, amiable & handsome.... I know not what she is worth ... it was enough for me to know that he loved her, that she was respectable and accomplished." Unbeknownst to Sarah Yorke, she had passed the test of acceptability.[15]

Sarah, born in 1803, was a member of an old and distinguished Pennsylvania Quaker family, but her parents were married at Christ Church (Episcopal) where later Sarah and her siblings were baptized.[16] Peter Yorke, her father, was both a sea captain and a wealthy merchant. However, shortly before his death in 1815, the family fortune was diminished by the loss at sea of two Yorke owned merchant ships. Her mother, Mary Haines Yorke, died in Philadelphia on May 31, 1820, leaving Sarah and her two sisters, Marion and Jane, orphans. Sarah then was seven. The three sisters were raised by two paternal aunts, Mrs. George Farquhar and Mrs. Mordecai Wetherill. One of the aunts probably was the old lady described in Sarah's introductory encounter with Andrew.[17]

Throughout her life, Sarah remained very close to her sister Marion Adams. When her husband died, Marion moved to The Hermitage. Jane Lockridge, the second sister, married well; consequently, she was dubbed "the rich sister." Jane's relationship with her two siblings became strained from her distant residence in Philadelphia; moreover, she was loyal to the Union during the Civil War. In contrast both Sarah and Marion were sympathetic to the Confederate cause.[18]

Sarah's biographical, interpersonal, religious, and economic history before her marriage to Andrew Junior is but barely documented. Many particulars from her first three decades of life remain lost to the historian. However, it is documented that after the death of their parents, the three sisters attended the French and English Boarding and Day School for Young Ladies in Philadelphia for seven years. A well-respected educator, Mrs. Mallon, presided over their education. There is no knowledge regarding any prior romantic involvement or social engagement by Sarah Yorke. It is curious that an attractive, amiable, educated, and well-spoken woman would wait until the age of twenty-eight to marry a younger man. However, her future mate was more than abundantly eager to fulfill both his responsibility to his father and to his amorous desires.[19]

Their romance was impulsive and impetuous; their engagement was brief. Sarah and young Andrew wed in Philadelphia on November 24, 1831. The bride was twenty-eight and the groom just two weeks short of twenty-three, almost six years her junior. The pressures of the presidency prohibited Andrew Jackson's attendance at the marriage ceremony. He was represented by his friend, the artist Ralph E.W. Earle; the president's gift to his new daughter-in-law was a pearl ring. The newlyweds immediately departed Philadelphia for the White House.[20]

Andrew Jackson and Sarah Yorke Jackson immediately bonded. The president embraced her as his daughter, and she regarded him as the father who for many years had been absent from her life. Sarah's initial assessment by others in the White House was that she "was small, of dark complexion, gentle voice and gentle manner. Except as the wife of the President's son, she would have been inconspicuous in the gay company that centered about Emily Donelson and Mary Eastin." The groom and bride were welcome guests during the Christmas festivities that delighted all within the presidential mansion. The ever-perceptive Emily Donelson in a letter to her sister concurred with this description and with her uncle's approbation, "She is quite pretty, has black hair and eyes and is about an inch lower than myself—she is quite agreeable and we are all very much pleased with her, and Uncle seems very much pleased."[21]

"Very much pleased" was Andrew Jackson's verdict which he proclaimed in a flurry of letters during November and December 1831. In letters to close friend Judge John Overton and relatives Samuel Jackson Hayes and William Donelson, he wrote repeatedly that Sarah was "accomplished," "pretty," "amiable," with whom "he was well pleased." His letter to William Donelson concluded, "I have no doubt from her amiable disposition she will endeavor, in all things, to add to my happiness."[22]

Sarah's arrival affected the old general's life in many ways. He became relieved that this little daughter would be a positive influence upon Andrew Junior, who was sometimes less than responsible and frequently without organization. Her amiable disposition would add to Jackson's happiness within the White House and to the graceful ambience of his beloved Hermitage. Most importantly, Sarah's hoped-for fertility would assure the Jackson lineage. This narrative previously recorded the president's message to a friend, when contemplating the possibility of Junior marrying, which said, "It is the only hope by which I look to a continuation of my name."[23]

Jackson's hope was fulfilled; Sarah and Andrew raised his three grandchildren who survived to maturity. Rachel, the couple's first born, was so named in remembrance of Andrew Jackson's treasured wife. Rachel was born November 1, 1832. Little Rachel soon became her grandfather's "little pet." Sarah would give birth to five children; all were born at The Hermitage. However, two boys, the youngest, perished before their first birthday.[24]

Sarah and Junior departed Washington for The Hermitage in April 1832. He carried with him a long memorandum from his father that listed all his advice regarding the proper management of the plantation. Although Andrew Jackson expressed occasional annoyance at his son's minor management mistakes and near-absent communications, the president approved Junior's careful supervision of Rachel's grave and his plans for new stables. It is alleged that at this time the famous guitar shaped entrance drive lined by cedar trees was designed. Whose idea it was is unknown, but Sarah played the guitar.[25]

Sarah was well aware that her father-in-law, although unspoken, had bestowed upon her the responsibilities of mistress of the mansion. She would enjoy this role and frequently wrote to the president about her activities and plans. Jackson reciprocated with frequent letters:

> It gave me much pleasure that you had reached so near The Hermitage, ...where I hope you may reach in health & safety, and find it as comfortable a home, as I think you will"; "say to Andrew not to be so lazy [sic] in writing me"; "I will endeavor to visit & spend a short time with you this Summer.... I am sure you & myself can arrange a system of neatness and oconomy [sic] in Housekeeping, that will be satisfactory and pleasing to all—you must engage Andrew's attention to this part of domestic economy, by which your labours will be lightened, by his attention to the servants & seeing that your orders are duly executed"; "and when you leave the House will have to see that all furniture for the table is locked up, but what may be necessary, for such company as may be passing.[26]

Andrew Jackson happily anticipated his biannual visit to his home in summer of 1832, "for now there was a daughter at The Hermitage to welcome him." His anticipation was more than satisfied during his Tennessee stay. Jackson delayed his return to Washington for a week for the wedding of Thomas Jefferson Donelson and Emma Farquhar that took place on September 17, 1832. Emma Farquhar, a cousin of Sarah, previously accompanied the young Jacksons on their journey to Tennessee after their Christmas in the Executive Mansion. Emma quickly fell in love with Junior's cousin, Thomas Jefferson Donelson, and then married him. The cousins' wedding celebration probably occurred at The Hermitage; President Jackson by happy habit gave the bride away, thereby delaying his return to Washington. In the White House, Old Hickory was much invigorated by his trip to the beloved Hermitage, possibly a result of its new aura under Sarah Jackson, its new mistress.[27]

During the 1832–3 winter in Washington, and despite his re-election and upcoming inauguration, Old Hickory complained of headaches and loneliness. He wrote to the distant Sarah, "This day I am left alone." Circumstances soon changed for the better, lifting his pre–inauguration lethargy upon the White House arrival of Junior, Sarah, and the new little Rachel. His first grandchild was only four months old. She "became the pride and joy of Andrew Jackson to the day of his death."[28]

"The sight of his little grandchild did much to renew his sagging spirits." However, Jackson was perturbed through the spring of 1833 by worries over the health of the ailing Sarah and Rachel, "the d'r little pet." He urged his son to take them to Philadelphia for a medical examination by the president's favorite medical consultant, Dr. Philip Syng Physick, "whose advice on her situation I am very desirous should be had, his skill and experience, if anything is wrong, will, by taking it in time, perfectly restore her, when if neglected now, may destroy her health in time." Jackson admonished his son to take Dr. Physick's advice and not to neglect it. Fortunately, the president's fears were unfounded, since "Sarah has quite recovered."[29]

On July 4, 1833, the recently re-elected president returned to Washington from a lengthy political trip to the northeastern United States. He was both exhausted and very ill. Emily Donelson and Sarah Jackson ministered to his physical needs; together they nursed him back to recovery. The year of 1833, being an odd-numbered year, denoted the Rip Raps as the location for his summer vacation. Jackson convalesced by the seashore in the company of his two nurses, Emily and Sarah. Little Rachel and three of Emily's children with their nurse completed the presidential party.[30]

Thereafter the young Jackson family returned to The Hermitage. The president lamented their absence, especially Rachel's, in letters to his son: "I cannot tell why, unless being very lonesome at night not hearing the prattle of little Rachel," and to Sarah, "I dreaded the long travel for our sweet little pet ... she is given to us as a blessing."[31]

XIII—Sarah Yorke Jackson: His "Daughter" 167

Although Jackson was confident that Sarah was a competent household administrator, it is unlikely that he hoped that his daughter-in-law would be a positive factor in her husband's management of the entire Hermitage plantation. As a stereotype of an antebellum Southern plantation owner, Jackson undoubtedly believed that this responsibility was a man's work, although his dearly departed Rachel clearly was burdened with some plantation responsibilities during his many absences as a warrior and as a politician.

Junior's administrative performance was scrutinized from afar and occasionally found deficient by his father. He admonished his son for neglect of their enslaved people, complained about the services of the plantation overseer, and was upset over Junior's neglect of a payment to Mr. Hibbs and his incompetence in finalizing a land purchase from Mr. Hill. Any involvement by Sarah in her husband's business decisions is unrecorded.[32]

The president considered Emily Donelson to be a most excellent First Lady since she was a very agreeable woman and had been raised to entertain large numbers of guests. However, as Remini speculated, Jackson sometimes wished that Sarah could serve as the White House Hostess, and then his granddaughter would be around him all the time.[33] During the 1833–4 winter, Sarah was pregnant again. Her father-in-law feared for her health during this second pregnancy. April 1834 was marked by the birth of a healthy boy, Andrew Jackson III. The proud grandfather rejoiced that at last there was a grandson to carry on his name.[34]

Summer 1834 was the time for President Andrew Jackson's biannual vacation at The Hermitage. When he arrived on August 5, he immediately went to visit his grandson. Andrew III was "a very large fat baby, a veritable Hercules." Sarah slowly recovered from her second childbirth and suffered several relapses of illness. She nursed her infant son as often as her strength allowed; she prohibited anyone else from nursing, even when a severe attack confined her to bed a few weeks after Jackson's arrival. During her mother's illness, Rachel clung to Jackson for security every waking moment. Her grandfather described the little girl as "sprightly as a fairy" and "wild as a little partridge." Andrew invariably referred to his grand daughter as his "little pet."[35]

Jackson had barely returned to the White House before a catastrophic fire almost consumed The Hermitage. The destructive fire broke out by accident at four o' clock in the afternoon of Monday, October 13, 1834. Neither Andrew nor Sarah were at home when the conflagration began. The mansion's roof was ignited "by sparks or soot of the chimney" in the dining room that rose upwards. A stiff northeast wind quickly spread the fire. Finally, the roof of the mansion collapsed. Fortunately, no one died or was injured by the inferno.[36]

The fire was first noticed by the household servants of the burning mansion, who spread the alarm. Joseph Reiff and William C. Hume rushed to the burning structure; they were carpenter-contractors who were building the nearby Poplar Grove home for Emily and Andrew Jackson Donelson. The two carpenters, the servants of The Hermitage, and William Donelson's farmhands who were working in the nearby fields, combined to save as much as possible. When Sarah arrived at the scene, she "acted with firmness and gave every necessary direction to save the furniture." For his part, Andrew Junior blamed his servants for the calamity.[37]

Through the combined efforts of many, most of the downstairs belongings were pulled clear, but much of the upstairs furniture was partially damaged or burned. One significant casualty were many letters of Rachel Jackson. Fortunately, the general's papers were saved, as well as Rachel Jackson's wardrobe. The president, when he learned of the tragedy, was resigned: "The Lord's will be done. It was he that gave me the means to build it and he has the right to destroy it, and blessed be his name." The Hermitage's brick walls resisted the flames, leading to a decision by Jackson to rebuild on the same spot. His beloved Rachel had selected the original location; of course, he would honor her initial decision. In the fire's aftermath, Sarah became distraught. The president's sole worry after the disaster focused upon his dear Sarah, writing in a letter to his son, "I am fearful that the fatigue & alarm may be injurious to our dear Sarah's health—let not the loss trouble you & her for one moment."[38]

The fire and smoke damage to the Jacksons' mansion made it uninhabitable. As a result, Sarah Jackson and her two children chose to live at the White House, where they settled on November 26, 1834. The six children of Sarah and Emily enlivened the presidential house during the 1834–35 Christmas season, much to the great delight of its indulgent paterfamilias. At some point during this cheerful period, Andrew Jackson promised his daughter-in-law, "You, my dear, are mistress of the Hermitage, and Emily is hostess of the White House."[39]

Sarah Yorke Jackson enthusiastically assumed this responsibility almost immediately. In Washington, she embarked on a shopping spree for personal items that resulted in a $345.80 bill. Her benefactor, the president, paid the bill. She then traveled to Philadelphia to purchase replacements for The Hermitage's damaged and destroyed furniture. From seven Philadelphia merchandisers she bought wardrobes, bedsteads, dressers, tables, chairs, rugs, drapes, and other sundry items. The cost was $2,303.77. Jackson had dispatched William Berkeley Lewis, his trusted friend and adviser, to accompany Sarah. The capable Lewis was far more experienced in purchasing. Perhaps the president also desired a trained eye to oversee his daughter-in-law's free-spending habits.[40]

For the most part, Andrew Junior remained in Nashville at the rebuilding site. Andrew Jackson wanted his son to assume full responsibility for the project. The ubiquitous W.B. Lewis, a more conscientious letter writer than Junior, kept the White House informed about the progress of the reconstruction. On January 1, 1835, a contract was signed with the aforementioned Joseph Reiff and William C. Hume for the restoration of The Hermitage. Overruns for the cost and delays of the completion date inevitably followed. Weather disruptions and a shortage of competent workers were the reasons. The final cost was $6,425, and the date of completion was the summer of 1836.[41]

Andrew Junior's days of loneliness away from his family while organizing the reconstruction of the Jackson home apparently necessitated surveillance from the White House. His father often admonished Andrew for tardy, if at all, correspondence, "you might write a few lines to your D'r Sarah.... Your own interest is involved." Sarah seemingly expressed worries about Junior's drinking habit, since he replied to her that he would adhere to his promise to remain sober. In Nashville the ever-supportive Major Lewis monitored Junior's sobriety; this honest watch dog subsequently reported that he was pleased with the young man's behavior.[42]

The president always expressed his loneliness whenever Sarah and her two children departed from Washington. "We are very loansome [sic] now, only Mr. Earl, Mrs. Donelson and myself and Mrs. D's three small children." While The Hermitage remained unoccupied, Sarah occasionally left the White House for Philadelphia, where her family resided. Her April 1835 visit had a dual purpose: to assist during her cousin Emma's confinement and to have Rachel reexamined by Dr. Physick. The young girl's health apparently was good.[43]

The president enjoyed his fourth and final vacation at the Rip Raps in July 1835, where his close family embraced him: Sarah, Junior back from Tennessee, their two children, and Emily Donelson with her four. Six servants accompanied the party to ensure the family's health and comfort. Upon their return to the White House, the young Jacksons again visited the Yorke family in Philadelphia. Sarah's bond with the senior Andrew continued to tighten. Andrew Jackson's frequent correspondence with his daughter demonstrated their affectionate intimacy; he always used the possessive "our" when referring to Sarah's children. After the latest Philadelphia visit, his son returned to Nashville while his daughter brought her children back to the White House.[44]

Emily Donelson's worsening tuberculosis forced her departure from the White House for her Tennessee home. From October 1836 to the end of Jackson's presidential administration in March 1837, Sarah assumed the duties of the sole presiding lady of the White House. Sarah probably assumed some of the home's social and personal responsibilities even earlier. She "arrived at the White House on November 26, 1834. She immediately began to take on the role as co-hostess of the White House along with the President's niece Emily Donelson. It was the only time in history when there were two women simultaneously acting as White House Hostess." This arrangement was potentially awkward, but the two young mothers, both of an amiable disposition, made it work relatively smoothly.[45]

On March 6, 1837, after the inauguration of Martin Van Buren, Jackson's much desired successor, the ex-president set out for home with his son, Sarah, their two children, and several servants. They were joined on their journey by the surgeon general of the Army, Thomas Lawson. President Van Buren assigned this duty to Doctor Lawson as a final act of fealty to his predecessor.[46]

Life at The Hermitage for the eight years until its patriarch's death in 1845 was characterized by his daughter's physical and emotional support. It was also marked occasionally by Jackson's political campaigning, more by his declining health, and frequently by his son's inconsistent estate management and financial incompetence. Junior's money woes were both persistent and profound. His father authorized a $6,000 loan to pay his debts: "No matter how many debts Andrew Junior incurred, his father never deserted him." On one occasion, Jackson's intervention saved Junior from bankruptcy. On another occasion the ex-president was compelled to borrow $10,000 from his friend Francis P. Blair to save the Jackson landholdings.[47] After the president's death, Sarah regretted the absence of his wise counsel given her during their past walks around The Hermitage plantation.[48]

The old general, probably influenced by the devout Presbyterian practice of Elizabeth his mother and Rachel his deceased wife, was admitted into the Presbyterian Church on July 15, 1838, together with his daughter Sarah and a "beloved niece." Each evening at The Hermitage, Andrew Jackson professed his Christian devotion during a prayer service with Sarah and his grandchildren. He first read a Bible chapter, distributed a hymn, and kneeling, led his family in prayer.[49] The old general's piety inspired his daughter's religious outlook. In 1857, she wrote Andrew Jackson III, "I regret continually that I had so little conversation with you on religious subjects while you were here with us." Many subsequent letters to her son were full of religious allusions. One letter stated, "Put it in Christ, he is all in all, and in him alone is all your hope."⁵⁰

Sarah and her widowed sister, Marion Adams, nursed Andrew Jackson, often before, and constantly during his terminal illness. Marion and her three children lived at The Hermitage, moving there shortly after the president's retirement. In addition, his adored Rachel, approaching her teenage years, frequently visited and comforted her grandfather.

Visitors often interrupted Old Hickory's rest. One caller was a painter from France. King Louis Philippe had dispatched painter George Healy to fashion portraits of significant Americans to be hung in his royal gallery. When Healy completed Jackson's likeness, the dying man asked the painter for a personal favor, to make a portrait of his "dear child," Sarah. Healy complied, thereby forcing Henry Clay, the next significant American on Louis Philippe's list, to wait. Undoubtedly, Jackson was amused by his perpetual enemy's inconvenience.[51]

On his deathbed, Andrew Jackson turned to Sarah first and thanked her for all her kindness, especially during his long illness. Then he said farewell to Marion Adams, then Junior, then his grandchildren, then the children of Mrs. Adams. At the time of death, Junior supported his father's head while Sarah held his hand. Right after Jackson's demise, Sarah developed "spasms," then fainted, and needed to be carried from the room to be bathed in camphor. Her husband "seemed bewildered."[52]

Andrew Jackson's will left Junior The Hermitage estate as well as his plantation in Mississippi, all his enslaved people, all household furniture, his entire store of farming tools, and all the estate's livestock. To Sarah he bequeathed the enslaved girl Sarah, Hannah, a house slave, and two of Hannah's children. He explained therein his generosity towards "his daughter": "This gift and bequest is made for my great affection to her as a memento of her uniform attention to me and kindness on all occasions, and particularly when worn down with sickness, pain and debility. She has been more than a daughter to me, and I hope she never will be disturbed in the enjoyment of this gift and bequest by any one." Finally, the three children of Andrew and Sarah received individual gifts of enslaved people.[53]

The years that followed the death of Andrew Jackson were disappointing at best for Andrew Jackson, Jr. The generous estate left him by his father gradually dwindled until he lost his old home, The Hermitage; his family was forced into an almost impoverished condition. These sad events were the theme that scored the remaining twenty years of Junior's life. He had inherited $150,000 in 1845, but ten years later he was $100,000 in debt. In 1855 his creditors threatened to foreclose.[54]

His business ventures uniformly were failures. He invested in lead mines in Kentucky, iron works also in Kentucky, and farms in Mississippi, all of which resulted in borrowing and increased indebtedness. The state of Tennessee offered to buy The Hermitage in 1856 for $50,000 with the understanding that the Jacksons could occupy it for two years past the date of sale, and the agreement stipulated that the family would pay rent. The sale was made, and some of the proceeds were to pay Andrew Jackson's long-term loan from his loyal friends Francis Blair and John C. Rives. The balance of this debt was never paid.[55]

In 1859, the Jackson family made the painful decision to move from their iconic Tennessee home to their Mississippi properties. Junior's ill-fortune continued; his newly repaired farmhouse in Mississippi was destroyed by fire. Sarah intermittently resided in Mississippi, but she often returned to Nashville. The Jacksons reestablished their residence at The Hermitage in 1860. This time Tennessee permitted the family to live there until their deaths.[56]

Meanwhile, Sarah and her husband were able to witness the growing up of their children.

Rachel, the "little pet," attended school at Belmont in Loudon County, Virginia; she married Dr. John M. Lawrence in a brilliant affair at The Hermitage on January 25, 1853. Junior and Sarah Jackson led an active social life for a while. Junior often hunted and fished with his son-in-law. Andrew Jackson III, the eldest son, graduated from West Point and commenced a military career. Samuel, their third child, assisted his father in renewing the farm in Mississippi and helped to settle a portion of Junior's debts. During the Civil War, Samuel fought bravely, rose through the Confederate officer ranks, but died on September 27, 1863, from wounds suffered in the Battle of Chickamauga. Their fourth child, Thomas, died at birth, and their fifth, Robert, only survived five months. One complication soured the family harmony: Dr. Lawrence was besieged by claimants who held his father-in-law's unpaid bills.[57]

The Jacksons reoccupied the mansion in 1860. The ensuing Civil War was inevitably unkind to the family. Junior continued to own enslaved people. Sarah and the children strongly supported the Confederacy. Lieutenant Samuel Jackson, CSA, died at the Battle of Chickamauga. Colonel Andrew Jackson III, CSA, was imprisoned in a Union camp for eight months. Union General George Thomas placed guards around The Hermitage for the protection of the Jackson family and for the preservation of the historic mansion.[58]

In April 1865, as the Civil War ended, Junior, 56 years of age, died following a strange mishap. He perished soon after his hunting gun accidently discharged while he was climbing over a fence. The bullet wound in his hand became infected, "and he died of what was called lockjaw." Lockjaw was archival term for tetanus.[59] Andrew Jackson Junior expired on April 17, six days after the accident, after severe suffering. His widow wrote Andrew III before the death, "He is suffering very much, but the doctor thinks he may be able to save part of his fingers, perhaps three and his thumb, but it is uncertain ... it continues to bleed...." This was not the last time that a physician's optimistic prognosis would be refuted by reality.[60]

Sarah's life was beleaguered by the legacy of her husband's indebtedness. Bankruptcy, the threat of homelessness, and impoverishment, were all constant concerns. Her anxieties flowed from her pen onto letters that she wrote to her children. She counseled Andrew III, "to avoid the quicksands your father has been ruined on"; "Your Pa's ... all combine to make my life any thing but happy"; "I am wary of debt. My life has been a never-ending and unvarying scene of trouble and mortification on account of debt, officers of every grade to insult us and lawsuits continually."[61]

Sarah died in Nashville on August 23, 1887, twenty-two years after the passing of her husband. Her state of health was rarely a complaint in her many letters to her children. However, as she aged, an occasional lament appeared in letters to others. She wrote to Mary Anne Atkinson, "but my health is so feeble, or I should say that my nervous system is feeble ... and I am almost unable to guide my pen." Two years before her death, Sarah wrote her new daughter-in-law of "loss of sight and unsteadiness of hand."[62]

Andrew Jackson III and his family lived at The Hermitage until 1893. In June 1889, the state of Tennessee suddenly terminated Jackson III's position as a tenant farmer. In addition, the state invoiced him a considerable amount of money to reinstate the prior relationship. The Ladies Hermitage Association was formed in 1889; it slowly assumed control of the mansion. However, Andrew Jackson III had difficulties with this arrangement, and he and his wife vacated The Hermitage in 1893.[63]

XIV

Mary Ann Eastin
His Favorite Niece and Other Favored Young Women

"On last evening was consummated the marriage of your son Lucius to my favorite niece Mary Eastin...."
—Andrew Jackson letter to William Polk,
April 11, 1832 *Jackson Papers. Volume X*, 229

"I am grieved My Dear Uncle to find your mind still harassed by this subject & likely to continue so, much aggravated by the idea that your connections have deserted you."
—Mary Ann Eastin (Nashville) letter to
Andrew Jackson (White House),
December 5, 1830, *Jackson Papers.*
Volume VIII, 648–9

Andrew Jackson wrote in his April 1832 letter to William Polk, "On last evening was consummated the marriage of your son Lucius to my favorite niece Mary Eastin...."[1] During his long life, Jackson in his characteristic patriarchal, yet chivalrous manner, treated young women with affection and courtly respect. He, always monogamous and ever faithful to Rachel, often assumed the role of *gallant* around young ladies, especially those members of the extended Donelson family.

Abundant nieces and grandnieces of Rachel and by marital extension to Andrew Jackson sprouted upon the branches of the fecund family tree of the Donelsons. A genealogical table revealed a count of at least thirty-three women, including Emily Donelson, Mary Coffee, Mary McLemore, and Mary Anne Eastin.[2]

Who was Mary Ann Eastin? Why did her uncle bestow upon her

XIV—Mary Ann Eastin: His Favorite Niece

his favoritism? The answers to these questions will comprise this chapter's narrative.

Mary Ann, usually addressed as "Mary" by her Uncle Jackson, was the close companion and confidante of her three-year older aunt Emily Donelson. She lived in the White House with Aunt Emily during much of President Jackson's first term. In the void left by her great-aunt's demise, Mary Ann's effusive personality and vibrant behavior enlivened the gloomy atmosphere of the White House. Moreover, it lifted the unhappiness of its presidential occupant. Finally and most importantly, this niece acted as the conduit between Andrew and Emily Donelson during their mutual alienation over the Eaton Affair. For these deeds, the president was extremely grateful.

A plethora of "Rachels" both occupy and complicate the Donelson genealogical chart. Rachel, Andrew Jackson's wife, had the benefit of ten siblings, one of whom was her brother John. John Donelson and his wife were the parents of thirteen children, including daughters Emily and Rachel. This Rachel, Emily's sister, married William Eastin and bore him several children, one of whom they named Mary Ann. Rachel Donelson Eastin was sixteen years older than her sister Emily Donelson who became Andrew Jackson's Surrogate First Lady. Therefore, Mary Ann Eastin was the niece of Emily; she always referred to her as "Aunt Emily," although she was only three years younger.[3]

Rachel Donelson Eastin died in Nashville after the birth of her daughter, yet another "Rachel." Andrew Jackson rushed to his niece's deathbed from an Alabama visit but arrived too late. Subsequently, William Eastin placed the care of his surviving children with Mary Purnell Donelson, his mother-in-law and the children's grandmother. Mary Ann (1810–1847), Susanna (1812–1824), Elizabeth Donelson Eastin (1817–1839), and John Donelson (1820) were afterwards raised at The Mansion, adjacent to The Hermitage, by John and Mary Purnell Donelson.[4]

Mary Ann, only twelve years old when her mother died, was entrusted to the care of her maternal Donelson grandparents. At the same time, these Donelsons continued to raise their thirteenth and youngest child, fifteen-year-old Emily Tennessee. The two young ladies bonded and became confidantes. Both were educated at the Nashville Female Academy, an elite boarding school for girls, where they were tutored in all the finer things of life. A significant exception was dancing, considered a sin by the Academy's overseers. During school holidays, both girls spent many weeks at The Hermitage where Andrew and Rachel made great pets of them.[5]

The Nashville Female Academy was founded in 1816; it opened for its first classes with sixty-five enrollees in August 1817. The student population increased to one hundred by the time Emily was a student, Hostilities forced its closing during the Civil War, and it was never fully reopened. An academy enrollment advertisement listed the subjects that Emily and Mary Ann were taught as prospective Southern belles: "Reading, writing, English Grammar, English, Arithmetic, Composition, History, Geography, Ancient, Modern with the Use of Globes, Rhetorick, Logic, Moral Philosophy, Natural Philosophy, Chemistry, Astronomy, Botany and Mythology, Plain Sewing, Filigree, and all kinds of Ornamental needlework, Embroidery, Tambouring, Rug Work etc. etc.... Drawing and Painting."[6]

The death of Rachel Jackson in December 1828 made Emily Donelson the inevitable choice to become the mistress of the White House. She thus became the third woman not married to the president to fulfill this role.[7] It was likewise inevitable that Emily, barely twenty-one, would invite Mary Ann Eastin, her intimate friend, confidante, niece, and near-sister, only eighteen, to accompany her to the White House. The new Surrogate First Lady unquestionably required the support and empathy of a steadfast female companion during her uncle's first term. Emily needed to overcome the challenges of motherhood, her husband's professional difficulties, the "Eaton Malaria," and her lengthy banishment to Tennessee. Together the two not only endured but conquered these obstacles, and acting in concert, they enlivened not only the atmosphere of the White House but also the spirits of its principal occupant.

Young Mary Ann's personality endeared her to the Jacksons. Rachel, prior to her death, wished the young woman to accompany her to the White House in 1829; also, according to Jackson biographer James, the teenager was considered "a great pet of the General." Jackson, when his 1823–4 senatorial term in Washington separated him from Rachel, became very concerned over his wife's well-being and expressed his appreciation for Emily's and Mary's attention to Mrs. Jackson: "I feel grateful to my young female friends for their attention to Mrs. J. that her spirits should be kept up is altogether important to her health and nothing is likely to obtain this as the company of her young female friends."[8] Several years later, after Mary Ann left the White House for Tennessee to accompany Emily during her banishment, gloom pervaded Jackson's White House. The unhappy president acutely missed "a genial and sweet Mary Eastin."[9]

After her father, William Eastin, died, the president wrote John Coffee, "...poor Mary has felt her bereavement severely, but I have tendered to her all the consolation in my power 'that I would be a father to her as long as I lived.'" "Until the marriage of his adopted son and the coming of Sarah Yorke into his life, Mary Eastin, more than any other of

Rachel's nieces, held the place of daughter in the heart of Andrew Jackson. Beautiful and sprightly, her ingenuous letters to her uncle and his replies show the place she had in his affections."[10]

Miss Eastin was described as "pretty," and with aunt Emily, "both excellent and esteemed ladies. Unaffected and graceful in manner, amiable, and purely feminine in disposition and character and bight and self possessed in conversation, they were fair representatives of the ladies of Kentucky and Tennessee." Mary Ann was also depicted as "genial and sweet."[11]

Biographer James dubbed Mary Ann "The Cumberland Cinderella," and quoted her teenage delight over her bedroom in the Executive Mansion: "I have a room fit for a Princess with silk curtains, mahogany furniture, a carpet such as you Tennesseans have in your parlor, and a piano."[12] She pulled her aunt Emily from a sickbed for a pre–inauguration shopping spree. The two ladies entered Abbott's, a chic Washington store, where they spent extravagantly on expensive items—cologne, soap, jewelry, good black veils, and yards of black satin, which Mary fashioned into a dress to be worn at the inauguration ball.[13]

Emily Donelson and Mary Ann Eastin remained close companions during the Jackson political era until Mary's wedding in April 1832. They were inseparable during the first three years of the Jacksonian presidency. The two stood stalwartly side by side for hours greeting guests at the 1829 inauguration ball and at the January 1830 White House Levee. Meacham appraised the two's gracious behavior, "They affected no superiority, showed no pride, and from their behavior no one would have supposed that they belonged to the family of the Chief Magistrate of a great nation. Their honor sat so easy on them that they seemed not to know it.... Perfect good breeding ... taught them from their earliest infancy both by precept and example by their Aunt, the good, the amiable, and ever to be lamented Mrs. Jackson."[14]

When travelling, if Emily appeared, Mary was present nearby. Together they visited Martha Jefferson Randolph when Thomas Jefferson's daughter visited the capital city. In July 1829, the two women were part of the presidential party that visited Charles Carroll, the last surviving signer of the Declaration of Independence, at his Maryland home. On their return to the White House, the two young women visited the family of Louis McLane in Delaware. McLane was a future secretary of the treasury in the Jackson cabinet. On a subsequent occasion, the duo went to New York City to visit Mary Ann Lewis, the daughter of their uncle's political confidante. On this journey, the ladies were chaperoned by Andrew Jackson Junior.[15]

Miss Eastin, pretty, amiable, lively, spirited, and still somewhat of an ingénue, did not lack for the attention of eligible young men. This attraction was noted early by her Aunt Emily. In a letter to her mother during the arduous journey to the first Jackson inauguration, Emily wrote, "Mary has enjoyed herself very much and is surrounded with beaux." Later in 1829, on a trip to Wilmington and Philadelphia, Emily was accompanied by Mary, Major Abraham Van Buren, the son of the then secretary of state, and Samuel Jackson Hays. Emily named the major as Mary's beau and assumed the role of chaperone.[16]

Parties aplenty enlivened the Executive Mansion when Emily and Mary Ann were in residence; the ambience of youthful frolic and fun brought happiness to the patriarch of the residence. The two ladies engineered the festivities; the party regulars in addition to the two hostesses included Cora Livingston; the daughters of cabinet members John Branch and John Berrien; Andrew Donelson's brother, Daniel Smith Donelson; and the aforementioned Abraham Van Buren. Daniel Smith successfully wooed Margaret Branch; their wedding in the bride's native North Carolina soon followed. Aunt Emily and her protégé Mary Ann made certain to visit the beneficiaries of their matchmaking, calling on Daniel and his bride in their Cumberland, Tennessee, home. The friendship with the Branch and Berrien daughters probably irked the president, although he remained silent. Both their fathers, Attorney General Berrien and Secretary of the Navy Branch, became irreconcilable enemies of President Andrew Jackson.[17]

During the White House parties, Abraham Van Buren was very attentive to the lively Mary, although Mary was probably unserious, since the popular teenager "had a beau for every day of the week." Whether the president and his foremost political ally reviewed the romantic flirtation between their young family members is unknown, except for a cryptic conclusion to a letter from Jackson to Van Buren, then in England: "Miss Eastin has promised to write you soon & Mrs. Donelson says she will endeavour to make the young Lady of which you speak worthy of your son." Both married successfully, but not to each other. Abraham Van Buren's future bore interesting coincidences to that of the young Donelsons. Like Andrew, Abraham became the confidential secretary to a president, his father, Martin Van Buren. Moreover, he chose as his wife Angela Singleton, who became like Emily the White House Hostess of a widower president, once again Van Buren.[18]

Mary Ann, ever-supportive and loyal to her Aunt Emily, was drawn into the Margaret Eaton unpleasantness, even though she was not an actor in the drama, only at best a supernumerary. The annoying clerical meddler, the Reverend Ezra Stiles Ely, was the first to attach her to the matter in his March 1829 letter to the president, writing, "I do not presume to ask my venerable friend any thing more than this, that you will not expect Mrs. Donelson and Miss Easton [sic], your lovely nieces to return the civilities of Mrs. Eaton."[19]

Martin Van Buren, the secretary of state, aimed to use the diplomatic skills inherent in his position to resolve the conflict between the president and his niece over the question of Mrs. Eaton. The forty-six-year-old Van Buren attempted to dissuade Mrs. Donelson, less than half his age, from her obstinate alienation from the wife of the secretary of war.

The meeting occurred in the White House in November 1829. Emily's constant consort, Mary Eastin, also attended. The secretary's calm persuasion being ineffective, he became argumentative and assertive. Mary, whose sympathy for her aunt was abundant, sensed Emily's rising fury, and sought to hide her own emotion by gradually withdrawing herself from Van Buren's sight to within the embrasure of the window. She sobbed aloud. At this point, at the sound of Mary's crying, the Secretary realized the effect his words were having on Emily and withdrew from the room.[20]

The favorite niece of Andrew Jackson became his informant and liaison to Emily Donelson during her 1830–31 Tennessee banishment from Washington. A correspondence of seven letters, five from Jackson and two from Eastin, were transmitted between Washington and Nashville during these months.

The president apparently desired a woman's sounding board for emotional comfort, support, and justification for his actions. His beloved Rachel was deceased, while Emily was both alienated and the source for much of his emotional turbulence. Mary Ann, an intimate of her aunt and a loyal, affectionate, uncritical, and warm niece to Uncle Jackson, now her surrogate father, became his appropriate selection for this mission. Moreover, he knew that Mary Ann would be a more satisfying correspondent over these issues than would Emily, who likely would be more direct and possibly even abrasive.

Mary Ann's response to her uncle's assignment can only be surmised in the absence of any written documentation. She may have been honored that the president confided in her, and even astonished by his trust in her opinion and discretion. The delicacy of her situation surely disquieted her as the chosen intermediary between two whose love and loyalty she cherished. Jackson by indirection assumed that Mary would share his correspondence with her Aunt Emily. He affectionately buttressed his niece's courage and determination in fulfilling this role, writing, "I assure you Mary I never did complain of you—yours was a course of profound discretion, & has made you many friends here."[21]

Jackson's letters typically were prefaced by appeals for his correspondent's sympathy for his loneliness: "Andrew Jackson Donelson has informed you that the House appears lonesome ... it would give me great pleasure that you & Emily with the sweet little ones were here."[22] Her uncle made certain to emphasize his grief over the loss of Rachel which was compounded by his physical sufferings: "My health is not very good." In addition, he underlined his sadness over Rachel's death, saying that he wished he would join her in the grave to escape the wickedness he saw all around him.[23]

The body of these letters was devoted to the perfidy of his enemies, the unassailable justice of his actions, and the mistaken opinions of Andrew and Emily Donelson: "I shall forever much regret that Emily & you did not at first pursue my advice, it was then in your power ... put down, that wicked political combination of Slanderers, & to have prevented those disagreeable consequences that have ensued." The letter continued with a long attack upon John C. Calhoun, although he was unnamed.[24] In a later letter, the president emphasized the Donelsons' errant behavior: "My Dr. Mary, I shall ever regret the time ... when the gossips of this city obtained the ear of my Dr. Emily and Andrew, caused them to throw aside my council, attend to that of strangers, and listen to slander...." Jackson used the axiom, "A house Divided against itself cannot stand," which he repeated later.[25] He employed this axiom as proof for his actions many times.

Miss Eastin's responding letters were affectionate, gentle, and sincere, writing, "I am grieved My Dear Uncle to find your mind still harassed by this subject & likely to continue so, much aggravated by the idea that your connections have deserted you." Moreover, she was very grateful for his affection and for giving her a place in his family. Expressing her understanding of his political adversaries, she was sympathetic to his unpleasant turmoil that arose with the beginning of the Congressional session.[26]

In a June 1831 letter, the niece congratulated her uncle for his successful dismantling of the intractable Cabinet, writing, "...ensuring the future happiness, harmony & prosperity of your administration." She continued, "I have the satisfaction to tell you that I have just received the dress you were so kind as to send me." Finally, she filled her letter with copious amounts of flattery for her dear uncle.[27]

When the Donelsons returned to the White House in September 1831, Emily predicted that Mary, her companion, who enjoyed "a beau for every day of the week," would have a White House wedding before too long. Emily was prescient.[28] A proposal was soon forthcoming. Not long after Mary was engaged "to a very clever and highly respected

XIV—Mary Ann Eastin: His Favorite Niece

officer of the Navy, by the name of Finch." Friends and family were disappointed that their beautiful sprite would marry someone not only older, but also destined to be absent on sea duty for long periods of time. The wedding was scheduled for Valentine's Day, 1832. The future bride shopped for her trousseau in New York City. Her squire there was Jackson's friend, former assistant secretary of state and the son of Alexander Hamilton, James A. Hamilton.[29]

These plans were shortly abandoned; Mary broke her engagement and instead married a younger Tennessean, Lucius J. Polk, a cousin of future President James K. Polk. Lucius had previously met his future bride at The Hermitage; for him, it had been love at first sight. When news of Miss Eastin's first engagement reached Polk, he immediately rode to Washington with a counter proposal.

The President gave his favorite niece away to Polk in the East Room of the White House on April 10, 1832. Mary Ann's bridesmaids were her young friends, Mary McLemore and Cora Livingston. Her wedding ceremony was the fourth to be held in the White House.

"Jackson had long loved Mary as much as he loved Emily, sometimes finding the more easygoing Mary more approachable and arranged to pay for a White House ceremony."

The bills from paying for Mary Eastin's and Andrew Junior's weddings left the president "short of funds for the following year."[30] Mary Ann Polk set out from the White House to live with her husband in Tennessee. Jackson missed her, but not so great as when Sarah departed on her occasional trips.[31]

The affectionate correspondence between the president and his favorite niece restarted after the new Mrs. Polk settled in her new home. Two months after her wedding, she wrote Jackson to reassure him of her safe arrival. Moreover, she becalmed his concern by attesting that his new daughter-in-law, Sarah Yorke Jackson, was very pleased with her new home, The Hermitage. She closed, "Every body is very anxious to know when you are coming out this summer. I hope you will be able to do so, for it will be such a gratification to your friends as well as to your self." Her uncle responded to the new Mrs. Polk at the end of his Tennessee vacation, that he was happy, "so long as you are situated on your farm, enjoying the calm of retirement, with the affections of your dear husband." The same November 1832 communication expressed Jackson's satisfaction, "that Lucius possessed the temper, the disposition, and all those amiable qualities necessary to make the married state a paradise." In December 1832, Mary Ann congratulated the president on his reelection and closed by stating that the triumph of our friend Mr. Van Buren is complete.[32]

In 1833, Jackson corresponded with his grand-niece, writing, "I am happy to find that you were invited to the wedding of our mutual friend Miss Mary Coffee. You are not so good at guessing as I am, or you would have guessed A.J. Hutchings as the happy man." Mary Coffee was the daughter of John Coffee, the president's revered friend. Andrew Jackson Hutchings was his grand-nephew, whom the Jacksons had raised since the age of five. The wedding occurred in Alabama; Mary Ann's attendance was doubtful.[33]

In 1836, Old Hickory, during his final stay at The Hermitage while president, felt compelled to visit Mary Coffee at her Alabama home. He asked Andrew Jackson Donelson to leave his very sick wife to accompany him to Mary Polk's home in Columbia, Tennessee, from which he planned to travel to Alabama. Donelson left the president in Mary's care and returned home alone.[34]

Lucius Junius Polk was a wealthy cotton planter and owner of enslaved people in Columbia, Tennessee. Mary Ann's marriage apparently was content, and she bore many children. Their union saw the birth of eight children spaced evenly on a regular basis, every second year. She died in 1847 at thirty-seven years of age.[35]

Other Ladies

Besides Mary Eaton, several other young women were frequent guests at the festive White House parties; these ladies were relatives or friends of Emily Donelson. They not only enlivened the milieu of the Executive Mansion, but also buoyed the spirits of its most important inhabitant. Their presence certainly uplifted the mood of its Surrogate First Lady, whose responsibilities could be burdensome. However, their influence upon the president was otherwise minimal, and far peripheral to the central impact of Emily or even that of Jackson's favorite niece.

Mary McLemore (1816–1873)

This Mary was one of many children of Elizabeth Donelson and her husband, John Christian McLemore. An unwinding of the entangled Donelson family genealogy shows the following:

Elizabeth was Emily Tennessee's sister and Mary was Emily's niece. She was raised in the Nashville home of her parents and was part of a happy group with Mary Eastin, Mary Coffee, and Elizabeth Martin. "Their greatest delight were the long visits one and all in turn paid Uncle and Aunt Jackson at the Hermitage."[36]

She accompanied Emily and Andrew Donelson on their triumphant return to the White House in September 1831, but soon departed for Philadelphia in their company to pursue training with the harp.[37] She soon reappeared at the White House where "Mary Coffee, Mary McLemore and Aunt Emily seem to enjoy themselves very well at the swirl of Washington parties." She replaced her newly-wed cousin Mary Eastin as the new White House belle.[38]

Mary remained at the White House to attend her great-uncle's second inauguration and to shine at the inaugural ball. Afterwards she returned to Tennessee with John Coffee and her cousin Mary Coffee. She soon married Dr. James Monroe Walker of a distinguished Virginia family. The ceremony occurred at the McLemore home in Nashville. The bride was seventeen. Dr. Walker was a graduate of the Transylvania Medical School; he joined the medical practice of the familiar Dr. Samuel Hogg.[39]

Mary Coffee (1812–1839)

This Mary was the daughter of Mary Donelson, who was a sister of Emily Tennessee and General John Coffee, Andrew Jackson's most dependable friend. As such she was a niece of Emily Donelson and a grandniece of the president. She was one of the three Marys with Mary McLemore and Mary Ann Eastin who grew up around The Mansion and The Hermitage.

She also attended the Nashville Female Academy where, "In 1827 little Mary Coffee was mastering the delightful style which later gave such piquancy to her letters concerning passing events."[40] Mary likewise enjoyed herself at the same parties attended by aunt Emily and cousin Mary McLemore.

Mary Coffee returned to the Coffee plantation in Alabama where she further endeared herself to Uncle Jackson by falling in love with, and then marrying, the owner of the adjacent plantation on November 14, 1833. The owner was Andrew Jackson Hutchings, a ward of Andrew and Rachel, whose life had been nurtured through college and into his maturity by Jackson. Earlier Jackson had counseled "Little Hutchings" on choosing a mate. The President congratulated his ward on his judgment and prudence, writing, "I view her as a treasure to your welfare and happiness in this world, and by her gentle conduct will lead you in the paths of virtue thru this life and prepare you for a better beyond the grave."[41]

Thereby Old Hickory indirectly accomplished the union of his Donelson grandniece with his ward. A second role, that of medical advisor, unfortunately followed several years later. Mary became seriously ill with tuberculosis; her main symptom was severe back pain. Jackson, then an ex-president, advised Hutchings to employ the following armamentarium: camphor, Epsom or Harrodsburgh salts, a bag of hot ashes, and Matchless Sanative. "Doctor" Andrew's pharmacy was ineffective. Mary Coffee Hutchings perished in early December 1839.[42]

Cora Livingston (1806–1873)

Cora was the daughter of Secretary of State Edward Livingston and his beautiful Creole wife, Louise de Castera. The Livingston family moved from Louisiana to Washington when her father was elected as Louisiana senator in 1829. She soon became a close friend of Emily and was part of her party group. She was called "the beauty from the Crescent City," and attracted the capital city's eligible bachelors to the White House drawing rooms. Her close camaraderie with others of the party group resulted in her being named a godmother to Emily's daughter, Mary Rachel, and serving as a bridesmaid at the wedding of Mary Ann Eastin.[43]

General Jackson was introduced to Cora when he defended New Orleans from the British; her father was a significant aide to the general. The Crescent City beauty was as dear to the president as any of his young connections. He watched her success in Washington with increasing satisfaction. Miss Livingston married young American diplomat Thomas Barton in April 1833. The festivities were held in the White House at Jackson's expense. As a parting gift to the young couple, Jackson assigned young Barton as the aide to Edward Livingston so they could accompany Livingston to Paris, where he would serve as the new U.S. ambassador to France.[44]

Mary Ann Lewis (1814–1866)

The Jacksons took in several children of William Terrell Lewis, a former North Carolina legislator and vast landowner in the Tennessee territory. When William Terrell Lewis died in 1813, he left his two daughters, Margaret and Myra, under the Jacksons' care.

Both sisters married in 1813. Margaret married her cousin, William Berkley Lewis, and Myra married John H. Eaton. Both husbands became close political allies of Andrew Jackson.

Mary Anne Lewis, the daughter of William B. and Margaret Lewis, came to stay at The Hermitage and became a "special pet" of Rachel Jackson. Later, in the White House, Mary "always added sparkle to the surroundings." The president urged Emily Donelson and Andrew Junior

XIV—Mary Ann Eastin: His Favorite Niece

to visit Miss Lewis in New York City in September 1831, explaining, "She is a sweet disposition, and I am sure will make a very fine and elegant woman, it is said here she is esteemed as one of the Belles of New York—I have no doubt but that she would make a sweet and affectionate companion."[45]

She married Joseph Pageot, a French diplomat and secretary of the French Legation, in 1832 at the White House, an event made possible by President Andrew Jackson. The couple's first born, a son, was named Andrew Jackson Pageot. It has been suggested that Mary Anne Pageot, since Jackson favored her, served an influential diplomatic role when France failed to repay debts in a timely manner, although there is no direct evidence.

XV

Andrew Jackson's Women
A Summary of Their Influence

Andrew Jackson was a man of significant complexity and frequent, sometimes glaring, inconsistencies. Fatherless at birth and orphaned at the age of fourteen, he transplanted himself to middle Tennessee, still on the American frontier. He arrived in Nashville as a young attorney, where he successively became a judge, businessman, plantation patriarch, congressman, senator, general, politician, and a twice elected president of the United States.

As a general he decisively defeated the Creek Nation in 1813–4, overwhelmed a tested British army in New Orleans in 1815, and was the primal force that led Florida into union with the United States.

As a politician, he was the founder of the Democratic party and the overseer of a significant increase in white male suffrage. As a president, he reduced government corruption, and he was a firm steward of federal expenses to the degree that he zeroed out the national debt. Moreover, his successes included the abolition of the National Bank, the peaceful solution of the nullification crisis with South Carolina after the state surrendered to federal sovereignty, and an important expansion of foreign trade with the United States.

However, this chapter is not intended to be a paean to a monument of Andrew Jackson. The man had glaring character flaws and perpetrated erroneous policies. He was a slaveholder until the day of his death; he routinely bought, sold, gifted, and bequeathed enslaved Blacks. Jackson had an ingrained animus towards Indians, considering them a lower class of humans. The infamous Trail of Tears is part of his legacy.

Andrew Jackson was a man whose frequently uncontrollable anger led to violence, gunfights, and duels. He killed a man in a duel; during the Creek Campaign, he ordered a deserter to be shot; and during the

First Seminole War, he executed British citizens Alexander Arbuthnot and Robert Ambrister.

The previous chapters are devoted to six women who enhanced Jackson's good qualities and may have, to some degree, quelled his destructive impulses. Three ladies, Elizabeth Hutchinson Jackson, Rachel Donelson Jackson, and Emily Donelson, were of most importance. Margaret Timberlake Eaton, the most colorful of the six, infused both controversy and determination into much of Jackson's first presidential term. Sarah Yorke Jackson provided heirs, solace, and comfort to the aging ex-president. Mary Ann Eastin assisted in the pivotal reconciliation of Jackson with Emily Donelson.

If Elizabeth Jackson, his mother, had not been felled by "ship's fever" in Charleston, South Carolina, and had returned to the Waxhaws to reunite with her surviving son, would her survival have changed the course of Andrew Jackson's career?

Elizabeth had already instilled in him the Scots-Irish qualities of determination, persistence, loyalty, courage, quickness to anger, and a truthful directness instead of subtlety in expressing his opinion. Her hatred of the British was ingrained into his persona by the death of his two brothers, the assault upon him by a British officer, his imprisonment, and his contagion of smallpox.

Andrew was his mother's favorite of her three sons. She gave him a better education than his siblings in the hope that Andy would become a minster. Possibly disappointed by his selection of the law, she very likely would have accepted it, supported his legal education, and welcomed his profession as an attorney.

Their previous home, the James and Jane Crawford homestead, was shattered. Jane, her sister, died around 1780. James, her brother-in-law, died battling the British. Elizabeth would have no home to return to, other than a possible residence with one of her surviving sisters. Andrew's reverence for his mother should have compelled him to live with, and probably support, her in the Waxhaws, at least for a while. Since Elizabeth had previously had fled to North Carolina, a new residence with Andrew in that state was possible while he studied the law and began his legal career. However, if Elizabeth still lived, any travel over the Allegheny Mountains to a new start in Tennessee seems most improbable.

If Rachel Jackson lived and accompanied her husband to the White House, would Jackson's first term have been affected?

Mrs. Jackson would be First Lady and the president's official White House Hostess. Emily Donelson would be relegated to the role of Rachel's assistant. Rachel, the hostess of the Hermitage, a center for family and political assemblies, possessed both the skills and the experience to manage the White House. For tiring ceremonial occasions, including inauguration balls, levees, dinners, etc., Emily certainly could substitute if necessary. Rachel had the congenial skills to control and the Donelson family stature to demand the respect of niece Emily. President Jackson, comfortable in the presence of his wife and no longer so lonely, may have less time or reason to be consumed by the travails of Margaret Eaton. Additionally, Rachel assuredly could control and minimize the Emily-Margaret feud. The intensity of the Eaton Affair likely would be lessened.

If Rachel Jackson survived a four-year term, would Jackson have competed for re-election?

Rachel did not appreciate the social routine of the nation's capital city. She experienced several months in Washington during Jackson's completion of his senatorial term in 1824–5. Rachel wrote her sister May Donelson with her weariness, "We got two or three invitations a day sometimes." Her husband contemporaneously agreed, "I have resisted all those invitations Except the 8th January."[1] A ball was held on that date at General Brown's home to mark the twentieth anniversary of the victory of Andrew Jackson at New Orleans. Brady speculated, "The expense and social whirl in the city upset her, especially the extravagance in dressing and running out to parties. At the Hermitage she was accustomed to a peaceful existence." In Mrs. Jackson's words, "The play-actors sent me a letter, requesting my countenance to them. No. A ticket to balls and parties. No, not one."[2]

Whether Rachel, if alive, were inclined to remain in the White House for an additional four years either as a recluse like First Ladies Elizabeth Monroe and Letitia Tyler, or a returnee to home like Floride Calhoun, separated from her husband in Washington, is unknowable. What is known is that Andrew Jackson, a man of determination, pride, and persistence, would run for reelection.

Would the ladies of Washington have accepted Rachel Jackson as First Lady?

The ladies of Washington were the white elite and middle-class women of the city, members of local families and female kin of government officials. Collectively, they were the social arbiters who controlled the parlors where both political deals and reputations were made. "Washingtonians still enjoyed mocking her country ways, and joked about her smoking her pipe in the White House."[3] Catching a glimpse of Rachel during her 1824–5 Washington visit, Louis McLane told his wife,

XV—A Summary of Their Influence 189

she "is an ordinary looking old woman."[4] Mrs. Jackson likely would be tolerated by the Washington Ladies, but unlikely to be much admired.

What were the negative consequences, if any, of The Eaton Affair, upon Andrew Jackson's first term?

The curator of The Hermitage best answered,

> I think the Eaton affair was disruptive of Jackson's first term. It was a huge distraction at a time when many were already a little suspicious of Jackson as an outsider. Did it stop legislation or cause Jackson to change his opinions? No, but it was one of several things that happened during the first term that kept things from running smoothly. Jackson could have ignored it but he let his friendship with the Eatons keep him from focusing on the big picture.[5]

What were the positive effects, if any, of Emily Donelson's return as Surrogate First Lady upon Andrew Jackson's second term?

Emily and her circle of young women enlivened the dour, otherwise womanless, White House gloom, making it a more congenial, and very amiable, place to work. Moreover, her children thrilled the president, warmed his heart, and evaporated the pall of his loneliness. His successful opposition to National Bank renewal, the peaceful conclusion of the South Carolina nullification crisis, and the passage of the Indian Removal Act marked his second term as noteworthy and accomplished.

Sarah Yorke Jackson filled in as White House Hostess after Emily Donelson's illness, brought order to Andrew Junior's disheveled life, assured the continuation of the Jackson name, and competently managed The Hermitage. Thereby, she made Jackson's post-presidential decade as comfortable and fruitful as possible. Mary Ann Eastin Polk importantly calmed the Andrew Jackson–Emily Donelson relationship.

Chapter Notes

Preface

1. Robert Remini, *Andrew Jackson: The Course of American Empire 1767–1821*, Vol. I, 1.
2. Jon Meacham, *American Lion. Andrew Jackson in the White House*, xviii.
3. Presidential Historians Survey, 2017: Total Scores/Overall Rankings, C-Span, https://www.c-span.org/presidentsurvey2017/?page=overall.
4. Louis Jacobson, and Sarah Wavehoff, "What's Up with Donald Trump and Andrew Jackson?" Politifact: Accessed 8 December 2019. https://www.politifact.com/truth-o-meter/article/2017/may/02/whats-up-with-donald-trump-andrew-jackson/.
5. Andrew Burstein, *The Passions of Andrew Jackson*, xiv.
6. Remini, 42.

Chapter I

1. Harry Watson, *Andrew Jackson vs. Henry Clay: Democracy and Development in Antebellum America*, 21. Advice attributed by Elizabeth Jackson to Andrew Jackson.
2. definition of Scots-Irish
3. Jim Webb, *Born Fighting: How the Scots-Irish Shaped America*, 185–6.
4. William Cobbett, *Life of Andrew Jackson, President of the United States of America*, iv.
5. James Leyburn, *The Scotch-Irish: A Social History*, 67.
6. *Ibid.*, xv.
7. H. Tyler Blethen & Curtis W. Wood Jr., *From Ulster to Carolina: The Migration of the Scotch-Irish to Southwestern North Carolina*, 3.
8. Leyburn, 67.
9. *Ibid.*, 68.
10. *Ibid.*, 83.
11. Webb, 87.
12. H.W. Brands, *Andrew Jackson: His Life and Times*, 10.
13. Blethen, 6.
14. Webb, 115.
15. Blethen, 13.
16. *Ibid.*, 6.
17. Blethen, 19.
18. Webb, 116; Leyburn, 158.
19. Leyburn, 168.
20. *Ibid.*, 27.
21. *Ibid.*, 63, 68, 70.
22. Cobbett, *Life of Andrew Jackson*, viii.
23. Leyburn, *The Scotch-Irish*, 185.
24. "Carrickfergus," Wikipedia.org.
25. Robert Remini, *Andrew Jackson: The Course of American Empire 1767–1821*, Vol. I, 2.
26. "Battle of the Boyne." BBC. The Battle of the Boyne was fought along the Boyne River, thirty miles north of Dublin. King William I, the English king, Protestant army defeated the deposed King James II's Catholic army.
27. "Family Group Sheet of Andrew Jackson and Elizabeth Hutchinson Family," Western Kentucky History and Genealogy, Westernkyhistory.org. The article lists the birth order of Hutchinson children; the numbers of Hutchinson sisters may be greater since a "Sally" is listed but is otherwise unidentified.
28. Paul McClure, *Hutchinson Family*

Notes—Chapter I

Record, 13 a–g; "Elizabeth 'Betty' Jackson," Geni.com.
29. Parton, *The Life of Andrew Jackson*, Vol. I, 37.
30. Remini, Vol. I, 2.
31. Parton, 30.
32. Remini, Vol. I, 2.
33. Brands, *Andrew Jackson*, 11.
34. Remini, Vol. I, 2.
35. Parton, 46–7.
36. Blethen, *From Ulster to Carolina*, 22.
37. Hutchinson Family Records.
38. Parton, 46–7.
39. Remini, Vol. I, 2.
40. Brands, 12.
41. "[P]robably landed in Pennsylvania." Remini, Vol. I, 3; "They landed near Newcastle, on the Delaware River, and settled near Lancaster, Pennsylvania, among other Scots-Irish immigrants." Hutchinson Family Records; Reference is to the previous travels of the Hutchinson sisters; as stated in the text, Elizabeth and Andrew's sea and land route are unconfirmed.; Cobbett, *Life of Andrew Jackson*, 11. alternatively declared that the Jacksons landed in Charleston, South Carolina, before they trekked westward to settle in the Waxhaw region; John Eaton, 5, agrees with Cobbett, writing in his Jackson campaign biography, "Landing at Charleston, in South Carolina, he [Andrew Jackson] shortly purchased a tract of land, in what was then called the Waxhaw settlement."; Booraem, *Young Hickory: The Making of Andrew Jackson*, 1. They landed in Charleston, South Carolina, like many other Ulstermen since the South Carolina government offered free land, a tax exemption, and free tools to Protestant settlers; Burstein, *The Passions of Andrew Jackson*, 7, listed both alternatives, but favored Pennsylvania.
42. Remini, Vol. I, 3; Hutchinson Family Record.
43. "Waxhaw people." Wikipedia.org.
44. Meacham, *American Lion: Andrew Jackson in the White House*, 8; Booraem, 8–9, for locations of the farms of the Hutchinson sisters.
45. Marquis James, *The Life of Andrew Jackson*, 9; Brands, *Andrew Jackson*, 15.
46. Parton, *Life of Andrew Jackson*, 52; Remini, Vol. I, 5.

47. Parton, 52–5. The author made the incredible assertion that Jackson may have made a mistake in this "fact of this kind." As proof of the birth at the McKemy house, Parton quoted witnesses, all second hand, who recalled that this home was where the future president was born.
48. "Whether the birth took place in North or South Carolina has occupied historians for generations." Meacham, *American Lion*, 9.
49. Remini, Vol. I, 4–5.
50. Brands, *Andrew Jackson*, 16; James, *The Life of Andrew Jackson*, 10.
51. Marsha Mullin, The Hermitage personal correspondence, 18 July 2017.
52. Laura-Eve Moss, The Andrew Jackson Papers Project personal correspondence, 13 July 2017. Jackson's own belief that he was born in South Carolina is buttressed by the fact that no one challenged it during his lifetime. If there were grounds for such a challenge, "I would have particularly expected them to be raised in response to AJ's nullification proclamation, which essentially was a personal plea to his fellow South-Carolinians." The idea of North Carolina only appeared in the mid-1850s from tales of descendants of people who had been living at the time of AJ's birth.
53. Remini, Vol. I, 5.
54. Brands, 17.
55. "burned with a zeal..." "snapping blue eyes" "brisk little body," James, 5–6; "had grown stout." Remini, Vol. I, 5:
56. Sheila Ingle. "Elizabeth Hutchinson Jackson."
57. "Waxhaw uncles and aunts apparently did not take a good deal of interest in him. They had their own children, their own problems, their own lives." Meacham, *American Lion*, 10; Uncle Robert "is credited with giving Andrew his first gun and contributing to his love of horses." "Presidential Lore: Andrew Jackson and the Crawford Family of Salisbury." *Salisbury Post*.
58. Remini, Vol. I, 5–6; Meacham, 9, 19; Brands, 17.
59. Stephenson affidavit.
60. Booraem, *Young Hickory*, 22.
61. *Ibid.*, 27–8; 33–4.
62. "often would he spend the winter's evenings..." Cobbett, *Life of Andrew Jackson*, 12.

63. Remini, Vol. I, 15; Meacham, *American Lion*, 11.
64. "Huey Jackson was dying..." Booraem, 47; Ingle.
65. Booraem, 45–95.
66. *Ibid.*; Brands, *Andrew Jackson*, 30.
67. Remini, Vol. I, 23.
68. Webb, *Born Fighting*, 186.
69. Meacham, 37.
70. John Eaton, *The Life of Major General Andrew Jackson*
71. Booraem, *Young Hickory*, 108.
72. Meacham, *American Lion*, 10, 19; Brands, 27.
73. Remini, Vol. I, 12.
74. Rachel Jackson to Katherine Duane Morgan, 18 May 1825.
75. Remini, Vol. I, 24–5.
76. Meacham, 4.

Chapter II

1. Patricia Brady, *A Being So Gentle: The frontier Love Story of Rachel and Andrew Jackson*, 59–60
2. Hendrik Booraem, Young Hickory. The Making of Andrew Jackson.
3. *Ibid.*, 136.
4. *Ibid.*, 123, 136, 148.
5. *Ibid.*, 132, 139.
6. *Ibid.*, 133, 181; James Parton, *Life of Andrew Jackson*, 150–1, Overton's quote.
7. *Ibid.*, 189–90, 193.
8. Remini, Vol. I, 40–1.
9. *Ibid.*
10. Katherine W. Cruse, *An Amiable Woman: Rachel Jackson*, 3; Patricia Caldwell, *General Jackson's Lady*, 14: The family history prior to their residence in Maryland is vague, "but it is generally understood that Capt. John Donelson, father of (John Donelson), came to America from London about 1716, with his father Patrick Donelson." "Patrick Donelson and his son John were engaged in the shipping business, first settled in Delaware. There John Donelson, the first, married Catherine Davies."
11. Brady, *A Being* So *Gentle*, 14.
12. Caldwell, *General Jackson's Lady*, 14.
13. Cruse, *An Amiable Woman*, 3.
14. Brady, *A Being So Gentle*, 105.
15. Caldwell, *General Jackson's Lady*, 15–19.
16. *Ibid.*, 57.
17. Brady, *A Being So Gentle*, 14
18. Cruse, *An Amiable* Woman, 3.
19. *Ibid.*; Caldwell, *General Jackson's Lady*, 19.
20. *Ibid.*, 20–1.
21. Cruse, *An Amiable Woman*, 3.
22. *Ibid.*, the youngest daughter and eighth of eleven children; Brady, *A Being So Gentle*, 13, ninth of eleven children; Caldwell, *General Jackson's Lady*, 6, tenth child and fourth daughter of eleven children.
23. Brady, *A Being So Gentle*, 14.
24. Caldwell, *General Jackson's Lady*, 8.
25. *Ibid.*, 13.
26. *Ibid.*, 59.
27. Parton, *Life of Andrew Jackson*, 126–7. Parton estimates its length to be two thousand miles; Brady, *A Being So Gentle*, 62 provides a more plausible calculation of one thousand miles.
28. Parton, *Life of Andrew Jackson*, 126–7; Brady, *A Being So Gentle*, 62; Caldwell, *General Jackson's Lady*, 62–76.
29. Caldwell, *General Jackson's Lady*, 62–76.
30. Brady, *A Being So Gentle*, 16, Describes the dimensions of *The Adventure*; Parton, *Life of Andrew Jackson*, 126, "black eye, black haired..."
31. Bill Bays, *James Robertson, Father of Tennessee and Founder of Nashville*, 125.
32. Caldwell, *General Jackson's Lady*, 30–1.
33. Bays, *James Robertson*, 185.
34. *Ibid.*, 85.
35. Brady, *A Being So Gentle*, 32.
36. Caldwell, *General Jackson's Lady*, 101.
37. Brady, *A Being So Gentle*, 53.
38. Cruse, *An Amiable Woman*, 4; Caldwell, *General Jackson's Lady*, 101.
39. Caldwell, *General Jackson's Lady*, 106.
40. *Ibid.*, 108.
41. *Ibid.*, 109.
42. *Ibid.*, 112.
43. *Ibid.*, 118, date of Robards arrival in Nashville.
44. *Papers of Andrew Jackson*, Vol. I, xxiii; Parton, *Life of Andrew Jackson*, 132, description of Nashville in 1788.

45. Caldwell, *General Jackson's Lady*, 115–6; Parton, *Life of Andrew Jackson*, 133.
46. Caldwell, *General Jackson's Lady*, 113–5.
47. *Ibid.*, 118.
48. Brady, *A Being So Gentle*, 42; Caldwell, *General Jackson's Lady*, 119; Parton, *Life of Andrew Jackson*, 150–1.
49. Caldwell, *General Jackson's Lady*, 119; Parton, 150–1.
50. Brady, *A Being So Gentle*, 46–7.
51. *Ibid.*, 49; Caldwell, *General Jackson's Lady*, 123–7.
52. Caldwell, *General Jackson's Lady*, 123–7.
53. Ann Toplovich, "Marriage, Mayhem, and Presidential Politics: The Robards-Jackson Backcountry Scandal," 3–22.
54. Parton, *Life of Andrew Jackson*, 152, Overton quote; Caldwell, *General Jackson's Lady*, 138, Overton's visit to the Robards home, 122, Assembly of Virginia granting Robards the right to sue for divorce.
55. Caldwell, *General Jackson's Lady*, 137–8.
56. Brady, *A Being So Gentle*, 57.
57. Caldwell, *General Jackson's Lady*, 146, 149.
58. John Overton alleged that, Jackson "hastened back to Natchez ... and married the woman he had innocently and unintentionally caused much loss of peace and unhappiness." Remini, Vol. I, 61; "Although they later claimed to have been married in Natchez..." Brady, *A Being So Gentle*, 49; "...the Natchez marriage, other than the bare statement that it took place...", Caldwell, *General Jackson's Lady*, 139.
59. Caldwell, *General Jackson's Lady*, 139.
60. *Jackson Papers* I, 18 January 1794, 44.
61. Brady, *A Being So Gentle*, 59–60.
62. *Jackson Papers* I, 3 August 1792, 36–7.
63. *Ibid.*, 10 September 1792, 38.
64. *Ibid.*, 2 March 1794, 45–6.
65. Caldwell, *General Jackson's Lady*, 166.
66. *Jackson Papers* I, 9 June 1795, 59; 1 July 1796, 94–5.
67. *Ibid.*, 12 December 1794, 52.
68. Caldwell, *General Jackson's Lady*, 163.
69. *Jackson Papers* I, 223n.
70. Caldwell, *General Jackson's Lady*, 173, 182.
71. *Ibid.*, 183.
72. Parton, *Life of Andrew Jackson*, 337.
73. Caldwell, *General Jackson's Lady*, 169.
74. *Ibid.*
75. *Jackson Papers* I, 26 January 1798, 174.
76. *Ibid.*, 17 January 1799, 223.
77. *Ibid.*, 26 January 1798, 174; 17 January 1799, 223.
78. *Ibid.*, xxiv–xxv.

Chapter III

1. *Jackson Papers* I, 375–7, Jackson to Sevier, 9 October 1803.
2. *Jackson Papers* II, xiii.
3. Remini, One, 132, 420 acres ten miles from Nashville; Parton, *Life of Andrew Jackson*, 307; Brady, *A Being So Gentle*, 87, for description of the log cabin; Caldwell, *General Jackson's Lady*, 208–11, purchase from Nathaniel Hays. Poplar Grove was their first,
4. Caldwell, *General Jackson's Lady*, 350.
5. *Collins English Dictionary*, Online ed. "Hermitage."
6. Caldwell, *General Jackson's Lay*, 211–2. Burr's influence may be apocryphal since no other reference for either Burr's involvement or Mrs. Prevost could be unearthed by the author; "Rural retreat", Marsha Mullin, personal correspondence, Laura Eve Moss, personal correspondence; A September 1804 letter was addressed to Andrew Jackson at the Hermitage.
7. "...little boys who came to live with them for months at a time ... Rachel's brother Sam's three—John Samuel, Andrew Jackson. and Daniel Smith Donelson ... children of his friend Edward Butler ... Edward George Washington and Anthony Wayne Butler, boys of four and one...", Brady, *A Bing So Gentle*, 89.
8. Remini, Vol. II, 132.
9. Eaton
10. Brady, *A Being So Gentle*, 39–41;

Notes—Chapter III

Jackson Papers letter to Waightstill Avery, 12 August 1788.
11. Jackson Williams, *Dueling in the Old South*, 5,13.
12. *Ibid.*, 69.
13. Remini, Vol. I, 113.
14. H.W. Brands, *Andrew Jackson: His Life and Times*, 105–9; Parton, *Life of Andrew Jackson*, 234; Brady, *A Being So Gentle*, 80–1.
15. Parton, *Life of Andrew Jackson*, 164; Brady, *A Being So Gentle*, 80–1; Brands, *Andrew Jackson: His Life and Times*, 105–9.
16. Caldwell, *General Jackson's Lady*, 187; Parton, *Life of Andrew Jackson*, 234; Brands, *Andrew Jackson: His Life and Times*, 105–9.
17. *Jackson Papers* I, letter to Sevier, 2 October 1803, 367–8.
18. *Ibid.*, Sevier to Jackson, 2 October 180, 368.
19. *Ibid.*, 375–7, Jackson to Sevier, 9 October 1803, 375–7
20. Remini, Vol. I, 123; Bradley J. Birzer, "Andrew Jackson's Duel with John Sevier."
21. *Jackson Papers* II, Background, 66–7; Memorandum 67–9, 28 July 1805; letter Thomas Overton to Andrew Jackson, 69–70, 1 August 1805.
22. *Ibid.*, 82–3, Swann to Jackson, 12 January1806; Remini, Vol. I, 128.
23. Parton, *Life of Andrew Jackson*. 295–306; Remini, Vol. I, 124–143; Brands, *Andrew Jackson*, 131–8.
24. Caldwell, *General Jackson's Lady*, 228.
25. "...polluted mouth and pronounced it in a most lascivious way," Parton, *Life o Andrew Jackson*, 268–9; Remini, Vol. I, 136.
26. Brands, *Andrew Jackson*, 131–8.
27. *Jackson Papers* II, 97–8: Charles Dickinson letter to Thomas Eastin, 21 May 1806.
28. *Ibid.*, 98: Andrew Jackson letter to Charles Dickinson, 23 May 1806.
29. Parton, *Life of Andrew Jackson*, 295.
30. *Ibid.*, 296–7.
31. "nearly a month before he could move...", Remini, Vol. I, 142: ; Parton, *Life of Andrew Jackson*, 304
32. Ludwig M. Deppisch, "Andrew Jackson and American Medical Practice," 131.
33. *Ibid.*, 134–5.
34. Caldwell, *General Jackson's Lady*, 225, 232.
35. Remini, Vol. I, 143.
36. Parton, *Life of Andrew Jackson*, 305.
37. Remini, Vol. I, 144.
38. *Jackson Papers* 58; 110: Andrew Jackson letter to William Preston Anderson, 25 September 1806.
39. A.M. Phadke et al: "Smallpox as an Etiologic Factor in Male Fertility," 802–4; Malpani, "How Do Infections Cause Male Infertility."
40. Ludwig M. Deppisch, *The Health of the First Ladies: Medical Histories form Martha Washington to Michelle Obama*, 15.
41. Caldwell, *General Jackson's Lady*, 241, Elizabeth Donelson was too ill to raise twins.; Linda Bennett Galloway, *Andrew Jackson Junior: Son of a President*, 12–13; *Jackson Papers* II, 218, adoption.
42. *Jackson Papers* I, 325, 3 January 1801.
43. *Jackson Papers* II, 535, 3 February 1806: Hay's affidavit; "John Caffrey," Geni.com.
44. Remini, Vol. I, 132–5; *Jackson Papers* I, 262; *Jackson Papers* II, 6.
45. *Jackson Papers* II, 437, Andrew Jackson to Rachel Jackson 13 October 1813; 487, Andrew Jackson to Rachel Jackson 14 December 1813.
46. *Ibid.*, 572. 4 December 1812.
47. *Jackson Papers* I, 172–3, Andrew Jackson to Robert Hays, 5 January 1798; 443, Andrew Jackson to Alexander Donelson, 18 October 1797; *Papers*, II, 558, 2 February 1819; Papers II, 536, purchased 367 acres from Severn for $200, 11 February 1806.
48. *Jackson Papers* I, 34, partners in mercantile business, lawyer, three children became wards, candidate for state attorney general; *Papers*, II, 204, death at Jackson's home in 1804.
49. *Jackson Papers* I, 26, land transactions; I, 433, surety bond, 17 February 1790.
50. *Jackson Papers* II, 444. Andrew Jackson letter to Rachel Jackson, 4 November 1813.
51. Remini Vol. I, 160–1.
52. *Jackson Papers* II, 535n.
53. *Ibid.*, 172–4.

54. Remini, Vol. I, 181–3.
55. Ibid., 183.
56. Ibid., 184.
57. Ibid., 185; Caldwell, *General Jackson's Lady*, 262; Parton, *Life of Andrew Jackson*, 393; Brands, 188–191.
58. Deppisch, *Tennessee Quarterly*, 139.
59. Ludwig M. Deppisch, "Andrew Jackson's Exposure to Mercury and Lead: Poisoned President?"
60. Remini, Vol. I, 185.

Chapter IV

1. Remini, *Andrew Jackson*, Volume One, 192.
2. Ibid., 221.
3. Ibid., 225.
4. Ibid., 318.
5. Ibid., 319.
6. Reid died on January 18, 1816 from influenza. "It was not until May, after consideration of several candidates, that Jackson and his advisers settled upon John Henry Eaton for the task." *Jackson Papers* IV, 3.
7. "John Henry Newman," Wikipedia.
8. Remini, Vol. I, 323–4, 340, 390.
9. Ibid., 350.
10. Ibid., 364.
11. Ibid., 371–7.
12. Cynthia Kierner, *Beyond the Household: Women's Place in the Early South, 1700–1835*, 17.
13. Andrew Jackson to Rachel, 8 January 1813, *Jackson Papers* II, 354: Send the wagon load of pork; "and the hands out under him and his sole control, and kept constantly employed at gathering the crop until it is in": Andrew Jackson (Camp Blount) to Rachel, 11 October 1813, *Jackson Papers* II, 436; "have as much land cleared as he can, take care of my stock, and see that you are comfortable," Andrew Jackson (Fort Strother) to Rachel, 29 December 1813, *Jackson Papers* II, 516.
14. Patricia Brady, *A Being So Gentle*, 139.
15. Andrew Jackson Chikasaw Council House) to Rachel, 18 September 1816, *Jackson Papers* IV, 62.
16. *Jackson Papers* II, 271. Selection of site for slave quarters to be constructed; Andrew Jackson to Rachel, 1 March 1813, *Jackson Papers* II, 216. While on a military march, discussed price ($500) for selling a slave, but left the resolution of the matter to her.
17. Brady, *A Being So Gentle*, 128–9.
18. Marsha Mullin, chief curator *The Hermitage*, personal communication to the author, January 9, 2020.
19. Andrew Jackson to Hutchings, 18 April 1833, Remini, Vol. I, 69.
20. Brady, *A Being So Gentle*, 128. Rachel was tasked with the health of Junior and the slaves in addition to herself; "kiss our little son for me," Andrew Jackson (Natchez) to Rachel, 17 December 1811, *Jackson Papers* II, 273; "kiss Andrew," Andrew Jackson (Jackson Headquarters) to Rachel, 22 February 1813, *Jackson Papers* II, 370; "Kiss my little Andrew for me," Andrew Jackson (Camp Jackson) to Rachel, 1 March 1813, *Jackson Papers* II, 373; "Kiss Andrew for me," Andrew Jackson (Fort Deposit) to Rachel 9 December 1813, *Jackson Papers* II, 478.
21. "I have only to add a renewal of my prayers to the Sovereign..." Andrew Jackson (Natchez) to Rachel, 15 February 181–, *Jackson Papers* II, 364; "Say to my Son if he will learn his Book..." A. Jackson to Rachel, home of Judge Harry Toulmans, 13 March 1816, *Jackson Papers* IV, 14.
22. Remini, Vol. I, 193.
23. Parton, *Life of Andrew Jackson*, 430 Creek Indians refusal to care for Lincoya; "Keep Lincoya in the house—he is a Savage," A. Jackson to Rachel, Fort Strother, 29 December 1813, *Jackson Papers* II, 516.
24. Parton, *Life of Andrew Jackson*, 439–40. Background on the Jacksons' care of Lincoya; "how thankful I am to you for taking poor little Lincoya home and clothing him." A. Jackson (Chickasaw Council House) to Rachel, 18 September 1816, *Jackson Papers* IV, 62.
25. See Chapter III for more information.
26. "If you continue in the notion of moving, I think you would be pleased with it. Society is in a more miserable condition in that country [Nashville] ... nothing but jealously, slander, & envy ... the most of the inhabitants having lately emigrated there for the purpose of becoming politicians, each is endeavoring to aggrandize

Notes—Chapter IV

himself." Alexander Donelson to Andrew Jackson, 9 October 1811, *Jackson Papers* II, 266–7.

27. *Jackson Papers* II, 408. Battle background; "made at me and gave me five slight wounds." Thomas Hart Benton to the Public, Franklin TN, 10 September 1813, *Jackson Papers* II, 425–7.

28. Remini, Vol. I, 207; "Oh, my unfortunate Nephew." Rachel to Andrew Jackson, 10 February 1814, Remini, Vol. I, 209–10.

29. "...when I tell you how gratified it is to me that in all your..." Rachel to Andrew Jackson Donelson, 19 October 1818, *Jackson Papers* IV, 244–5.

30. Remini, Vol. 3, 49.

31. Ludwig M. Deppisch, "Andrew Jackson's Exposure to Mercury and Lead: Poisoned President?"

32. *Ibid.*; Deppisch, "Andrew Jackson and American Medical Practice."

33. A. Jackson (Chikasaw Council) to Rachel, 18 September 1816, *Jackson Papers* IV, 62; *Ibid.*, 63. Dr. Bronaugh (1788–1822), an army surgeon and later Surgeon General of the Division of the South, served as aide to Jackson in Florida in 1821. He died from yellow fever during an epidemic in Pensacola.

34. Remini, Vol. I, 223–4.

35. *Ibid.*, 320.

36. "I can now scarcely write with a pain in my left side..." Andrew Jackson to Isabella Butler Vinson, 9 May 1817, *Jackson Papers* IV, 115; "I have enjoyed only tolerable health..." Andrew Jackson (Huntsville) to Rachel, 11 June 1817, *Jackson Papers* IV, 117:

37. "I have been so much exposed..." Andrew Jackson (Fort Montgomery) to Rachel, 2 June 1818; Remini, Vol. I, 364–5. letter of resignation to President Monroe.

38. Remini, Vol. III, 135.

39. Andrew Jackson to Isaac Shelby, 7 July 1818, *Jackson Papers* IV, 219; Andrew Jackson to Andrew Jackson Donelson, 14 July 1818, *Jackson Papers* IV, 222; Andrew Jackson to James Monroe, 19 April 1818, *Jackson Papers* IV, 38–9.

40. Remini, Vol. I, 378–9.

41. Andrew Jackson to Andrew Jackson Donelson, 17 May 1819, *Jackson Papers* IV, 299: Dr. Bronaugh accompanied Jackson during the Creek War. This physician was burdened by a phonetically challenging surname. Dr. Samuel Hogg was the Jackson family physician at The Hermitage.

42. Andrew Jackson to Andrew Jackson Donelson, 23 July 1819, *Jackson Papers* IV, 303.

43. "...yesterday was the first day in twelve that I could sit up long enough to write a letter..." Andrew Jackson to George Gibson, 7 September 1819, *Jackson Papers* IV, 318; "I was taken very ill & confined to my bed for ten days." Andrew Jackson to Andrew Jackson Donelson, 17 September 1819, *Jackson Papers* IV, 322–3.

44. "This is my birthday..." Andrew Jackson to George Gibson, 15 March 1820, *Jackson Papers* IV, 363.

45. Cynthia A. Kierner: *Beyond the Household: Women's Place in the Early South, 1700–1835*, 141–2: The contrast between Anglican and Presbyterian devotion; "A prominent Presbyterian clergyman argued..." Kierner, 144.

46. "On the paternal side she was the granddaughter of Catherine Davies, who was the sister of Reverend Samuel Davies." Michelle Gullion, private correspondence to the author, 25 August 2017.

47. Brady, *A Being So Gentle*, 109.

48. Remini, Vol. I, 59–60.

49. "Rachel's fervor was the bedrock of her life." Brady, *A Being So Gentle*, 183.

50. *Ibid.*, 161.

51. "But my blessed redeemer is making intersession..." Rachel to Andrew Jackson, 8 February 1813, *Jackson Papers* II: 361–2; "Angels wafted Her on their Celestial wings." Rachel to Ralph Eleazar Whitesides, 2 February 1819, *Jackson Papers* IV, 272; "She seemed as if she slept in Jesus." Rachel to William Davenport, 18 March 1819, *Jackson Papers* IV, 277.

52. "I thank you for your prayers..." Andrew Jackson to Rachel, 8 September 1813, *Jackson Papers* II, 54–5; "I have only to add a renewal of my prayers to the Sovereign..." Andrew Jackson (Natchez) to Rachel, 15 February 1813, *Jackson Papers* II, 364.

53. Remini, Vol. II, 62–3.

54. See Chapter V for a more complete narrative.

55. Remini, Vol. I, 403: Rachel in New Orleans and Pensacola; Remini, 408:

"Undoubtedly at Rachel's urging, Jackson also cracked down on all ungodly..."
56. Brady, *A Being So Gentle*, 175–183.
57. Remini, Vol. II, 85.

Chapter V

1. Remini, Vol. I, 209–10.
2. Remini, Vol. II, 7.
3. Rachel to Latitia Dalzell Chambers, 12 August 1824, *Jackson Papers* V, 432.
4. Caldwell, *General Jackson's Lady*, 236–7; "Rachel was now an extremely stout, dark-complexioned," Remini, Vol. I, 315–6.
5. Andrew Jackson to Rachel Jackson, August 10, 1814, Jackson Papers Huntington Library.
6. Edward Branley, "NOLA History: New Orleans in 1812"; Rachel Jackson (New Orleans) to Robert Hays, New Orleans, 5 March 1815, *Jackson Papers* III, 297–8.
7. Rachel Jackson to Mrs. Eliza Kingsley, New Orleans, 27 April 1821, Remini, Vol. I, 31.
8. Remini, Vol. I, 194–5.
9. Remini, Vol. I, 195; *Nolte Memoirs*, 238–9.
10. *Nolte Memoirs*, 238.
11. Brady, *A Being So Gentle*, 149.
12. *Ibid.* 152, 153.
13. Remini, Vol. I, 381.
14. Patricia Bauer, Encyclopedia Britannica. Conflict between U.S. armed forces and the Seminole Indians of Florida that is generally dated to 1817–18 and that led Spain to cede Florida to United States.
15. Remini, Vol. I, 382. Andrew Jackson remained in the army because of the possibility of a war with Spain; 402, date of retirement from the army.
16. Andrew Jackson (Nashville) to Andrew Jackson Donelson, 1 March 1821, *Jackson Papers* V, 24.
17. Andrew Jackson (Hermitage) to John Coffee, 11 April 1821, *Jackson Papers* V, 27.
18. *Jackson Papers* V, 29.
19. "Andrew Jackson Hutchings was left behind." Brady, *A Being So Gentle*, 159; "Andrew Jackson's Children," The Hermitage. Hutchings' biography.
20. *Jackson Papers* I, 417–422. Genealogy of the Donelson Family.
21. Brady, *A Being So Gentle*, 162
22. *Ibid.*
23. Remini, Vol. I, 408; *Jackson Papers* V, 79–82.
24. Brady, *A Being So Gentle*, 163–4.
25. Remini, Vol. I, 408.
26. Remini, Vol. I, 422–4.
27. *Jackson Papers* V, 11 May 1821, Andrew Jackson to John Coffee, 41.
28. "We all enjoy good health." Andrew Jackson to John Coffee, Pensacola, 26 July 1821, *Jackson Papers* V, 83; "The ladies are in good health." Andrew Jackson to Robert Butler, Pensacola, 27 July 1821, *Jackson Papers* V, 85; "Mrs. Jackson is only in tolerable health." Andrew Jackson to James Jackson, Pensacola, 2 August 1821, *Jackson Papers* V, 91–2.
29. Andrew Jackson to James Monroe, Hermitage, 5 October 1821, *Jackson Papers* V, 110.
30. Brady, *A Being So Gentle*, 167.
31. Caldwell, *General Jackson's Lady*, 381.
32. Remini, Vol. II, 7.
33. Jerry Trescott, "The Architecture of the Hermitage Mansion."
34. Remini, Vol. I, 379–80.
35. Trescott, "Architecture."
36. "My health is improving, but I find it very difficult to get clear of the cough." Andrew Jackson to Andrew Jackson Donelson, Hermitage, 26 April 1822, *Jackson Papers* V, 177; "I have been lately taken with a violent Lax..." Andrew Jackson to Andrew Jackson Donelson, Hermitage, 2 May 1822, *Jackson Papers* V, 193–4; "My cough has considerably abated..." Andrew Jackson to Andrew Jackson Donelson, Hermitage, 28 June 1822, *Jackson Papers* V, 193–4.
37. Remini, Vol. 2, 7.
38. *Ibid.*, 52; The 17th Amendment to the U.S. Constitution provided for the direct popular election of senators in 1913.
39. Andrew Jackson (City of Washington) to Rachel Jackson, 7 December 1823, *Jackson Papers* V, 322–3.
40. Andrew Jackson to John Overton, 8 November 1823, *Jackson Papers* V, 316.
41. "I assure you he is in most excellent health." John Henry Eaton to Rachel

Jackson, DC, 18 December 1823, *Jackson Papers* V, 325–7; "Genl. Jackson's health is most excellent. The climate agrees well with him, and he seems in better health than he has been since the war.... If the Genl. had remained at home..." John Henry Eaton (Washington) to Rachel Jackson, 8 February 1824, *Jackson Papers* V, 353–4.
42. Andrew Jackson to Rachel Jackson, Washington City, 21 December 1823, *Jackson Papers* V, 330–1.
43. Caldwell, *General Jackson's Lady*, 386.
44. Andrew Jackson (Washington City) to Rachel Jackson, 21 January 1824, *Jackson Papers* V, 345–6.
45. Andrew Jackson (Washington City) to Andrew Jackson Donelson, 18 January 1824, *Jackson Papers* V, 339–340; Andrew Jackson (Washington City) to Andrew Jackson Donelson, 6 March 1824, *Jackson Papers* V, 372–3; Andrew Jackson (Washington City) to Andrew Jackson Donelson, 4 April 1824, *Jackson Papers* V, 388–9.
46. Cheathem, *Old Hickory's Nephew*, 36–9.
47. Brady, *A Being So Gentle*, 183.
48. Cheathem, *Old Hickory's Nephew*, 37.
49. Caldwell, *General Jackson's Lady*, 384; Andrew Jackson (Washington City) to Rachel Jackson,11 December 1823, *Jackson Papers* V, 324–5.
50. Caldwell, *General Jackson's Lady*, 392.
51. *Jackson Papers* V, 371.
52. Rachel Jackson (The Hermitage) to Latitia Dalzell Chambers, 12 August 1824, *Jackson Papers* V, 432.
53. Caldwell, *General Jackson's Lady*, 324; Brady, *A Being So Gentle*, 184; Remini, Vol. 2, 84: The journey from The Hermitage to the capital took twenty-eight days.
54. Cheathem, *Old Hickory's Nephew*, 35.
55. Brady, *A Being So Gentle*, 184–5.
56. Caldwell, *General Jackson's Lady*, 386; Brady, *A Being So Gentle*, 189.
57. Caldwell, *General Jackson's Lady*, 399.
58. Rachel Jackson (Washington City) to Elizabeth Kingsley, 23 December 1824, *Jackson Papers* V, 456–7.

59. Brady, *A Being So Gentle*, 192: reached home on April 13, 1825.

Chapter VI

1. "To me the *Presidential charms* by the side of a *happy retirement from Public life* are as the tale of the candle and the substantial fire, the first of which it is sad is soon blown out by the wind but the latter is only increased by it." Rachel Jackson to Katherine Duane Morgan, 18 May 1825, *Jackson Papers* VI, 72.
2. "The 1824 Election and the 'Corrupt Bargain,'" ushistory.org.
3. Remini, Vol. II, 96: health; Rachel couldn't be happier upon return and believed
4. Brady, *A Being So Gentle*, 175.
5. Remini, Vol. II, 117.
6. June 1826, *Jackson Papers* VI, 182.
7. *Jackson Papers* VI, 252, note: Jackson's violent 1819 threat against Senator John Eppes.
8. Andrew Jackson to Thomas Patrick Moore, 31 July 1826, *Jackson Papers* VI, 194–5.
9. *Ibid.*, 252
10. *Ibid.*, xv.
11. Degregorio, *U.S. Presidents*, 112.
12. Brady, *A Being So* Gentle, 196.
13. See Chapter V.
14. *Jackson Papers* VI, 407: Andrew Jackson was aboard the *Pocahontas* to New Orleans to celebrate 13th anniversary of battle. His absence lasted from December 27, 1827 until early February 1828. Rachel's accompaniment is noted in a February 6, 1828 letter between Andrew Jackson and John Coffee.
15. *Jackson Papers* VI, xvi; 69.
16. Caldwell, *General Jackson's Lady*, 407–9.
17. See Chapter V.
18. Brady, *A Being So Gentle*, 175.
19. *Jackson Papers* VI, 118.
20. "Since my arrival home have been attacked with a renewal of the complaint I had when I left you—which has been increased by the fatigues I have encountered since is came home—first the renewed attention of the citizens to me—and then to Lafayette—I am now in dry-dock for repairs..." Andrew Jackson

Notes—Chapter VI

to Richard Keith Call, 7 May1825, *Jackson Papers* VI, 68.

21. "Owing to the fatigue I underwent on my Journey home, brought on me a severe affliction that confined me for many days: The arrival of Genl Lafayette aroused me from my bed to hail him welcome, which retarded my recovery, and has prevented me until now.... My general health is good, my affliction arose from fatigue & riding on horseback, which occasioned an inflammation in the rectum, which communicated to the bladder, & affected the prostate glands—rest has removed all pain." Andrew Jackson to Samuel Swartwout, 16 May 1825, *Jackson Papers* VI, 70–1.

22. "I intended setting out on Sunday next for your house, but from a very sudden attack of the bowels, & I might add severe, I find that I cannot be able to ride that Journey so early." Andrew Jackson to John Coffee, 24 April 1828, *Jackson Papers* VI, 447.

23. "I am seriously afflicted with a return of my old bowel complaint, from which I am just recovered, but am much debilitated." Andrew Jackson to James K. Polk, 3 May 1828, *Jackson Papers* VI, 451–2.

24. "I must be excused—having lost many of my teeth it is with great difficulty I can articulate..." Andrew Jackson to Robert Paine et al, 30 September 1826, *Jackson Papers* VI, 220.

25. "My health is not good, however, I complain not, because I know, it would be grateful to my enemies..." Andrew Jackson to William Berkeley Lewis, 10 December 1827, *Jackson Papers* VI, 404.

26. "...but mine (health) has been a little impaired, by hard and close labour & confinement, still, I trust providence will spare me until my enemies are prostrate." Andrew Jackson to John Coffee, 20–24 February 1828, *Jackson Papers* VI, 418.

27. *The Western Journal of Medicine and Surgery* 6(3) (1842): 151–5. Death of Dr. Samuel D. Hogg, 151–5.

28. Andrew Jackson to Andrew Jackson Donelson., 17 May 1819, *Jackson Papers* IV, 299.

29. Andrew Jackson to John Coffee, 1 December 1825, *Jackson Papers* VI, 124–5.

30. *The Western Journal of Medicine and Surgery* 6(4) (1842) 252–6: Miscellaneous Cases of Samuel Hogg late of Tennessee.

31. *Jackson Papers* VI, 11–12; "Evoking Andrew's reputation for violence, gossips claimed that he had driven Rachel's husband away and then lived with her for several years before she was divorced." Brady, *A Being So Gentle*, 178.

32. Brady, *A Being So Gentle*, 179.

33. *Ibid.*, 187.

34. Caldwell, *General Jackson's Lady*, 397; Andrew Jackson (Washington) to Charles Pendleton Tutt, 9 January 1825, *Jackson Papers* VI, 12.

35. Brady, *A Being So Gentle*, 205.

36. *Ibid.*, 212.

37. *Jackson Papers* VI, xv.

38. Andrew Jackson to William Berkeley Lewis., 12 December 1826, *Jackson Papers* VI, 240–1.

39. Remini Vol. II, 119.

40. *Jackson Papers* VI, 240–1.

41. Edward Butler (Cincinnati) to Andrew Jackson, 11 January 1827, *Jackson Papers* VI, 260.

42. John Henry Eaton to Andrew Jackson, 22–26 December 1826, *Jackson Papers* VI, 245–6.

43. David Heidler, and Jeanne Heidler, *Henry Clay: The Essential American*, 207.

44. *Jackson Papers* VI, 314–5.

45. *Ibid.*, 498.

46. Caldwell, *General Jackson's Lady*, 412.

47. Rachel Jackson to Elizabeth Courts Love Warren, 18 July 1827, *Jackson Papers* VI, 367–8.

48. Remini, Vol. II, 143.

49. Andrew Jackson to Richard Keith Call, 14 August 1828, *Jackson Papers* VI, 49–4.

50. "...for the day of retribution & vengeance must come." Andrew Jackson to Richard Keith Call, 3 May 1827, *Jackson Papers* VI, 315–6; "...still when Mrs. J. Character was so basely attacked, it was more than my mind could bear to hear it, and not redress it—I hope providence will spar me to that day, when I can freely act, when retributive Justice will await the actors in this vile procedure..." Andrew Jackson to John Coffee, 12 May 1828, *Jackson Papers* VI, 458.

51. John Eaton (Washington) to Rachel Jackson (Hermitage), 7 December 1828, *Jackson Papers* V, 543.
52. Remini, Vol. II, 7-8.
53. Andrew Jackson (Washington) to Rachel, 12 April 1824, *Jackson Papers* V, 393.
54. "She kept him informed of every ache and pain she suffered, and especially how grieved she was over his absence," Remini, Vol. II, 66; "but I trust that kind providence will soon relieve you from the pain that the inflammation of your eye must inflict—with what pleasure would I apply the cooling ash was I with you...." Andrew Jackson (Washington) to Rachel, 21 January 1824, *Jackson Papers* V, 345.
55. "Mrs. J has regained her health," Andrew Jackson to Richard Keith Call, 7 May 1825, *Jackson Papers* VI, 71; "Mrs. Jackson's health is perfectly restored, as soon as we got on the mountains," Andrew Jackson to Samuel Swartwout, 16 May 1825, *Jackson Papers* VI, 71.
56. "Mrs. J's indisposition prevents me and will prevent me this winter from visiting," Andrew Jackson to John Coffee, 1 December 1825. Doctor Hogg is identified as her treating physician. *Jackson Papers* VI, 124; "Mrs. J has just recovered from a severe illness which has confined her for six weeks," Andrew Jackson to George Winchester, 15 January 1826, *Jackson Papers* VI, 13; "Mrs. J. has had a severe illness, her health is measurably restored altho her complection remains somewhat sallow...," Andrew Jackson to Richard Keith Call, 9 March 1826, *Jackson Papers* VI, 150.
57. "Mrs. J's physician has advised her to visit the Harrodsburg springs this season for her health," Andrew Jackson to William B. Keene, 16 June,1827, *Jackson Papers* VI, 344; Miles Blythe McCorkle identified as the physician.; McCorkle is further referenced as a physician to The Hermitage in a letter to Andrew Jackson Junior from Andrew Jackson (Washington), 19 August 1829. *Jackson Papers* VII, 384; Harrodsburg Kentucky was the site of an exclusive spa that was located there from 1820–1853.
58. "We enjoy good health" Andrew Jackson to William Robinson (upon return from New Orleans), 3 February 1828, *Jackson Papers* VI, 413; "Mrs. J. is still good."; Andrew Jackson to John Coffee, 20–24 February 1828, *Jackson Papers* VI, 418; "Mrs. Jackson is well," Andrew Jackson to James Alexander Hamilton, 29 April 1828, *Jackson Papers* VI, 449.
59. Remini, Vol. II, 149.
60. Caldwell, *General Jackson's Lady*, 418.
61. Rachel Jackson to Louise Moreau Davezac de Lassy Livingston, 1 December 1828, *Jackson Papers* VI, 536.
62. Remini, Vol. II, 150.
63. Remini, Vol. II, 150–1; Caldwell, *General Jackson's Lady*, 425–6.
64. Caldwell, *General Jackson's Lady*, 425–8; Remini, Vol. II, 151.
65. Heiskell, Dr. Henry Lee, *Jackson Papers* VI, 517, Doctor's bill.
66. Andrew Jackson to Richard Keith Call, 22 December 1828, *Jackson Papers* VI, 546–7.
67. Andrew Jackson to Jean Baptiste Plauche. 27 December 1828, *Jackson Papers* VI, 547
68. Remini, Vol. II, 153–4.
69. *Ibid.*, 155.

Chapter VII

1. Harlow Giles Unger, *The Last Founding Father. James Monroe and a Nation's Call to Greatness*, 298–303.
2. *Ibid.*, 303.
3. Andrew Jackson to Andrew Jackson Donelson, 18 January 1824, *Jackson Papers* V, 340.
4. *Jackson Papers* I, 417–421.
5. Inman, *Brothers and Friends*, 45.
6. *Ibid.*, 81. surveyor; *Ibid.*, 85. justice of the county court.
7. "present me to Capt. John Donelson & family," Andrew Jackson to Rachel, *Jackson Papers* V, 323; "present me affectionately to Miss E. to my old friend Capt. J. D...." Andrew Jackson to Andrew Jackson Donelson, *Jackson Papers* V, 354–5.
8. Andrew Jackson (Washington) to John Donelson (Tennessee), 9 February 1824, *Jackson Papers* V, 354–5.
9. Pauline Wilcox Burke, *Emily Donelson of Tennessee* Volume 1, 1–4.
10. *Ibid.*, xi.
11. Andrew Jackson to John Coffee, 14

March 1822, *Jackson Papers* V, 158; Act of Congress, 24 May 1824, *Jackson Papers* VI, 108: Congress granted the heirs of John Donelson the right to claim 5000 acres of public land in Alabama or Mississippi; Andrew and Rachel Jackson to John Donelson, Deed, 22 October 1824, *Jackson Papers* V, 572. For their one-tenth share of 5000 aces granted to the heirs of John Donelson (1718–1786); John Donelson, Memorandum, April, 1825, *Jackson Papers* VI, 558. Memorandum by John regarding the survey of a tract of land for AJ and the heirs of Samuel Donelson.

12. Burke Volume I, xi–xii.
13. *Ibid.*, 36.
14. *Ibid.*, 68.
15. Burke, *Emily Donelson of Tennessee* 39.
16. Burke, Vol. I, xii—xiii, Emily's education; 70–1. Old log house school, Nashville Academy.
17. *Ibid.*, 106.
18. *Ibid.*, 109.
19. *Ibid.*, 114–17; Andrew Jackson to John Coffee, 20 September 1824, "Rachel Jackson, wife of William, is no more, she departed this life on the 16th ... the very day on which A & E Donelson were to be married ... what was to be done in this distressing circumstance was vey perplexing. It was at length concluded to let the parson perform the ceremony & *it was done.*", *Jackson Papers* V, 440.
20. "...treat me as their child." Burke, Vol. I, 123
21. *Ibid.*, 122.
22. *Ibid.*
23. *Ibid.*, 144–5. Capt John retreated into the woods.
24. Papers VI, 18: January 2, 1825: letter from Andrew Jackson (Washington City) to John Coffee, 2 January 1825, *Jackson Papers* VI, 18:
25. Andrew Jackson (Hermitage) to John Coffee, 24 April 1825, *Jackson Papers* VI, 65.
26. Burke, Vol. I, 137.
27. *Ibid.*, 142–3; Mark B. Cheathem, *Old Hickory's Nephew*, 37. 348 and a quarter acres adjoining The Hermitage.
28. Burke, Vol. I, 129–30.
29. *Ibid.*, 152.
30. Cheathem, *Old Hickory's Nephew*, 34–5.
31. *Ibid.*, 51.

Chapter VIII

1. *The Autobiography of Peggy Eaton*, 6.
2. Laura-Eve Moss, personal communication.
3. Phillips, *That Eaton Woman*, 2–4; *Autobiography*, 2.
4. "[A] devout Methodist who attended church regularly." Philips, 5; "whose intimate she became." Pollack, *Peggy Eaton*, 68–9.
5. Philips, 5–6; *Autobiography*, 6–7: quote about her brothers.
6. Phillips, 5.
7. Phillips, 2–5; Pollack, 21. Increased prosperity for O'Neale's Franklin House, possibly due to Vice President Clinton's demise on the premises.
8. Pollack, 8.
9. Pollack, 11.
10. Phillips, 10–11.
11. *Ibid.*, 11. On May 16, 1812, Margaret danced at the White House. The ebullient Dolley not only awarded her first prize in all five categories of dance but also placed a gold crown on her head.
12. *Ibid.*, 21; 34. Peggy O'Neale Timberlake was no longer welcome at the President's house.
13. *Ibid.*, 13–15.
14. Pollack, *Peggy Eaton*, 27.
15. Phillips, *That Eaton Woman*, 15; "No one stepped beyond the bounds of propriety." Phillips, 21.
16. Pollack, 28; Phillips, 16.
17. *Autobiography*, 14; "Previously Peggy had rejected suitors, an army colonel, two members of Congress, and an official of the British legation." Pollack, 22.
18. *Autobiography*, 16–17.
19. Pollack, 29, 33; Phillips, 17–20; *Autobiography*, 17–18.
20. The date of their engagement is disputed. Pollack, 39, asserts this date; Phillips, 27, uses "the spring of 1817." Margaret (*Autobiography*, 20) dates their meeting to "her sixteenth year." According to Wikipedia's article, "Peggy Eaton," "About 1816, at age 17, Margaret O'Neale married 39-year-old purser in the Navy." Pollack's chronology to this author is the most accurate.
21. "Peggy Eaton," Wikipedia.
22. *The Autobiography of Peggy Eaton*, 22.

23. Pollack, 39, 43–4; Phillips, 22–25; *Autobiography*, 22–3.
24. Pollack, 45–6.
25. Phillips, 24.
26. Pollack, 47–8.
27. Phillips, 26; "loved his spontaneity, succumbed to his unconscious, flexible, golden charm, and felt responsibility in regulating his life-work..." Pollack, 49.
28. Phillips, 31.
29. *Ibid.*, 29–30.
30. Remini, Vol. 2, 53–4. Eaton accompanied Jackson to Washington in Nov/Dec 1823 by horseback and stagecoach. Both were U.S. senators from Tennessee and both lodged at the O'Neale's boarding house.
31. Pollack, *Peggy Eaton*, 54.
32. *Ibid.*, 55.
33. Phillips, *That Eaton Woman*, 33; Pollack, 58.
34. Phillips, 33–35.
35. Pollack, 59.
36. State legislatures appointed Tennessee's two United States senators until the Seventeenth Amendment to the U.S. Constitution was ratified in 1913. The Amendment provided for a direct popular vote to elect senators.
37. Phillips, 42.
38. *Ibid.*, 43.
39. Pollack, 64–5. "Call propositioned her, which she rejected with 'much seeming indignation.'" Remini, Vol. 2, 404n.
40. Phillips, 43–4; Pollack, 64–5.
41. Phillips, 45; Pollack, 66.
42. Phillips, 42.
43. Pollack, 62–3.
44. Phillips, 45.
45. Phillips, 51–2; Pollack, 68–9.
46. Phillips, 41.
47. *Ibid.*, 46.
48. *Ibid.*, 52.
49. Pollack, 74.
50. Phillips, 52.
51. "A shipmate officer..." Phillips, *That Eaton Woman*, 52; *The Autobiography of Peggy Eaton*, 37. Discussion of asthma. Commodore Patterson quote; Pollack, *Peggy Eaton*, 76. Timberlake's will.
52. Phillips, 53.
53. *Ibid.*, 54.
54. *Autobiography*, 36.
55. *Ibid.*, 67.
56. Eaton to Andrew Jackson, Washington, 7 December 1828, *Jackson Papers* VI, 541–2.
57. Phillips, 55; *Autobiography*, 70–71.
58. "I guess you forgot that when you went to Florida, General." Phillips, 29; Pollack, 51.

Chapter IX

1. Andrew Jackson (Hermitage) to John Coffee, Hermitage, 7 January 1829, *Jackson Papers* VII, 12–13.
2. Andrew Jackson (White House) to the Marquis de Lafayette, 17 April 1829, *Jackson Papers* VII, 163.
3. Andrew Jackson (White House) to Hardy Murfree Cryer, 16 May 1829, *Jackson Papers* VII, 222–3.
4. Andrew Jackson (White House) to Mary Letitia Kirkman Call, 4 February 1830, *Jackson Papers* VIII, 66. Mary was the wife of Richard Keith Call, the president's friend and former military aide. She knew Rachel since the Calls were married at The Hermitage in 1824.
5. Andrew Jackson (White House) to Robert Minns Burton, 29 May 1830, *Jackson Papers* VIII, 303–4. He regretted not answering letter of December 1829. "...occasioned tears to flow, which will never cease to flow, for departed worth..." Burton had married a niece of Rachel Jackson.
6. Mark Cheathem, *Old Hickory's Nephew*, 57.
7. *Ibid.*, 58–9.
8. See Chapter VIII.
9. Cheathem, *Old Hickory's Nephew*, 60.
10. Queena Pollack, *Peggy Eaton. Democracy's Mistress*, 109.
11. Pauline Wilcox Burke, *Emily Donelson of Tennessee* Vol. I, 120–1.
12. *Ibid.*, 121–2.
13. *Ibid.*, 122
14. Cheathem, 66–7.
15. James, *The Life of Andrew Jackson*, 510.
16. Cheathem, 60.
17. *Ibid.*, 67–8.
18. *Ibid.*, 69; "a disposition not to be intimate with her." Pollack, *Peggy Eaton*, 110.
19. *The Autobiography of Peggy Eaton*, 91–2.

20. John Marszalek, *The Petticoat Affair*, 86–7; Cheathem, *Old Hickory's Nephew*, 75. Van Buren in 1830 endeavored to smooth hard feelings by visiting Emily in the White House.
21. Margaret O'Neale Timberlake Eaton to Andrew Jackson, 9 June 1830, *Jackson Papers* VIII, 357–8.
22. Cheathem, 75–6.
23. *Ibid.*, 77–9.
24. Pollack, *Peggy Eaton*, 84.
25. Andrew Jackson to John Coffee, 10 March 1829, *Jackson Papers* VII, 104–5.
26. Rev. Ezra Stiles Ely (Philadelphia) to Andrew Jackson, *Jackson Papers* VII, 101–104.
27. Andrew Jackson to John Coffee, 22 March 1829, *Jackson Papers* VII, 108–9.
28. Andrew Jackson to Rev. Ely, 23 March 1829, *Jackson Papers* VII, 113–118.
29. Andrew Jackson to John Coffee, 30 May 1829, *Jackson Papers* VII, 249–50.
30. *Jackson Papers* VII, 113–118.
31. "John Christmas McLemore," Tennessee Encyclopedia. In addition to his popularity and impressive good looks, McLemore's rise to prominence benefited from his marriage to Elizabeth Donelson, daughter of John Donelson, a longtime friend of Andrew Jackson. Before 1820 Jackson and McLemore cooperated in land development in northern Alabama with fellow brother-in-law and Jackson favorite General John Coffee; "John Christmas McLemore," Geni.com. Father of Mary Ann McLemore, John Coffee McLemore, Andrew Jackson McLemore, Catherine Donelson McLemore, Emily Donelson McLemore, Alexander Donelson McLemore, and one other.
32. Andrew Jackson to John Christmas McLemore, *Jackson Papers* VII, 183–5;
33. Andrew Jackson to R.K. Call, Florida, 18 May 1829, *Jackson Papers* VII, 226–8.
34. R.K. Call to Andrew Jackson, 28 April 1829, *Jackson Papers* VII, 187–8; Call to Jackson, 23 July 1829, *Jackson Papers* VII 341–5.
35. Andrew Jackson to R.K. Call, 23 July 1829, *Jackson Papers* VII, 341–5.
36. Rev. Ely (Philadelphia) to Andrew Jackson, 2 May 1829, *Jackson Papers* VII, 197–8; Ely to Jackson, 30 May 1829, *Jackson Papers* VII, 251.
37. "She assured me that there was not a word of truth in the story—no such occurrence ever had taken place in her house ... I also understood that Mrs. Timberlake's Father and Husband were with her at the time." Samuel Fisher Bradford (Philadelphia) to Andrew Jackson, 10 October 1829, *Jackson Papers* VII, 490; "attests to Mrs. Eaton's purity and calls upon AJ's friends to stand with Eaton against vile calumny." Peter Brady to William Berkeley Lewis, 16 September 1829, *Jackson Papers* VII, 757; "Testifies to Mrs. Eaton's good character and reproves her traducers." James Inslee Anderson to Andrew Jackson, 15 October 1829, *Jackson Papers* VII, 763; Andrew Jackson to Ezra Stiles Ely, 12 January 1830, *Jackson Papers* VIII, 28–30. Ellsworth Hyde denies in a letter to Andrew Jackson the previous slanderous statements alleged to him by the Reverend Campbell. Further Jackson refuted another Campbell charge alleged to "a pious matron of the Washington Methodist Church." "She had long known Mrs. Eaton, and that she never in her life knew anything ... prejudicial to her character as a lady."
38. Marszalek, *The Petticoat Affair*, 92–4.
39. Eaton, 106–110.
40. Andrew Jackson, Statement of Interview with John Nicholson Campbell, *Jackson Papers* VII, 405–10. Used Ely since a friend of Jackson would pass along Campbell's information regarding charges against Margaret before Eaton was appointed to the cabinet. Campbell discussed deceased Dr. Elijah R. Craven. Jackson rebutted that doctors were bound not to breach patient confidentiality and that such a doctor would be considered a base man in public. Campbell replied that Craven "accidently happened in;" AJ found that absurd. Then Campbell insisted on 1821; AJ responded that he had visited the Eatons and a sick Margaret showed him Timberlake's account books. Then Campbell accused Jackson of misunderstanding the date. Finally Campbell said that Francis Scott Key told him that his proof was sufficient; Andrew Jackson to John Nicholson Campbell, 10 September, *Jackson Papers* VII, 423–4. After September 13 interview, Atty. Key visited Jackson with proposal to discontinue any action until Mr. Ely has arrived. "I have

determine to call my cabinet together that evening with Ely and C." Jackson brought Eaton into his cabinet "with a full persuasion that the cause of virtue ... would be benefitted by it." At the cabinet meeting, Ely recanted his report of the Eaton's misbehavior in NYC, and praised Jackson's handling of the controversy. Jackson closed by condemning the stealthy attacks on Eaton. He declared "his entire conviction that Mrs. Eaton was a virtuous and persecuted woman."

41. Andrew Jackson to John McLemore, *Jackson Papers* VII, 429–30. (Footnote to undated letter.)

42. "Campbell refused to speak and his security from challenge as a minister." Footnote to letter, Reverend John Campbell to Andrew Jackson, 19 October 1829, *Jackson Papers* VII, 499–500.

43. "...with a Reverend Gentleman at their head, has formed a determination to put Mrs. Eaton out of society." Andrew Jackson to Samuel Swartwout, 27 September 1829, *Jackson Papers* VII, 452–4; Andrew Jackson enclosed papers related to the cruel persecution of Mrs. Timberlake, "the horror and disgust for a Clergyman who professes to be the ambassador of Christ. secret slanderer of his neighbor ... the Revd. Mr. Campbell I know will lie ... he will not only lie, but state falshoods [sic] for the basest purpose." Andrew Jackson to John Christian McLemore, 24 November 1829, *Jackson Papers* VII, 567–8.

44. Andrew Jackson to Ezra Stiles Ely, 12 January 1830, *Jackson Papers* VIII, 28–9; *Jackson Papers* VIII, 4. The president quit the Rev. Campbell's church.

45. Henry Watson, *Andrew Jackson vs. Henry Clay*, 54–5, 65.

46. Klotter, *Henry Clay*, 161.

47. Andrew Jackson to William Berkeley Lewis, Hermitage, 17 August 1830, *Jackson Papers* VIII, 485.

48. "[G]reat exertions have been made by Clays friends to raise a clamour about my taking Major Eaton into my cabinet ... the object was to intimidate me, from the selection, & thereby destroy Major Eaton." Andrew Jackson to John Coffee, 19 March 1829, *Jackson Papers* VII, 104; "Much pains was taken to prevent me from taking Mr. Eaton into the Cabinet, his wife was assailed secretly, in the most shameful manner, & every plan that Clay and his minions, could invent to deter me, in hopes that I would be intimidated and drop Eaton..." Andrew Jackson to John Coffee, 22 March 1829, *Jackson Papers* VII, 108–9; "This lady says Mr. and Mrs. Clay spoke in the strongest and most unmeasured terms of Mrs. Eaton." "I have not the least doubt but that every secret rumor is circulated by the minions of Mr. Clay for the purpose of injuring Mrs. Eaton and through her Mr. Eaton..." Andrew Jackson to Ezra Ely, 23 March 1829, *Jackson Papers* VII, 113–18; "But these satellites of Clay ... and their slanders are falling upon their own heads— There is no respectable strangers who do not call upon Mrs. & Major Eaton..." Andrew Jackson to John Christmas McLemore, 3 May 1829, *Jackson Papers* VII, 200; "...that very charge that calumny has set on foot against Mrs. Eaton has vanished upon enquiry..." Andrew Jackson to John Coffee, 30 May 1829, *Jackson Papers* VII, 249; "That the hired slanderers of Mr. Clay should have attempted to destroy Major Eaton and through him to reach me..." Andrew Jackson to Richard Keith Call, 5 July 1829, *Jackson Papers* VII, 326.

49. "...the base hypocrisy of this *great secret agent*..." Andrew Jackson to John Coffee, 10 April 1830, *Jackson Papers* VIII, 183; "the combination & conspiracy to injure & prostrate Major Eaton— and injure me—I see the *great Magicians* hand in all of this." Andrew Jackson to William Berkeley Lewis, Franklin, 28 July 1830, *Jackson Papers* VIII, 455.

50. Irving Bartlett, *John C. Calhoun: A Biography*, 190–2.

51. Ibid., 193.

52. vide infra.

53. Marszalek, *The Petticoat Affair*, 51.

54. Ibid., 54–5.

55. Pollack, *Peggy Eaton*, 88.

56. "List of United States Congresses: Twenty First Congress," Wikipedia.

57. "I have been crowded with thousands of applications for office, and if I had a tit, for every applicant to suck the Treasury pap, all would go away well satisfied..."Andrew Jackson to John Coffee, 22 March 1829, *Jackson Papers* VII, 108; "It seems to me from the thousands that

Pres for office, that every man who voted for the cause of the people, think they ought to be rewarded with office." Andrew Jackson to Ralph Eleazar Whitesides Earl, 16 March 1829, *Jackson Papers* VII, 98.

58. Andrew Jackson to R.K. Call, 18 May 1829, *Jackson Papers* VII, 226. Call returned to Florida from Havana with documents regarding fraud in the State of Florida. Jackson mentioned Navy Dept Auditor who committed fraud; Andrew Jackson, report, 10 September 1829, *Jackson Papers* VII, 426. Report of Spanish solders from Havana landing in Mexico; Andrew Jackson to Anthony Butler, 10 October 1829, *Jackson Papers* VII, 487. Discussion of the replacement of the American consul to Mexico; *Jackson Papers* VII, 529. Alludes to the U.S. treaties with France.

59. Samuel Ingham to Andrew Jackson, 27 November 1829, *Jackson Papers* VII, 580.

Chapter X

1. John Marszalek, *The Petticoat Affair*, 108–9.
2. "Floride Calhoun," Wikipedia; Patricia G McNeely, *Andrew Jackson, John C. Calhoun, and the Petticoat Affair*, 63–4: second cousin marriages not uncommon in South Carolina.
3. McNeely, *Petticoat Affair*, 67.
4. McNeely, *Petticoat* Affair, 6, 87: In November 1829, a guest at a WH dinner told AJ that Calhoun had not been his champion in the FL matter; 90: Calhoun's position on nullification gave AJ something else to pin on Calhoun; 114: In early 1832, AJ nominated Van Buren to be minister to London. Calhoun killed the nomination with his tie-braking vote on January 24, 1832; 164–5: Floride and Margaret Eaton.
5. *The Autobiography of Peggy Eaton*, 88–9.
6. Marszalek, *Petticoat Affair*, 109–110.
7. Ibid., 110–111.
8. Ibid., 112–113.
9. *Jackson Papers* VIII, 49, 24 January1830, 49: Andrew Jackson to Martin Van Buren.
10. Marszalek, *Petticoat Affair*, 116–118.
11. *Jackson Papers* VIII, late January 1830, 51–54.
12. *Jackson Papers* VIII, 56–57: Memorandum of Interviews with John Branch, Samuel Delucenna Ingham, and John Macpherson Berrien. AJ met individually with the three on January 29 and 30, 1830. This Memorandum most likely was written in summer 1831 after the cabinet dissolution.
13. *Jackson Papers* VIII, 2 January 1830, 5: letter from Andrew Jackson to Susan Wheeler Decatur. In a previous letter, Mrs. Decatur has enclosed an anonymous note warning her not to associate with Mrs. Eaton. "I perfectly agree with you that the anonymous letter you enclose me, is evidence not only of a malicious and vindictive community in this district, but also of a corrupt and profligate community. I believe no lady has been more basely slandered or cruelly persecuted than Mrs. Eaton."
14. *Jackson Papers* VIII, 29 May 1830, 303: Andrew Jackson letter to Robert Mims Burton. Burton had married Martha H. Donelson, daughter of Rachel's brother William. "...the secrete & wicked combination to destroy E for political effect, by which, it was to injure me for having taken Major Eaton into my Cabinet..."
15. *Jackson Papers* VIII, 57.
16. *Jackson Papers* IX, 19 June 1831, 314–5: Letter Andrew Jackson to John Coffee.
17. Robert Remini, *Andrew Jackson Volume Two*, 165.
18. *Jackson Papers* VII, 31 July1829, 348–9: Letter Andrew Jackson to RK Call: "...the confidence I had in Mr. Berin (sic) rectitude..."
19. *Jackson Papers* VIII, 16 April 1830, 196–8: Letter Berrien to Andrew Jackson.
20 *Jackson Papers* IX, June 15, 1831, 310–11: Letter Andrew Jackson to Berrien: There was no dissatisfaction with the Attorney General's performance of his duties. However, "...the harmony in feeling so necessary to an efficient administration had failed in a considerable degree..."
20. Ibid., 19 July 1831, 405: Andrew Jackson's Memorandum of earlier interviews with Berrien, Branch, and Ingham.

21. Andrew Jackson to Van Buren: "I had a hope that Berrien would have retired like a Gentleman—but I fear he is a stranger to what constitutes one, as much as he is to truth.... They are a happy trio." *Jackson Papers* IX, 25 July 1831, 418; Andrew Jackson to Van Buren: "We all thought here that Berrien was retiring like a Gentleman—but it appears that birds of a feather flock together ... he is as regardless of truth as any other in society." 23 July 1831, 415; Andrew Jackson to Van Buren, the three conspired "...will be buried in the oblivion of forgetfulness, for the profligate & wicked course they have pursued." 8 August 1831, 472.

22. *Jackson Papers* IX, 523: 29 August 1831: Letter Andrew Jackson to Willie Blount: "The attempt of these Judas's (to destroy me) has failed." 523

23. *Jackson Papers* IX, 553, 6 September 1831: Letter Andrew Jackson to John Coffee: "I have had an unpleasant time with my late Cabinet, or rather the three Judases ... Ingham Branch and Berrien, attempted to make it, not only unpleasant, but injurious to me.... They came into my Cabinet by the recommendation of Eaton ... Berrien say he came into it, from assurances from his friends that Eaton would soon be forced out of it—and Branch has the unblushing affrontery (sic) to say, that he told me the appointment of Major Eaton would give my enemies an opportunity to assail me."

24. Letter R.K. Call (FL) to Andrew Jackson: "Major Eaton has certainly exposed most successfully the corruption of Mr. B and his want of very manly virtue. The latter, stand self convicted of the most palpable falsehood, and his character for truth and chivalry is equally tarnished," *Jackson Papers* IX, 7 November 1831, 671–2.

25. *Jackson Papers* IX, 438: 27 July 1831, 438: Andrew Jackson to Andrew Jackson Donelson.

26. *Jackson Papers* IX, 467: Note (2): Eaton challenged Berrien to a duel on July 25, charging that Berrien publication gave "countenance and sanction to base slanders" about Eaton's "domestic relations." Berrien replied on July 29 declining an immediate acceptance. In his September 13 Candid Appeal to the American Public, Eaton published his challenge and accused Berrien of refusing out of cowardice and a guilty conscience.

27. Jackson Papers IX, 672:

28. September 24, 1831. The National Intelligencer published Berrien's response to Eaton's Candid Appeal. Berrien accused Eaton of multiple falsehoods. He branded Eaton's demands and threats as 'idle bravado' and accused him of 'a palpable evasion of the combat, which he affected to invite." Berrien said that he had deferred, but not refused Eaton's challenge.

29. Robert Remini, *Andrew Jackson: Volume Two*, 164.

30. Marshall De Lancey Haywood, *John Branch. 1782–1863*, 1: Speaker of the North Carolina Senate three times, three times North Carolina Governor, member of the U.S. House of Representatives and U.S. Senate;14: just reelected as U.S. Senator.

31. *Jackson Papers* VII, multiple citations.

32. Haywood, *John Branch*, 21.

33. *Jackson Papers* VIII, 51–2: 27 January 1830: Letter John Branch to Andrew Jackson.

34. Jackson Papers VIII, 56: January 29–30, 1830 meetings with the three reprobates; *Ibid.*, 57: Memorandum.

35. *Jackson Papers* IX, 192–3: Branch letter of resignation; Andrew Jackson to Branch: "In accepting your resignation, it is with great pleasure that I bear testimony to the integrity and zeal with which you have managed the concerns of the Navy ... I have been fully satisfied." 20 April 1831,199; Letter Andrew Jackson to Andrew Jackson Donelson : "Gov. Branch, in whose friendship I have the fullest confidence." 20 April 1831, 200.

36. Haywood, *John Branch*, 22: Branch claimed offers of a diplomatic post and the Territorial Governor of Florida. The author could not verify this.; *Ibid.*, 46: Appointed Governor of Florida.

37. Andrew Jackson letter to Coffee: "This conduct of his gives to the world evidence of his weakness, if not his depravity." *Jackson Papers* IX, 26 May 1831, 268; Andrew Jackson letter to Coffee: "Branch has been dishonorable to the extreme." *Ibid.*, 19 June 1831, 314–5; Andrew Jackson to Van Buren: "three

Judases." *Ibid.*, 5 September 1831, 543; *Ibid.*, 534–7: Memorandum; Branch's recall of Eaton statement to Jackson; *Ibid.*, 553: Jackson's rebuttal to Branch.

38. William Armstrong Ingham, *Samuel Dulucenna Ingham*, 12.

39. *Ibid.*, 15.

40. *Jackson Papers* VII.

41. *Jackson Papers* VIII.

42. *Ibid.*, 2 April 1829, 171–3: Henry Petrikin (Harrisburg) to Andrew Jackson. Petrikin was editor of the *Bellefonte Patriot* and a member of the Pennsylvania state legislature.

43. *Jackson Papers* IX, 18 April 1831, 190–1, Ingham to Andrew Jackson: Ingham's befuddlement; Ingham to Andrew Jackson: "You have expressed your satisfaction with the manner in which I have discharged the duties ... and your conviction o the public confidence in my Administration of the Treasury Department." *Ibid.*, 19 April 1831, 194–5; *Ibid.*, 20 April 1831, 197–8: Andrew Jackson to Ingham with his rationalization of his purpose in requesting Ingham's resignation.

44. *Ibid.*, 324–5: June 20, 1831 letter Ingham to Andrew Jackson.

45. *Ibid.*, 314: Preface to June 19, 1831 letter Andrew Jackson to Coffee: discussion of *U.S. Telegraph* article, Ingham to Eaton: "It is too absurd to merit an answer."; *Ibid.*, 325–6 note: Eaton challenged Ingham to a duel.

46. *Ibid.*, 20 June 1831, 325–6: Ingham to Eaton: "I am not to be intimidated by threats," etc.; *Ibid.*, 325–6: June 20, 1831 letter Eaton to Ingham: "It proves to me that you are quite brave enough to do a mean thing..." etc.

47. Phillips, *That Eaton Woman*, 119.

48. *Jackson Papers* IX, 21 June 1831, 325–7: letter Ingham to Andrew Jackson: The five were Eaton; brother-in-law Philip G. Randolph; second auditor of the Treasury William B. Lewis; register of the Treasury Thomas I. Smith; and Treasurer of the United States John Campbell.

49. *Ibid.*, 30 June 1831, 355–6: Ingham to Andrew Jackson; Ingham presses for a legal investigation into the "assassination attempt" against him; *Ibid.*, 7 July 1831, 367: Nicholas Trist to Ingham: dismissed Ingham's claims of an assassination attempt.

50. *Ibid.*, 27 July 1831, 438: Andrew Jackson to Andrew Jackson Donelson: "I did not know that my Cabinet, like J.C. Calhoun was Smiling in my face & secretly endeavoring to destroy..."; *Ibid.*, 462: August 4, 1831 letter AJ to Benjamin Howard: "The whole career of Mr. Ingham since my election convinces me..."; *Ibid.*, 507: Andrew Jackson to Hardy Murfree Cryer: "So you See that the Secret attempts by Calhoun, thro' his tools, Ingham, Branch & Berrien, with all their notes & note Books, has done me no injury."

51. *Ibid.*, 27 July 1831, 438: letter Andrew Jackson to Andrew Jackson Donelson.

52. Mark B. Cheathem, *Old Hickory's Nephew. The Political and Personal Struggles of Andrew Jackson*, 89–90.

53. *Ibid.*, 65–6.

54. *Ibid.*, 86.

55. *Jackson Papers* VIII, xxix.

56. *Ibid.*, 21 July 1831, 436: Andrew Jackson (Hermitage) to William Berkeley Lewis.

57. *Jackson Papers* VIII, 3 August 1830, 462–3: Andrew Jackson (Hermitage) to John Eaton.

58. *Jackson Papers* IX, 1 September 1831, 576: Andrew Jackson to Nicholas Trist: "On my accepting his offer of the post..."; *Ibid.*: many Trist references in 1831; Remini, Vol. 3, 196, 398–9: 1832 references to Trist as secretary; Stephens, 84: "friend and secretary to Andrew Jackson."

59. *Ibid.*, 7 August 1830, 468–9: Andrew Jackson (Hermitage) to Lewis.

60. Phillips, *That Eaton Woman*, 109–110: Emily Donelson (Tennessee) to Andrew Jackson Donelson (White House).

61. *Jackson Papers* VIII, 25 August 1830, 501: Andrew Jackson (Franklin) to WB Lewis: "If Mrs. E would consent to remain until midwinter here, she would obtain a complete triumph..."; Marszalek, *The Petticoat Affair*, 135: Margaret's refusal to remain in Tennessee; *Ibid.*, 138: Margaret hosted a large Washington dinner party in December 1830.

62. *Jackson Papers* VIII, 24 October 1830, 578–81: Andrew Jackson (White House) to Mary Ann Eastin (Tennessee).

63. *Ibid.*, 25 October 1830, 581–4: Andrew Jackson Donelson (White House) to Andrew Jackson (White House).

64. Marsha Mullin, personal communication, 13 April 2020: "Emily's behavior may be explained as other than disloyalty..."
65. *Jackson Papers* VIII, 25, October 1830, 584: Andrew Jackson to Andrew Jackson Donelson; 27 October 1830, 586: Andrew Jackson Donelson to Andrew Jackson; *Ibid.*, 587: Andrew Jackson to Andrew Jackson Donelson; *Ibid.*, 30 October 1830, 592–3: Andrew Jackson to Andrew Jackson Donelson; *Ibid.*, 30 October 1830, 594–5: Andrew Jackson Donelson to Andrew Jackson; *Ibid.*, 30 October 1830, 595: Andrew Jackson to Andrew Jackson Donelson.
66. *Ibid.*,16 November1830, 628–9: Andrew Jackson to Andrew Jackson Donelson: "...you are welcome to withdraw."
67. *Jackson Papers* IX,1 January 1831, 4–5: Andrew Jackson to Mary Eastin: "...20 ounces of blood..."; *Ibid.*, 17 February 1831, 87–8: letter Andrew Jackson to Mary Eastin: "My health is not very good. I have been afflicted with headache for the last two or three days."
68. *Ibid.*, January 1 January 1831, 4: Andrew Jackson to Mary Eastin: "...it brought fresh to my recollection ... a bereavement which has left for me no prospect of happiness this side of the grave..."; *Ibid.*, 30 January 1831, 34: Andrew Jackson to Emily Donelson: "*She often hovers around me in my nightly visions*..."; *Ibid.*, 8 July 1831, 368: Andrew Jackson to Mary Eastin: "...the tomb of my dear departed, but ever to be lamented wife..."
69. *Ibid.*, xxviii: 1831 Chronology.
70. *Ibid.*, xxix: 1831 Chronology.
71. *Ibid.*, 11 July 1831, 378–9: letter Andrew Jackson to Andrew Jackson Donelson.
72. Phillips, *That Eaton Woman*, 113.

Chapter XI

1. The Hermitage, "Andrew Jackson' Children," The last of the children embraced by the Jacksons was Andrew Jackson Hutchings (1812–1841). Hutchings was the grandson of Rachel's sister and the son of a former business partner of Jackson's. Both of his parents died by the time he was five. So in 1817, little Hutchings, as the family called him, came to live permanently at The Hermitage. He attended school with Andrew Jr., and Lincoya. He then attended colleges in Washington and Virginia while Jackson was president. In 1833, he married Mary Coffee, daughter of Jackson's friend John Coffee, and moved to Alabama. Hutchings died in 1841.
2. *Ibid.*, 104, *Emily Donelson of Tennessee* Vol. I. Arrival at the nearly empty White House 5 September 181.
3. *Ibid.*, 104: Early June 1836: Emily whose health was not promising left for Tennessee with three of her four children. Official business forced Andrew Jackson and her husband to remain in the nation's capital.
4. Burke, 54: July 27, 1833: Leaning on Andrew Jackson Donelson and his son, the president set out for the Rip Raps. He was accompanied by Sarah with little Rachel, Emily with Jackson, Mary Rachel, and John Samuel, a nurse and two servants; *Ibid.*, 86–7: July 6, 1835, the president departed for the Rip Raps with Andrew Jackson Junior & family, the Donelson family minus Andrew Jackson Donelson who was detained at the White House by official business.
5. Burke, Vol. II, 2: September 18, 1831: The Donelson family traveled with Mary McLemore to Boston, and then were sightseeing in New York City for five days.
6. *Ibid.*, 68–9: Early July 1834: Emily with three children brought Elizabeth Martin to a visit with Lewis Randolph her fiancé. Randolph was the grandson of President Thomas Jefferson. Lewis and Elizabeth named their first borne Lewis Jackson Randolph. Ironically Andrew Jackson was no fan of Thomas Jefferson.
7. *Ibid.*, 59: quote from Harriet Taylor Upton, Our *Early Presidents: Their Wives and* Children, 373.
8. Remini, Vol. 3, 148. Raised to entertain large numbers of guests; *Jackson Papers* I, 419. Birth order of the children of Mary Purnell and John Donelson.
9. "model American home," Remini, Vol. III, 382; "a very agreeable woman," Remini, Vol. III, 148; "With quiet dignity, she assumed charge." Burke II, 7: "With quiet dignity, she assumed charge," Burke, Vol. II, 7.

10. James, *The Life of Andrew* Jackson, 668–9.

11. Cole, *The Presidency of Andrew Jackson*, 189; Remini, Vol. III, 382–3. Guista's preference for John Quincy Adams and his gift to the Adams' residence from the Jackson kitchen.

12. Burke, *Emily Donelson*, 130.

13. *Ibid.*, 164. Description of the levee; *Ibid.*,165. Praise of Emily and Mary excerpted from Caleb Atwater, *Remarks Made on a Tour to Prairie du Chen*, 269ff.

14. Andrew Jackson to Emily Donelson, 20 January 1831, *Jackson Papers* IX, 33–5; Alfred Balch (Louisville) to Andrew Jackson, 21 July 1831, *Jackson Papers* IX, 412.

15. Andrew Jackson to Mary Eastin, 1 January 1831, *Jackson Papers* IX, 4, "lost 20 ounces of blood" immediately after the New Year levee. The performer of the venesection is not identified.

16. "My health is not very good, I have been afflicted with headache for the last two or three days," Andrew Jackson to Mary Eastin, 17 February 1831, *Jackson Papers* IX, 87; "with a return of my severe headache, I have taken medicine to day...", Andrew Jackson to Andrew Jackson Donelson, 20 March 181, *Jackson Papers* IX, 152; The source of the arm pain most likely was the bullet impacted in his left shoulder joint. "I have been a great deal afflicted with my left arm since you left me" Andrew Jackson to Andrew Jackson Donelson, 19 April 1831, *Jackson Papers* Ix, 192.

17. Andrew Jackson to William Gray, 2 May 1831, *Jackson Papers* IX, 224–5. Wrote with thanks for a pot of Gray's ointment. A 1920 Dept of Agriculture chemical analysis of the potion revealed a mixture of linseed oil, lead soap, lead acetate turpentine and wax.; Martin Van Buren to Andrew Jackson, 29 July 1831, *Jackson Papers* IX, 446. The author was apprehensive of AJ's health. He advises rest and a trip to Virginia Springs; Hartwell Carver to Andrew Jackson, 26 December 1831, *Jackson Papers* IX, 918*n*, Carver recommended liverwort to treat AJ's bleeding from the lungs. The cause of the hemorrhage was Dickinson's bullet from the 1806 duel. Liverwort is a plant that is used for many medical maladies.

18. The President was visited "by my friend Judge Overton." He anticipated a rest from business and throng of strangers, but "the repainting of my dwelling, which was, I thought, very injurious to my health, & made me very subject to my excruciating headaches." Andrew Jackson (Rip Raps) to John Christmas McLemore, 27 June 1831, *Jackson Papers* IX 345:

19. "I returned day before yesterday from the Rip Raps; from the continued rains the Air was very humid, & I caught cold, & am troubled with a cough, but it is subsiding." Andrew Jackson to Andrew Jackson, Jr., 9 July 1931, *Jackson Papers* IX, 370; "I am not very well..." Andrew Jackson to Andrew Jackson Junior, 11 July 1831, *Jackson Papers* IX, 379; "I labor under a severe headache to day & you will excuse this scrall (sic)," Andrew Jackson to Martin Van Buren, 10 August 1831, *Jackson Papers* IX, 479.

20. "With yours of the 14th ulto, reached me I was confined to my bed with a severe illness—it was not shewn (sic) me until yesterday," Andrew Jackson to John Coffee, 3 October 1831, *Jackson Papers* IX, 598; "late indisposition which confined me to my bed for several days," Andrew Jackson to James Remwick Willson, 4 October 1831, *Jackson Papers* IX, 599; "severe indisposition since you left me, from which I have recovered, but have not yet regained my usual strength, but am fast improving," Andrew Jackson to Andrew Jackson Hutchings, 8 October 1831, *Jackson Papers* IX, 612; "I had an attack of the prevailing fever of this place, from which I have entirely recovered," Andrew Jackson to William Burke, 9 November 1831, *Jackson Papers* IX, 677.

21. Deppisch, *The Health of the First Ladies*, 27.

22. Burke, Vol. II, 5.

23. "I had an attack of the prevailing fever of this place, from which I have entirely recovered & feel more free from affliction than I have for the past ten years." Andrew Jackson to William Burke, 9 November 1831, *Jackson Papers* IX, 677; "I am perfectly recovered from the attack of fever, & my health strength is quite restored. I am more free from affliction than I have been for years." Andrew Jackson to Andrew Jackson Hutchings, 15 November 1831, *Jackson Papers* IX, 696.

24. Deppisch, Ludwig M., "Andrew Jackson and American Medical Practice."
25. James, *The Life of Andrew Jackson*, 390.
26. Burke, Vol. II, 17.
27. On a Steamer to Fredericksburg, "A well set up young man ... approached the President as if to greet him.... The young man thrust his fist violently into Jackson's face as if to pull his nose." The assailant was Robert R. Randolph, a former Navy Lieutenant whom the Navy has dismissed for stealing funds from his predecessor as purser, Margaret Eaton's first husband, Timberlake. Andrew Jackson: "I want no man to stand between me and my assailants, and none to take revenge on my account." Later Jackson claimed that had he been on his feet when Randolph attacked, "never would have moved with life from the tracks he stood in." No charges were pressed; the trial was delayed until his presidency concluded. Andrew Jackson refused to give evidenced Jackson kicked the table away. James, *The Life of Andrew Jackson*, 636–7; "President Andrew Jackson Attacked..." *The Microcosm, American and Gazette*, Providence, Rhode Island, 11 May 1833. The first attempt to do bodily harm to a President.
28. Remini, Vol. 3, 69–70.
29. Deppisch, "Andrew Jackson and American Medical Practice," 139–42.
30. James, *The Life of Andrew Jackson*, 641; Remini, Vol. 3, 77. John Warren was the Quincy family physician who twice bled Andrew Jackson in Boston.
31. James, *The Life of Andrew Jackson*, 645.
32. Deppisch, "Andrew Jackson and American Medical Practice," 142.
33. Burke, Vol. 2, 52–3.
34. Deppisch, "Andrew Jackson and American Medical Practice," 135–39.
35. *Ibid.*, 135.
36. *Ibid.*, 137–9.
37. Burke, Vol. II, 53. Andrew Jackson dispatched his Hermitage physician, Dr. Hogg to the ailing John Coffee's Alabama home. Hogg is described as a "good friend."; Andrew Jackson to Dr. Philip Synge Physick, May 1835, Remini, Vol. III, 238.
38. Burke, Vol. II, 54. Leaning on Andrew Donelson and Andrew Jackson, Jr., as he embarked. The president was accompanied by Sarah with little Rachel, Emily with Jackson, Mary Rachel, and John Samuel, a nurse and two servants; *Ibid.*, 55. Suffered a relapse. Length of stay at Rip Raps; Remini, Vol. III, 89. The party stayed at the Hygeia Hotel. Andrew Jackson in good spirits although his health was precarious and his feet and ankles were badly swollen.
39. Cole, *The Presidency of Andrew Jackson*, 221; James W. Clarke, *American Assassins: The Darker Side of Politics*. Housepainter and a certifiable paranoid schizophrenic. Even prosecutor Francis Scott Key (of National Anthem fame) agreed that Lawrence was not guilty by reason of insanity. He remained in a mental institution for the rest of his life. Deluded that he was Richard III, and Jackson was standing in the way of just compensation.
40. "My bowls..." Remini, Vol. III, 238; "Rush's Thunderbolts," Discovering Lewis and Clark. Constituents and history of Rush's Thunderbolt
41. James, *The Life of Andrew Jackson*, 712; Remini, Vol. III, 368; Remini, Vol. III, 370. Jackson said it was divine will. "A kind Providence..." Semi-comatose for several days, preventing Andrew Jackson Donelson from leaving.
42. Kate Dickinson Sweetser, *Famous Girls of the White House*, 107. "First Lady of the Land," "Her tact and charm of manner did much to make the Jackson Administration stand out as a brilliant one"; Meacham, *American Lion*, 137. "Close to Jackson, she and Andrew were able to cheer him most of the time, greeting his guests and presenting a gracious face to the outside world."
43. Burke, Vol. II, 32
44. *Ibid.*, 17–18. John Samuel Donelson; *Ibid.*, 65. Rachel Jackson Donelson.
45. Meacham, *American Lion*, 290.
46. Burke, Vol. II, 4–5: THE DYAS COLLECTION. COFFEE MS: 23 October 1831: "The city has been extremely dull since we have been here. Uncle seems quite happy and everything is moving harmoniously."
47. Burke, Vol. II, 29. Mary Coffee writes her sister of "everlasting parties"; *Ibid.*, 31. Mary Coffee, Mary McLemore, and their aunt Emily in social whirl;

Ibid., 27. Mary Coffee to mother regarding White House disputes between Emily and Mary McLemore.
48. *Ibid.*, 11, 12, 45.
49. *Ibid.*, 23–4.
50. *Ibid.*, 56. Mary Coffee engaged to cousin, Andrew Jackson Hutchings; *Ibid.*, 58. Mary McLemore engaged to Dr. James Wallace.
51. Burke, Vol. 2, 95; Meacham, *American Lion*, 318.
52. See Chapter VII.
53. "It was, it turned out, tuberculosis." Meacham, *American Lion*, 326.
54. Emily wrote her sister, "My health was so bad..." Meacham, 50; 168. In January 1831, she lost weight and reportedly looked like a specter.
55. "My health has been very delicate ... I had an attack of chills and fever." Meacham, 216. Burke, Vol. 2, 70. Illness in Tennessee during the 1834 summer.; *Ibid.*, 73. Emily concurred with Andrew Jackson Donelson's wishes, and left Tennessee in November for Washington.
56. Burke, Vol. 2, 86–7.
57. "I trust that Providence is equally kind to you and our dear children;" "Accept, my dear Emily, the constant prayers of an affectionate and devoted husband for your health and happiness." Andrew Jackson Donelson to Emily Donelson, 30 June 1836, 11 July 1836, *Emily Tennessee Donelson Papers*, Tennessee State Archives; Burke, Vol. II, 289, 293.
58. Meacham, *American Lion*, 326.
59. Andrew Jackson to Andrew Jackson Donelson, 13 October 1836, Burke Vol. II, 113–4; *Ibid.*, 116. Family members were distressed.
60. *Ibid.*, 124.
61. *Ibid.*, 117. Donelson sought Dr. Huntt's medical advice; "Dr. Sales has just been here." Emily Donelson to Andrew Jackson Donelson, 11 November 1836, Burke, 122.
62. Emily's "remains were deposited today by the side of her Father and Sister." Burke, 131.
63. *The Washington Globe*, 4 January 1837. Obituary of Mrs. Donelson.
64. Cheathem, *Old Hickory's Nephew*, 123. Donelson's grief and guilt. The president's regret; "to arrange his personal affairs for the trip back to The Hermitage." Cheathem, 125.

65. *Ibid.*, 144. Jackson's advice to Andrew Jackson Donelson, Elizabeth Martin Randolph genealogy and marriage to Randolph. Jackson's letter of marital advice to Donelson was sent 19 February 1840.
66. *Jackson Papers* I, 422. Andrew Jackson Donelson's family tree.
67. Meacham, *American Lion*, 309–10. Sale of Tulip Grove; Meacham, 140, 146, 210, 213, 244, 301, 309. references to Donelson's struggles with indebtedness.
68. Cheathem, *Old Hickory's Nephew*, 146–7. Van Buren; Cheathem, 213. John Eaton.
69. *Ibid.*, 170, 217. Chargé d'affaires to Texas; *Ibid.*, 208–238. Minister to Prussia; *Ibid.*, 262–278. *Washington Union* editor and part owner.
70. *Ibid.*, 287, 297.
71. *Ibid.*, 332.

Chapter XII

1. Burke, Vol. II, 2: Nasty Eaton passage: Eaton will soon be transferred to TN, "he will scarcely play a part of such consequence in the future political operations of our party." All sincere friends of AJ "must pity Eaton's situation at the same time they deprecate the injury which the Administration has sustained on his account."
2. Andrew Jackson to John Eaton, 23 October 1831, *Jackson Papers* IX, 638. Commission to serve with John Coffee to negotiate with the Chickasaws and Choctaws to move west of the Mississippi; See Chapter XI regarding Andrew Jackson Donelson's assignments from his uncle and others; *vide infra* Chapter XII regarding territorial governor to Florida and ambassador to Spain.
3. Meacham, *American Lion*, 213. Eaton's request for payment; Meacham, 283. John Eaton was Donelson's attorney to address his indebtedness.
4. Burke, Vol. II, 105. Summer 1836.
5. Eaton, *A Candid Appeal*; Marszalek, *The Petticoat Affair*, 189.
6. Phillips, *That Eaton Woman*, 129–30.
7. Marszalek, *The Petticoat Affair*, 197.

8. Andrew Jackson to John Coffee, 3 October 1831, *Jackson Papers* IX, page 598.
9. Pollack, *Peggy Eaton*, 107.
10. Phillips, *That Eaton Woman*, 131.
11. John & Margaret Eaton (Hermitage) to Andrew Jackson (Washington), 16 April 1832.
12. Pollack, *Peggy Eaton*, 188.
13. *Ibid.*, 189.
14. *Ibid.*
15. *Ibid.*, 190; Beardsley, "The 1832 Cholera Epidemic."
16. WB Lewis to John Overton, Washington, 2 December 1832.
17. *The Autobiography of Peggy Eaton*, 169–70. This may be apocryphal since Peggy wrote her autobiography from memory many decades later. The author was unable to locate documentation for this.
18. Pollack, *Peggy Eaton*, 190.
19. Marszalek, *The Petticoat Affair*, 208.
20. *Ibid.*, 211. Eaton and Call remained rivals. Margaret and Mary Call got along well; Pollack, 197. The Calls' daughter's description of Margaret.
21. Marszalek, *The Petticoat Affair*, 209–11.
22. *The Autobiography of Peggy Eaton*, 170.
23. Pollack, *Peggy Eaton*, 197.
24. Marszalek, *The Petticoat Affair*, 212–3.
25. *Ibid.*, 214. Eaton's confirmation was routinely approved by the Senate; Pollack, 198. Van Buren's thoughts on Eaton's very easy Senate approval.
26. Richard Rush to Andrew Jackson, 16 September 1836, quoted in Marszalek, 214; "He was a gentleman, a scholar, and a statesman..." *The Autobiography of Peggy Eaton*, 175.
27. "Maria Cristina de Borbon," Britannica, accessed 9 August 2019, https://www.britannica.com/biography/Maria-Cristina-de-Borbon; Pollack, *Peggy Eaton*, 198.
28. *The Autobiography of Peggy Eaton*, 187; Marszalek, *The Petticoat Affair*, 217.
29. Autobiography, 187; Marszalek, 217.
30. Pollack, 205–6.
31. *Ibid.*, 209: "There, thank God, I was beyond the reach of venom."; Autobiography, 195: "I should have liked to have spent my life in Madrid."
32. Marszalek, 221.
33. Pollack, 213.
34. Marszalek, 221: at first both Eatons were relieved to be recalled, then anger set in; Autobiography, 196: Eaton was treated not with insufficient consideration, "especially in view of the fidelity of his friendship to Mr. Van Buren."
35. Pollack, 218.
36. Degregorio, William A., 144.
37. Remini Vol. III, 466–7.
38. *Ibid.*, 592*n*.
39. Pollack, 218–9.
40. *Ibid.*, 221–2.
41. Leon Phillips, *That Eaton Woman*, 157. Houston, riding with dispatch from Texas, arrived a few hours too late.
42. Cheatham, *Old Hickory's Nephew*, 206.
43. *The Autobiography of Peggy Eaton*, 203. After Spain they lived with Mrs. O'Neale; Marszalek, *The Petticoat Affair*, 223. The Eatons moved in with Mrs. O'Neale to I Street house, once a part of the Franklin Hotel complex; Marszalek, 224. Same author contradicts his previous statement by asserting, "Her mother continued to live near them..." It is probable that that Rhoda lived with Margaret most of the time, other than the summer months in Franklin.
44. Marszalek, *The Petticoat Affair*, 223–4.
45. Marszalek, 224. After mid-1841, Margaret's health improved and did not suffer from the debilitating illnesses that earlier had crippled her; "Emily, 17, developed consumption.... Marszalek, 232; Worked among Washington's less fortunate, called "Alma Mater..." "I have never seen anyone so beautiful." Marszalek, 225.
46. Marszalek, 223–4.
47. Phillips, *That Eaton Woman*, 157.
48. Marszalek, 223.
49. Pollack, *Peggy Eaton*, 220; Marszalek, *The Petticoat Affair*, 226.
50. Pollack, 221–5: Marszalek, 226–7.
51. "...his heart gave out." Marszalek, 228; Pollack, 225. Death and inheritance of money, books, and wine.
52. *The Autobiography of Peggy Eaton*, 203.
53. Pollack, 231 & Marszalek, 229. Margaret's marriage; Marszalek, 229.

Became a pariah in Washington Society; Marszalek, 230. Antonio was an assistant librarian of the House of Representatives.
54. Marszalek, *The Petticoat Affair*, 231–2.
55. *Ibid.*, 233.
56. *Ibid.*, 234.
57. Pollack, *Peggy Eaton*, 272; "She was now old..." Marszalek, 235.
58. Pollack, 272.
59. "I am not afraid to die, but this is such a wonderful world to leave." Pollack, 278; Marszalek, *The Petticoat Affair*, 235–6. Buried next to John Eaton, daughter Margaret, and son-in-law John Randolph at Oak Hill Cemetery.

Chapter XIII

1. Galloway, *Andrew Jackson Junior*, 37.
2. *Ibid.*, 7; *Jackson Papers* I, 417: Severn Donelson was the brother of Rachel Jackson. The adoptee was biologically her nephew. Thomas Jefferson Donelson was Andrew Jackson Junior's twin brother.
3. Galloway, 13.
4. *Ibid.*, 23.
5. *Ibid.*, 28–9.
6. *Ibid.*, 30.
7. Andrew Jackson to Andrew Jackson, Jr., *Jackson Papers* VII, 22 July 1829, 340–1.
8. "You can judge of the anxiety I have that you should marry a lady that will make you happy which would add to mine," Andrew Jackson to Andrew Jackson, Jr., aboard Potomac, 26 July 1829, *Jackson Papers* VII, 345–6.
9. *Jackson Papers* VII, pp. 386–7: 20 August 1829 AJ (aboard Potomac) to Jr.: "Remember my son, that you are now the one solace of my mind..." Andrew Jackson (aboard the Potomac) to Andrew Jackson, Jr., 20 August 1829; *Jackson Papers* VII, 386–7; "I expected the result you name with Flora..." Andrew Jackson to Jr., 21 September 1829, *Jackson Papers* VII, 446–7.
10. Andrew Jackson to Jr., 22 July 1829, *Jackson Papers* VII, 340–1. Flora married a year later.
11. Galloway, *Andrew Jackson Junior*, 32–3. Andrew Jackson, Jr.'s romantic pursuit of Mary Smith and his rejection by her. The specifics of his breach of courtship etiquette may have been nothing more than not requesting her father to permit him to court the daughter; I am fearful that he has committed an error..." Andrew Jackson to Francis Smith, 19 May 1830, *Jackson Papers* VIII, 268–9.
12. Galloway, 34.
13. Remini Vol. II, 334.
14. Andrew Jackson to Junior, 27 October 1831, *Jackson Papers* IX 644.
15. "...to be married ... to a young lady of beauty and accomplishments..." Andrew Jackson to John Coffee, 20 November 1831, *Jackson Papers* IX, 700; "said to be by my friends who have wrote [*sic*] on the subject—accomplished, amiable, beautiful; These qualities must insure his happiness." Andrew Jackson to Andrew Jackson Hutchings, 15 November 1831, *Jackson Papers* IX, 696.
16. Marsha Mullin, personal correspondence, 21 April 2020. Church where Sarah's parents were married and where she was baptized.
17. Galloway, *Andrew Jackson Junior*, 34–5; "Sarah Yorke Jackson," Wikipedia. Several years of birth, 1803, 1804, 1806 have been attributed to Sarah Yorke. The position of the Jackson Papers and The Hermitage is that Sarah's birth occurred in 1803, as conveyed to the author in personal communications.
18. Sarah Yorke Jackson Papers The Hermitage, Tennessee.
19. *Ibid.*
20. Galloway, 34–5.
21. Sarah "was small, of dark complexion, gentle voice and gentle manner..." James, *The Life of Andrew Jackson*, 591; "She is quite pretty..." Galloway, 36.
22. "All well my daughter an accomplished and pretty girl with whom I am much pleased." Andrew Jackson to John Overton, 5 December 1831, *Jackson Papers* IX, 730; "My son has presented me with an accomplished daughter, pretty & well accomplished, with whom I am very much pleased." Andrew Jackson to Samuel Jackson Hays, 6 December 1831, *Jackson Papers* IX, 755; "My son has presented me with a daughter amiable and accomplished ... I am well pleased with his little Sarah; I have no doubt from her amiable disposition she will endeavor, in all

Notes—Chapter XIII

things, to add to my happiness." Andrew Jackson to William Donelson, 7 December 1831, *Jackson Papers* IX, 759.

23. Galloway, Andrew Jackson Junior, 37.

24. "Andrew Jackson Genealogy," Archives.com. Rachel was born November 1, 1832, Andrew Jackson III was born April 4, 1834, Samuel Jackson was born June 9, 1837. Both Thomas Jefferson Jackson (1841) and Robert Armstrong Jackson (1843) perished before their first birthday, Thomas on the day of his birth, Robert at five months.

25. Galloway, 38–41.

26. Andrew Jackson to Sarah, 6 May 1832, *Jackson Papers* X, 264: May 6, 1832 letter AJ to Sarah: "It gave me much pleasure that you had reached so near *The Hermitage* ... where I hope you may reach in health & safety, and find it as comfortable a home, as I think you will."; "say to Andrew not to be so lasy [sic] in writing me," Andrew Jackson to Sarah, 30 April 1832, *Jackson Papers* X, 257; "I will endeavor to visit & spend a short time with you this Summer ... I am sure you & myself can arrange a sys-tem of neatness and oconomy [sic] in Housekeeping, that will be satisfactory and pleasing to all—you must engage Andrew's attention to this part of domestic economy, by which your labours will be lightened, by his attention to the servants & seeing that your orders are duly executed." Andrew Jackson to Sarah, 10 June 1832, *Jackson Papers* X, 296; "and when you leave the House will have to see that all furniture for the table is locked up, but what may be necessary, for such company as may be passing." Andrew Jackson to Sarah, 21 June 1832, *Jackson Papers* X, 313.

27. "...for now there was a daughter at the Hermitage to greet him." Burke, Vol. 2, 22; Galloway, *Andrew Jackson Junior*, 38. Emma Farquhar, Sarah's cousin accompanied the Jacksons to Tennessee where she fell in love with Andrew's twin brother.; Burke, Vol. 2, 23–4, Galloway, 41. Wedding at Hermitage. Jackson gave the bride away; "Much invigorated by his trip to the beloved Hermitage." Burke Vol. 2, 24.

28. "This day I am left alone..." Andrew Jackson to Sarah, Tennessee in Burke, Vol. II.

29. Sarah gave birth on November 1, 1832 to a little Rachel, "who became the pride and joy of Andrew Jackson to the day of his death." Burke, 17. Burke, 37. Jackson's pre-Inauguration lethargy, lifted with the arrival of Junior, Sarah, and the new little Rachel. "The sight of his little grandchild did much to renew his sagging spirits." Galloway, *Andrew Jackson Junior*, 42; Jackson worried about the ailing Sarah and her daughter, Rachel, "the d'r little pet." He urged his son to take them to Philadelphia to be examined. Fortunately, "Sarah has quite recovered." Remini, Vol. 3, 51; Andrew Jackson to Andrew Jackson Junior, 2 April 1833 in *Correspondence of Andrew Jackson*, edited by John Spencer Bassett.

30. *Vide infra* for the travails of his political trip through the northeastern United States; "very ill," "Emily Donelson and Sarah Jackson did all within their power to minister to his needs." "...the good nursing of Sarah and his general strength helped him to recover." Burke, Vol. II, 52, Galloway, 45; Burke, Vol. II, 54. Accompanying Jackson to Rip Raps were Sarah, little Rachel, Emily with three of her children, a nurse, and two servants.

31. Galloway, 45. Sarah departed for Philadelphia to visit her family and to consult with Dr. Philip Synge Physic; "My spirits have been somewhat depressed since you and Sarah with my dear little Rachel left us. I cannot tell why, unless being very lonesome at night not hearing the prattle of little Rachel." Burke, Vol. II, 56; To Sarah, "I dreaded the long travel for our sweet little pet ... she is given to us as a blessing." Remini, Vol. III, 112.

32. Galloway, *Andrew Jackson Junior*, 47–9.

33. "Although Emily ... to be a most excellent 'First lady' since she was a very agreeable woman and had been raised to entertain large numbers of guests, AJ sometimes wished that Sarah could serve as his hostess. Then Rachel would be around him all the time." Remini, Vol. III, 148.

34. Burke, Vol. II, 65.

35. The little girl was "sprightly as a fairy" and "wild as a little partridge." Andrew III was "a very large fat baby, a veritable Hercules." Galloway, 51; Remini, Vol. III, 180–1. Sarah suffered severely

for postpartum weakness and fatigue. In her absence Rachel became very attached to Andrew Jackson; Andrew Jackson to Sarah Jackson, 6 October 1833, *Jackson Papers*; Andrew Jackson to Sarah, 13 October 1833; Andrew Jackson to Sarah, 23 January 1834. AJ's references to granddaughter Rachel as his "little pet."

36. Meachem, *American Lion*, 291, Remini, Vol. III, 184–6, James, *The Life of Andrew Jackson*, 678–9: date, source of fire. Meachem wrote that Sarah was at home, but the others disagreed and claimed that she was away from the house.

37. Remini, Vol. III, 184–6. Joseph Reiff and William C. Hume, William Donelson's servants; Stockley D. Donelson to Andrew Jackson, 14 October 1834, in Remini, Sarah acted with firmness and gave every necessary direction to save the furniture; Remini. Andrew Junior blamed the servants.

38. Remini, Vol. III, 184–6, James 678–9: List of saved and damaged contents; "The Lord's will be done. It was he that gave me the means to build it and he has the right to destroy it, and blessed be his name." Rachel had chosen the site, and that is here it will be rebuilt. Andrew Jackson, quoted in Remini, 184–6; "I am fearful that the fatigue & alarm may be injurious to our dear Sarah's health—let not the loss trouble you & her for one moment." Andrew Jackson to Junior, 25 October 1834 quoted in Remini.

39. "You, my dear, are mistress of the Hermitage, and Emily is hostess of the White House." Burke, Vol. II, 73.

40. Remini, Vol. III, 189. Sarah Jackson's purchases in Washington and Philadelphia; Remini, 189.

41. Galloway, 54. Lewis accompanied Sarah to Philadelphia; "William Berkeley Lewis," Wikipedia, accessed 17 September 2019, https://en.wikipedia.org/wiki/William_Berkeley_Lewis. for information regarding Lewis.

42. Galloway, *Andrew Jackson Junior*, 53–54; Remini, Vol. III, 190. Andrew Jackson admonished Junior for his lack of letters, "you might write a few lines to your D'r Sarah.... Your own interest is involved." Meachem, *American Lion*, 291; Galloway, 55. Sarah and Lewis concerned about Andrew Jr.'s affection for alcohol.

43. "We are very loansome [*sic*] now, only Mr. Earl, Mrs. Donelson and myself and Mrs. D's three small children." Burke, Vol. II, 84; Galloway, 56, Remini, Vol. III, 238. Rachel was examined by Dr. Physick; Remini, 238. Sarah in Philadelphia to assist sister Emma's confinement.

44. Burke, Vol. II, 86. Rip Raps with Andrew Jr., from Tennessee Sarah and two children, Emily with her four, and six servants; Burke, 89. Andrew Jackson was possessive, always referring to the children as 'our'.

45. Galloway, *Andrew Jackson Junior*, 57–8. From October 1836 to the end of Jackson's administration Sarah took over the duties of presiding lady of the White House; "Sarah arrived at the White House on November 26, 1834. She immediately began to take on the role as co-hostess of the White House along with the President's niece Emily Donelson." "Sarah Yorke Jackson," World Heritage Encyclopedia. "It was the only time in history when there were two women simultaneously acting as White House hostess." "Sarah Yorke Jackson," Wikipedia; "First Ladies Never Married to Presidents," National First Ladies Library.

46. Galloway, 57–8; Burke, Vol. II, 138. Surgeon General of the Army Thomas Lawson accompanied the ex-president to Tennessee.

47. "No matter how many debts Andrew Junior incurred, his father never deserted him." *Ibid.*, 60; *Ibid.* 61. Instead of Junior declaring bankruptcy, Andrew Jackson assumed his debts; *Ibid.*, 62. Andrew Jackson borrowed $10,000 from Francis P. Blair.

48. Sarah Jackson to Andrew Jackson III, Clifton, Mississippi, 19 February 1859, Sarah York Jackson Papers, The Hermitage.

49. Remini, Vol. III, 433. Description of Jackson leading the nightly prayer service; Remini, 447. On July 15, 1838, he was admitted into Presbyterian Church together with Sarah and a "beloved niece."

50. "I regret continually that I had so little conversation with you." Sarah Jackson to Andrew Jackson III, Hermitage, 16 May 1856, Sarah Yorke Jackson Papers, The Hermitage; "Put it in Christ," Sarah Jackson to Andrew Jackson III, 2 June 1863; Sarah Jackson to Andrew Jackson

III, Clifton, Mississippi, 19 February 1859.

51. Remini, Vol. III, 520; "Sarah Yorke Jackson," National First Ladies Library. After Jackson's retirement, Sarah's widowed sister and three children moved in; James, *The Life of Andrew Jackson*, 782. Healy painted Sarah's portrait forcing Henry Clay to wait.

52. Remini, Vol. III, 523. The order of farewells; Galloway, *Andrew Jackson Junior*, 63. Sarah and Andrew Jr., at the time of death; Meachem, *American Lion*, 345. Sarah became spasmodic, fainted, and needed to be revived by camphor.

53. Andrew Jackson's will and appendix, June 7, 1843, Basset, Correspondence VI, 220–223, quoted in Galloway, *Andrew Jackson Junior*, 64.

54. "The estate left him gradually dwindled until he lost his old home, the Hermitage, and was forced into an almost impoverished condition. These sad events set the tone of the remaining twenty years of his life." Galloway, 64; Galloway, 74. He had inherited $150,000 but ten years later he was $100,000 in debt. In 1855 his creditors threatened to foreclose.

55. *Ibid.*, 72. The Kentucky ironworks sold at less than anticipated. His family acknowledged that their financial situation was dire; *Ibid.*, 73. He owned lead mines in Kentucky- that never proved very profitable; *Ibid.*, 75–6. Sale of plantation to the State of Tennessee. Francis Preston Blair was both a friend and political ally of Andrew Jackson. John C. Rives was Blair's partner as published of *The Washington Globe*, a Jackson-friendly newspaper.

56. *Ibid.*, 78–9. In 1857, Jacksons decided to move to Mississippi. On April 4, 1858, the newly repaired house was destroyed by fire; *Ibid.*, 82. Decision to return to the Hermitage; *Ibid.*, 82–3. Confusion by author: "Doubtful whether Sarah ever left Tennessee.," Sarah returned to *The Hermitage* while Jr., remained in Mississippi to sell his property; Sarah Jackson Papers, The Hermitage, Tennessee. letters 1857–1860, Sarah Jackson to and from sons Andrew Jackson III and Samuel Jackson indicated an imprecise to and from Mississippi.

57. Galloway, *Andrew Jackson Junior*, 69. By 1851, Andrew Jackson III, 17, was a West Point cadet. Rachel was still in school at Belmont. January 25, 1855: Hermitage saw the wedding of Rachel to Dr. John M. Lawrence. A brilliant affair; *Ibid.*, 74: Active social life. Junior hunted and fished with son in law; *Ibid.*, 82: Son-in-law was besieged by his father-in-law's unpaid bills; *Ibid.*, 82–3. Samuel; *Ibid.*, 84: A fourth child Thomas had died at birth; "Samuel Jackson Genealogy," Geni.com. Death from wounds suffered at the Battle of Chickamauga.

58. *Ibid.*, 84.

59. Meacham, *American Lion*, 352; 18 April 1865, *Nashville Daily Press*. Lockjaw is a condition in which a person's jaw muscles spasm. The jaw may be "frozen" in a certain position which prohibits the ability to open the mouth wide. It is an early sign of tetanus.

60. Sarah Jackson to Andrew Jackson III, April 1865, Sarah Jackson Papers, The Hermitage, Tennessee.

61. "...to avoid the quicksands..." Sarah Jackson to Andrew Jackson III, 11 February 1856, Sarah Jackson Papers; "...anything but happy..." Sarah Jackson to Andrew Jackson III, 19 February 1857, Sarah Jackson Papers; "I am weary of debt..." Sarah Jackson to Andrew Jackson, 3 September 1860, Sarah Jackson Papers.

62. "...my nervous system is feeble..." Constant fears of impoverishment will do that to a person. Sarah Jackson to Mary Anne Atkinson, 30 October 1869, Sarah Jackson Papers; "...loss of sight..." Amy Rich of Hamilton, Ohio recently married Andrew Jackson III, Sarah Jackson to Amy Rich Jackson, 21 August 1885, Sarah Jackson Papers.

63. Sarah Jackson Papers, The Hermitage, Tennessee; Marsha Mullin, personal correspondence, 21 April 2020.

Chapter XIV

1. Andrew Jackson to William Polk, 11 April 1832, *Jackson Papers* X, 229.

2. *Jackson Papers* I, 417–422.

3. *Ibid.*, 417, 419.

4. Andrew Jackson to John Coffee, 21 December 1822, *Jackson Papers* V, 229, note 2; "Mary Ann Eastin Polk," Find a Grave. Eastin Siblings: added another sibling, Tabitha Eastin 1814–1816. The

Rachel Eastin whose birth felled her mother Rachel Jackson Donelson Eastin is listed only as being born in 1822. She is not mentioned elsewhere.

5. *Jackson Papers* I, 419. John and Mary Purnell Donelson genealogy; "Mary Ann Eastin," Geneology.com. National Female Academy, vacations at The Hermitage.

6. Erica Joy Rumbley, "Ornamental Music and Southern Belles at the Nashville Female Academy, 1816–1861"; Burke, 61. The Academy had opened in August 1817. Emily entered in 1820 to 1821. In 1817, about 65 students, which increased to 100 when Emily attended.

7. Dolley Madison frequently was social hostess for the widower president Thomas Jefferson. Elizabeth (Eliza) Kortright Monroe, the eldest daughter of James Monroe, directed the ceremonial and social functions of the White House for her ill mother Elizabeth Monroe.

8. Andrew Jackson to John Donelson, 9 February 1824, *Jackson Papers* V, 354.

9. "Mary Eastin, a pretty niece whom Rachel intended to take to Washington." James, *The Life of Andrew Jackson*, 475; "A great pet of the General." James, 512–3; Gloomy, Jackson missed "a genial and sweet Mary Eastin." Meacham, *American Lion*, 154.

10. "...poor Mary has felt her bereavement severely..." Andrew Jackson to John Coffee, 21 September 1829, *Jackson Papers* VII, 445; "Until the marriage of his adopted son and the coming of Sarah Yorke into his life, Mary Eastin, more than any other of Rachel's nieces, held the place of daughter in the heart of Andrew Jackson..." Burke, Combined Volume, 214–5.

11. "pretty," James, *The Life of Andrew Jackson*, 475; "both excellent and esteemed ladies..." Van Buren, in Burke, Vol. I, 209; "genial and sweet." Meacham, *American Lion*, 154.

12. Mary Eastin to Mrs. Stockley Donelson, 9 April 1829, in James, 513.

13. Meacham, *American Lion*, 51. Pre-Inauguration shopping spree at Abbott's; Burke, 125. Mary used the black satin for a dress which was probably worn at the Inauguration ball.

14. Meacham, 124.

15. *Ibid.*, 104. Martha Jefferson Randolph visited Washington, D.C. Jackson and Van Buren, breaking protocol, visited her first, followed by Emily and Mary; Burke, 149. In July 1829, Emily and Mary were members of the presidential party to visit Charles Carroll, and the two women visited the family of Louis McLane in Delaware on return; Burke, 224. Emily and Mary went on to New York City in charge of Andrew Jackson, Jr., and to visit Mary Ann Lewis.

16. On trip above, from Wheeling WV, Emily to her mother, "Mary has enjoyed herself very much..." Burke, 124; Joined Emily on trip to Wilmington and Philadelphia. "Emily's role just now was that of chaperone for Mary Eastin, whose beau, Major Abraham Van Buren, and young Samuel Jackson Hays made up the party." Burke, 15.

17. Burke, 163. Emily and Mary Ann's parties in the White House; Burke, 200. They visited Daniel and Margaret in the Cumberland.

18. "...popular Mary had a beau for every day of the week." Burke, 163; "Mrs. Donelson says she will Endeavour to make the young Lady of which you spoke worthy of your son." Andrew Jackson to Martin Van Buren, Washington, 19 December 1831, *Jackson Papers* IX, 779; "Abraham Van Buren," Wikipedia.org.

19. Ezra Stiles Ely to Andrew Jackson, 18 March 1829, *Jackson Papers* VII, 102.

20. Grasping Emily's fury, Mary "sought to hide her emotion by gradually withdrawing herself from sight in the embrasure of the window." Meacham, *American Lion*, 107; Burke, 155. The more Van Buren argued, the more agitated became Mary. Her sympathy for her aunt Emily finally got the better of her.

21. Andrew Jackson to Mary Ann Eastin, 1 January 1831, *Jackson Papers* IX, 4–6.

22. Andrew Jackson to Mary Ann Eastin, 24 October 1830, *Jackson Papers* VIII, 578–81.

23. "My health is not very good." Andrew Jackson to Mary Ann Eastin, 17 February 1831, *Jackson Papers* IX 87–8; 8 July 1831. Sadness over Rachel's death.

24. Andrew Jackson to Mary Ann Eastin, 24 October 1830, *Jackson Papers* VIII, 578–581.

25. Andrew Jackson to Mary Ann Eastin, 1 January 1831, *Jackson Papers* IX, 4–6; Jackson to Mary Ann Eastin, 10 May 1831, *Jackson Papers* IX, 140–3.
26. Mary Ann Eastin to Andrew Jackson, 5 December 1830, *Jackson Papers* VIII, 648–9.
27. Mary Ann Eastin to Andrew Jackson, 12 June 1831, *Jackson Papers* IX, 303–4.
28. James, *The Life of Andrew Jackson*, 513.
29. Burke, 228–9.
30. "How Many Weddings Have Been Held at the White House?" White House Historical Association. The Polk/Eastin wedding ceremony was the fourth to occur in the White House; "Jackson had long loved Mary as much as he loved Emily..." Meacham, *American Lion*, 202; James, 627. Jackson generously paid for both Mary Eastin's and Andrew Jackson Junior's marriages which encumbered him with debt for a year.
31. James, 596.
32. Mary Eastin Polk to Andrew Jackson, Willis Grove, 24 June 1832, *Jackson Papers* X 323; Andrew Jackson to Mary Ann Eastin Polk, 26 November 1832, *Jackson Papers* X, 619; Mary Ann Eastin Polk to Andrew Jackson, Willis Grove, 18 December 1832, *Jackson Papers* X, 735.
33. Burke, Combined Volume, 257. 1833 letter Andrew Jackson to Mary Eastin Polk.
34. *Ibid.*, 293.
35. "Mary Ann Eastin Polk," Find a Grave. Mary Ann's children were Sarah Rachel (1833), Mary Brown (1835), Emily Donelson (1837), William (1839), Eliza Eastin (1841), Frances Ann (1844), stillborn twins (1845), Susan Rebecca (1847), and George Washington (1847).
36. Burke, 113.
37. Burke, 222; Remini, Vol. II, 334.
38. Burke, 240. Washington parties; Burke, 234. White House Belle.
39. Remini, Vol. III, 49. Mary present at 1833 Inaugural Ball; Burke, 244. Returned to Nashville with the Coffees after the inauguration; Burke, 258. marriage to Dr. Walker.
40. Burke, 113.
41. Remini, Vol. III, 49. Marriage date, and Jackson's congratulation to Hutchings; *vide infra:* Jackson's prior advice to "Little Hutchings" regarding selection of a wife.
42. Remini, Vol. III, 453–4. Harrodsburgh salt was rock salt obtained from the region of Harrodsburgh, Kentucky. Andrew Jackson swore by the efficacy of Matchless Sanative for his entire life. Its principal component was cheap whisky.
43. Burke, 157; 163.
44. Burke, 257. Cora was as dear to Jackson as any of his young connections; Remini, Vol. III, 50. Marriage in the White House.; Remini, 59. Assigned to Livingston's staff when Livingston became Minister to France.
45. "Always added a sparkle..." Remini, Vol. III, 50. Jackson gave her a lovely wedding; "She is a sweet disposition..." Burke, 224.

Chapter XV

1. Remini, Vol. II, Andrew Jackson to John Coffee, 23 January 1825. "I have resisted all those invitations Except the 8th January" 407*n*; Remini, Vol. II, Rachel Jackson to Mary Donelson, 27 January 1825. "We got two and three invitations a day sometimes."
2. Brady, *A Being So Gentle*: "The expense and social whirl in the city upset her, especially the extravagance in dressing and running out to parties. At the Hermitage she was accustomed to a peaceful existence. The play-actors sent me a letter, requesting my countenance to them. No. A ticket to balls and parties. No, not one." 185.
3. Catherine Allgor, *Female Trouble: Andrew Jackson versus the Ladies of Washington.*
4. Remini, Vol. II, Louis McLane to his wife, She "is an ordinary looking old woman." 85.
5. Personal correspondence, Marsha Mullin to author, 26 May 2020.

Bibliography

Books

Allgor, Catherine. *Female Trouble: Andrew Jackson versus the Ladies of Washington* (The Gilder Lehman Institute of American History).
Ammon, Harry. *James Monroe: The Quest for National Identity* (Charlottesville: University of Virginia Press, 1990).
Bartlett, Irving H. *John C. Calhoun: A Biography* (New York: W.W. Norton & Co., 1993).
Basch, Norma. "Marriage, Morals, and Politics in the Election of 1828," In *Sexual Borderlands, Constructing an American Sexual Past,* edited by Kathleen Kennedy and Sharon Ullman, 83–114. (Columbus: The Ohio State University Press, 2003).
Bassett, John Spencer, ed. *The Correspondence of Andrew Jackson* (Washington: Carnegie Institution of Washington. 1928).
Bays, Bill. *James Robertson, Father of Tennessee and Founder of Nashville* (Bloomington IN: West Bow Press, 2013).
Blethen, H. Tyler, and Curtis W. Wood, Jr. *From Ulster to Carolina: The Migration of the Scotch-Irish to Southwestern North Carolina* (Raleigh: North Carolina Department of Cultural Resources, 2013).
Booraem, Hendrik. *Young Hickory: The Making of Andrew Jackson* (Dallas, TX: Taylor Trade Publishing, 2001).
Brady, Patricia: *A Being So Gentle: The Frontier Love Story of Rachel and Andrew Jackson* (New York: St. Martin's Press, 2011).
Brands, H.W. *Andrew Jackson: His Life and Times* (New York: Anchor Books, 2004).
Burke, Pauline Wilcox. *Emily Donelson of Tennessee, Vol. I* (Richmond, VI: Garrett & Massie, 1941).
Burke, Pauline Wilcox. *Emily Donelson of Tennessee, Vol. II* (Richmond, VA: Garrett & Massie, 1941).
Burke, Pauline Wilcox, and Jonathan M. Atkins. *Emily Donelson of Tennessee* (Knoxville: University of Tennessee Press, 2001).
Burstein, Andrew. *The Passions of Andrew Jackson* (New York: Vintage Books, 2004).
Caldwell, Patricia French. *General Jackson's Lady* (Nashville: The Ladies Hermitage Association, 1936).
Cheathem, Mark R. *Old Hickory's Nephew: The Political and Personal Struggles of Andrew Jackson Donelson* (Baton Rouge: Louisiana State University Press, 2007).
Clarke, James A. *American Assassins: The Darker Side of Politics* (Princeton, NJ.: Princeton University Press, 1982).
Cobbett, William. *Life of Andrew Jackson, President of the United States of America* (London: Boult-Cort, 1834).
Cole, Donald B. *The Presidency of Andrew Jackson* (Lawrence: University Press of Kansas, 1993).

Collins English Dictionary 13th edition.
Cruse, Katherine W. *An Amiable Woman: Rachel Jackson* (The Hermitage: The Ladies Hermitage Association, 1994).
Cunningham, Noble E., Jr. *The Presidency of James Monroe* (Lawrence: University Press of Kansas, 1996).
Deppisch, Ludwig M. "Andrew Jackson and American Medical Practice." *Tennessee Historical Quarterly.* 62(9), Summer 2003, 130–151.
Deppisch, Ludwig M. "Andrew Jackson's Exposure to Mercury and Lead: Poisoned President?" *JAMA* 282(6), August 1999, 569–571.
Deppisch, Ludwig M. *The Health of the First Ladies: Medical Histories from Martha Washington to Michelle Obama* (Jefferson, NC: McFarland, 2015).
Digregorio, William A. *The Complete Book of U.S. Presidents*, 4th ed. (New York: Wings Books, 1993).
Eaton, John Henry. *Candid Appeal to the American Public in Reply to Messrs: Ingham, Branch, and Berrien on the Dissolution of the Late Cabinet* (City of Washington: Globe Office, 1831).
Eaton, John Henry. *The Life of Major General Andrew Jackson* (Philadelphia: McCarty & Davis, 1828).
Eaton, Peggy. *The Autobiography of Peggy Eaton* (New York: Arno Press, 1980).
Galloway, Linda Bennett. *Andrew Jackson Junior: Son of a President* (New York: Exposition Press, 1966).
Haywood, Marshall De Lancey. *John Branch: 1782–1863, Governor of North Carolina. United States Senator, Secretary of the Navy, Member of Congress, Governor of Florida, etc.* (North Carolina Booklet, 1915).
Heidler, David S., and Jeanne T. Heidler. *Henry Clay: The Essential American* (New York: Random House, 2011).
Ingham, William Armstrong. *Samuel Dulucenna Ingham* (Self-published, 1910).
Inman, Natalie R. *Brothers and Friends: Kinship in Early America* (Athens: University of Georgia Press, 2017).
Jackson, Andrew. *The Papers of Andrew Jackson,* Volumes I–X, Edited by Daniel Feller, Harold D. Moser, Laura-Eve Moss, Thomas Coens et al. (Knoxville: University of Tennessee Press, 1980–2019).
James, Marquis. *The Life of Andrew Jackson* (Indianapolis: The Bobbs-Merrill Co., 1938).
Kierner, Cynthia A. *Beyond the Household: Women's Place in the Early South, 1700–1835* (Ithaca, NY: Cornell University Press, 1998).
Klotter, James C. *Henry Clay: The Man Who Would Be President* (New York: Oxford University Press, 2018).
Leyburn, James G. *The Scotch-Irish: A Social History* (Chapel-Hill: University of North Carolina Press, 1962).
Marszalek, John F. *The Petticoat Affair* (Baton Rouge: Louisiana State University Press, 1997).
McClure, Paul, ed. *Hutchison Family Record* (Frankfort: Kentucky Historical Society, 1970).
McNeely, Patricia G. *Andrew Jackson: John C. Calhoun and the Petticoat Affair* (Columbia, South Carolina: Self-published, 2018).
Meacham, Jon. *American Lion: Andrew Jackson in the White House* (New York: Random House, 2008).
The Memoirs of Vincent Nolte (New York: G. Howard Watt, 1934) Originally published in the United States in 1854.
Parton, James. *Life of Andrew Jackson*. Vol. I (New York: Mason Brothers, 1859).
Phadke A.M, and N.R. Samant, et al. "Smallpox as an Etiologic Factor in Male Fertility." *Fertility and Sterility* 24 (10), October 1873. 802–4.
Phillips, Leon. *That Eaton Woman* (Barre, MA: Barre Publishing, 1974).
Pollack, Queena. *Peggy Eaton: Democracy's Mistress* (New York: Minton, Balch & Co., 1931).

Remini, Robert V. *Andrew Jackson: A Biography* (New York: Macmillan, 2008).
Remini, Robert V. *Andrew Jackson: The Course of American Democracy 1833–1845* Volume III (Baltimore: Johns Hopkins University Press, 1984).
Remini, Robert V. *Andrew Jackson: The Course of American Empire 1767–1821* Volume I (Baltimore: Johns Hopkins University Press, 1977).
Remini, Robert V. *Andrew Jackson: The Course of American Freedom 1822–1832* Volume II (Baltimore: Johns Hopkins University Press, 1982).
Remini, Robert V. *The Battle of New Orleans* (New York: Viking, 1999).
Rogin, Michael Paul. *Fathers & Children: Andrew Jackson and the Subjugation of the American Indian* (New York: Vintage Books, 1975).
Rumbley, Erica Joy. "Ornamental Music and Southern Belles at the Nashville Female Academy, 1816–1861." *American Music* 33(2) July 2015, 219–250.
Saxton, Martha. *The Widow Washington: The Life of Mary Washington* (New York: Farrar, Straus and Giroux, 2019).
Schlesinger, Arthur M., Jr. *The Age of Jackson* (Boston: Little, Brown and Company, 1953).
Stephens, Rachel. *Selling Andrew Jackson: Ralph E. W. Earl and the Politics of Portraiture* (Columbia: University of South Carolina. 2018).
Sweetser, Kate Dickinson. *Famous Girls of the White House* (New York: Thomas Y. Crowley Company, 1930).
Thomas, Louisa. *Louisa: The Extraordinary Life of Mrs. Adams* (New York: Penguin Press, 2016).
Toplovich, Ann. "Marriage, Mayhem, and Presidential Politics: The Robards-Jackson Backcountry Scandal." *Ohio Valley History*, 5(4), Winter 2003, 3–22.
Traub, James. *John Quincy Adams: Militant Spirit* (New York: Basic Books, 2016).
Turnbow, Tony L. *Hardened to Hickory* (Self-published, 2018).
Unger, Harlow Giles. *The Last Founding Father: James Monroe and a Nation's Call to Greatness* (Philadelphia: Da Capo Press, 2009).
Watson, Harry L. *Andrew Jackson vs. Henry Clay: Democracy and Development in Antebellum America* (Boston: Bedford/St. Martin's, 1998).
Webb, Jim. *Born Fighting: How the Scots-Irish Shaped America* (New York: Broadway Books, 2004).
Widner, Ted. *Martin Van Buren* (New York: Henry Holt & Co., 2005).
Williams, Jack. *Dueling in the Old South* (College Station: Texas A&M University Press, 1980).

Newspapers

The Microcosm, American and Gazette, Providence, Rhode Island, 11 May 1833.
The Washington Globe: Obituary of Mrs. Donelson, 4 January, 1837.
Sides, Susan Goodman. "Presidential Lore: Andrew Jackson and the Crawford family of Salisbury." *Salisbury Post*, 19 March 2017.

Internet

"Andrew Jackson Genealogy." Achives.com. Accessed 12 October 2019. www.archives.com/genealogy/president-jackson.html.
Anthony, Carl. "First Ladies Never Married to Presidents: Sarah Jackson." National First Ladies Library. Accessed 16 October 2017. http.//www.firstladies.org/blog/first-ladies-nevr-married-to-presidents-sarah-jackson/.
Birzer, Bradley J. "Andrew Jackson's Duel with John Sevier." The Imaginative Conservative. Accessed 6 March 2018. http://www.theimaginativeconservative.org/2017/07/andrew-jackson-duel-john-sevier-bradley-birzrhml.

Bibliography

Branley, Edward. "NOLA History: New Orleans in 1812." Go NOLA. Accessed 18 June 2018. http://gonola.com/things-to-do-in-new-orleans/nola-history.

"Elizabeth 'Betty' Jackson." Geni.com, https://www.genl.com/people/Elizabeth-Betty-Hutchinson/60000000003113486794.

"Family Group Sheet of Andrew Jackson and Elizabeth Hutchinson Family." Western Kentucky History and Genealogy." Accessed 14 December 2017. http://westernkyhistory.org/livingston/andrewjackson.html.

"First Lady Biography: Rachel Jackson." National First Ladies Library, http://www.firstladies.org/biographies/firstladies.aspx?biography=7.

Glass, Andrew. "John Calhoun resigns as vice president, Dec. 28, 1832." Politico Published 27 December 2015. Accessed 22 February 2020. https://www.politico.com/story/2015/12/calhoun-resigns-as-vice-president.

"The Hermitage: Andrew Jackson's Children." Accessed 23 June 2018.; https://thehermitage.com/learn/andrew-jackson/family/children/.

"Historical Rankings of Presidents of the United States." Wikipedia. Accessed 20 December 2018. https://en.wikipedia.org/wiki/Historical_rankings_of_presidents_of_the_United_States#2018_Quinnipiac_poll.

Jacobson, Louis, and Sarah Wavehoff. "What's Up with Donald Trump and Andrew Jackson?" Politifact: Accessed 8 December 2019. https://www.politifact.com/truth-o-meter/article/2017/may/02/whats-up-with-donald-trump-andrew-jackson/.

"John Caffrey." Geni.com. Accessed 12 April 2020. https://www.geni.com/people/Capt-John-Caffrey-II/6000000008842206555.

"John Christmas McLemore." Geni.com. Accessed 28 February 2019. https://www.geni.com/people/John-McLemore/6000000011381072897.

"John Christmas McLemore." Tennessee Encyclopedia. Accessed 28 February 2019. https://tennesseeencyclopedia.net/entries/john-christmas-mclemore/.

Malpani, Anjruddha. "How Do Infections Cause Male Infertility?" Malpani Infertility Clinic. Accessed 28 February 2018. https://www.drmalpani.com/knowldge-center/aticles/68.

"Mary Ann Eastin." Geneology.com. Accessed 10 October 2019. www.genealogy.com/forum/syrnames/topics/eastin/72/.

"Peggy Eaton" Wikipedia. Accessed 29 Sptember2018. https://en.wikipedia.org/wiki/Peggy_Eaton.

Politics and the New Nation: 23d. "The 1824 Election and the 'Corrupt Bargain,'" ushistory.org. Accessed 6 August 2018. http://www.ushistory.org/us/23d.asp.

Pyle, G.F. "The Diffusion of Cholera in the United States in Nineteenth Century." Accessed 26 March 2020. https://onlinelibrary.wiley.com/doi/pdf/10.1111/j.1538-4632.1969.tb00605.

"Rush's Thunderbolt." Discovering Lewis and Clark. Accessed 7 July 2019. http://www.lewis-clark.org/article/2564.

"Samuel Jackson." Geni.com. Accessed 21 November 2019. https://www.geni.com/people/Samuel-Jackson/6000000001014542033.

"Sarah Yorke Jackson." Accessed 5 September 2019. self.gutenberg.org/article/sarah__yorke__jackson.

"Sarah Yorke Jackson." Wikipedia. Accessed 5 September 2019. www.wikipedia.org/wiki/Sarah_Yorke_Jackson.

"Waxhaw tribe." Wikipedia. Accessed 23 June 2017, https://en.wikipedia.org/wike/Waxhaw_tribe.

Letters

Michelle Gullion to author, 25 August 2017.
Rachel Jackson to Katherine Duane Morgan, 18 May 1825.
Laura-Eve Moss to author, 22 June 2017.

Laura-Eve Moss to author, 12 July 2017.
Laura-Eve Moss to author, 2019.
Laura-Eve Moss to author, 15 January 2020.
Marsha Mullin to author, 18 July 2017.
Marsha Mullin to author, 8 January 2020.
Marsha Mullin to author, 9 January 2020.
Marsha Mullin to author, 13 April 2020.
Marsha Mullin to author, 21 April 2020.

Other

Gallo, Anthony. *The Eaton Woman. A Two Act Historical Drama*, Play. Unpublished, 2014.
Trescott, Jerry. "The Architecture of the Hermitage Mansion." Uncompleted master's thesis, Middle Tennessee State University, 1987.
The Western Journal of Medicine and Surgery. Vol. 6(2), 1842. Death of Dr. Samuel D. Hogg, 151–155.
The Western Journal of Medicine and Surgery. Vol. 6(4), 1842. Miscellaneous Cases of Samuel Hogg late of Tennessee, 252–256.

Index

Adams, John Quincy 126; appointments by 72; campaign manager 78; defeat 73, 78; in presidential race 1824 69, 70, 72; staff 134; supporters 76
Adams, Louisa 84
Adams, Marion (Sarah Yorke Jackson's sister) 163, 171
Adventure (flatboat) 23
Alabama, Native American attacks in 48
American colonies, Scots-Irish migration and settlement in 7–9, 10, 11
American Consul in Havana 128
American frontier, infectious diseases of 49–50
American War of Independence 14–16
Anderson, James Inslee 111
Anglican Church 7, 20–21, 55
Anglican Protestantism 55
Arbuthnot, Alexander 68, 72, 187
Armbrister, Robert 68, 72, 187
Armstrong, John 47
Arnold, Thomas Dickens 78
Atkinson, Mary Anne 173
Avery, Waightstill 36

Baird, Timothy 43–44
Baldwin, Henry, Jr. 162
Bank of the United States 115
Barry, William T. 94, 120
Barton, Thomas 184
Belton, Francis 94
Benton, Jesse 44, 45, 46, 52, 72
Benton, Thomas Hart 44–45, 46, 51, 72
Berrien, John Macpherson 130; AJ break with 121–122, 126; AJ meeting with 123; cabinet resignation 120; children 178; criticism o 150; Eaton Affair, involvement in 114, 119
Blair, Francis P. 170, 172
Blount, Willie 121
Booraem, Hendrik 18

Boulanger, Joseph 133, 134
Bowman's Station, Kentucky 23
Boyne, Battle of the 9, 191n26
Bradford, Samuel Fisher 111
Brady, Patricia 56, 73
Brady, Peter 111
Branch, John 122–123; AJ break with 121; cabinet resignation 120; children 127, 178; criticism 150; Eaton Affair, involvement 114, 119; as Florida governor 152
Branch, Margaret 127, 178
Bronaugh, Dr. James Craine 52, 54, 62, 75
Buchignani, Antonio 158–159
Burke, Pauline 88–89
Burr, Aaron 34, 41
Burstein, Andrew 2
Burton, Martha H. Donelson (Rachel's niece) 120, 206n14
Burton, Robert Minns 104, 120
Butler, Anthony Wayne 35, 194n7
Butler, Edward 35, 43, 78, 194n7
Butler, Edward George Washington 35, 194n7
Butler, Robert 61
Butler, Thomas 43

cabinet (Jackson administration): discord 119; dissolution 130; dysfunctional nature 120–122; firings from 114; social functions 116; wives 117, 118
Caffrey, John (Rachel's brother-in-law) 42
Caffrey, Mary Donelson (AJ's sister-in-law) 42
Caldwell, Mary 28, 40
Caldwell, Patricia 27
Calhoun, Floride: as Eaton, M. detractor 114–115, 117; Eatons opposed by 130; Inaugural Ball, 1829 attended 106;

227

return home 188; Washington social functions, absence from 116
Calhoun, John C.: AJ alienation from 113–114, 117–118, 120, 132, 180; Eaton, E. statements rebutted by 150; Inaugural Ball, 1829 attended by 106; Ingham, S. appointment backed by 123; Ingham, S. as alleged tool of 125; opponents 124; resignation 117; as Van Buren, M. rival 117; Washington social functions, absence from 116
Call, Mary Letitia Kirkman 104, 152, 203n4
Call, Richard K. 50, 69, 123, 152; AJ, fallout with 155; correspondence 74, 80–81, 104, 113, 203n4; Eaton, J. supported by 121; Eaton, M., attempted seduction 98; Eaton, M. slandered by 110–111
calomel (mercurous chloride) 52, 74–75
Campbell, David 133
Campbell, John Nicholson 111, 112–113, 121–122
Candid Appeal to the American Public (Eaton) 149–150
Carlist Rebellion 153
Carroll, Charles 177
Carroll, William 44
Cartrickfergus, Northern Ireland 9, 10, 14
Carver, Hartwell 135
Castera, Louise de 184
Catholics 63
Charleston, South Carolina 10
Cheathem, Mark R. 127, 146–147
Cherokee Expedition 21
Cherokee tribe 23, 47, 53
Chickamauga, Battle of 141, 172
Chickasaw Nation, treaties with 54
Chickasaw tribe, removal of 149
Choctaw tribe, removal of 149
cholera pandemic, 1832 151
Church of England. *See* Anglican Church
Church of Scotland. *See* Presbyterian Church (Scotland)
Civil War 172, 176
Clay, Henry 77, 78, 126; as AJ's political opponent 69, 113; attacks allegedly instigated by 109–110, 111; corrupt bargain, role 70, 72; Eaton, M. criticized by 113; portrait planned 171
Clinton, DeWitt 95
Clinton, George 93, 95
Coffee, Andrew Jackson (Rachel's grand-nephew) 62
Coffee, John 183; as AJ's business partner 42; children 52, 132, 142, 182, 209n1; correspondence 62, 64, 74, 75, 80, 86, 89, 104, 109, 110, 113, 121, 123, 163, 176; doctors attending 139; fight, involvement 44, 86; Indian removal, role 149
Coffee, Mary (John Coffee's daughter/Emily's niece) 131, 132, 141, 142, 174, 182, 183–184, 209n1
Coffee, Mary Donelson (Emily's sister) 86, 183
consumption 157
"Corrupt Bargain" 69–70, 72
courts of law, alternatives to 35, 36
Craven, Dr. Elijah R. 99, 112, 204n40
Crawford, James (AJ's maternal uncle) 13
Crawford, Jane Hutchinson (AJ's maternal aunt) 9, 12
Crawford, Robert (AJ's maternal uncle) 13, 14
Crawford, Thomas (AJ's cousin) 15, 16
Crawford, Will (AJ's cousin) 18–19
Crawford, William (Secretary of Treasury) 69
Crawford family 15
Creek Indians: AJ campaigns against 38, 40, 45, 46–47, 52–53, 72, 186; Donelsons in campaign against 51; in Florida 47–48; massacre, 1813 46; treaties 47
Creek Nation: campaigns against 2, 42, 43, 51; defeat 46–47, 186
Creek War, officers in 42–43
Cryer, Hardy Murfree 104, 126

Davidson Academy (*later* Cumberland College) 161
Davies, Catherine 55
Davies, Samuel 55–56
Davis, Warren 139
Decatur, Stephen 71
Decatur, Susan 120
Democratic convention, 1832 151
Democratic party 186
deserters, execution of 72, 186
Dickenson, Charles 2, 38, 39–40, 52, 68, 78–79, 137
Dickenson, John 38
Dickson, Mary Florida ("Miss Flora") 161–162
Dickson, William 161
divorce 26, 27–28, 158
Dr. Rush's Thunderbolt 140
Donelson, Alexander (AJ's brother-in-law) 41, 43
Donelson, Alexander (John Donelson's son; AJ's nephew) 51, 54, 58

Index 229

Donelson, Alexander (Sandy) (AJ's nephew) 43
Donelson, Andrew Jackson (AJ's nephew) (Emily's husband): actions, rationale behind 129; AJ and Rachel's health problems, response to 140, 143, 144–145; AJ relations with 115, 126–127, 129–130, 140, 146–147, 180; AJ, value to 104; at AJ's death 156; as AJ's namesake 62; AJ's presidential campaign aided by 90; as AJ's secretary 43, 51, 92, 103, 104, 108, 126, 127–128, 129, 132; biographies 127, 146–147; children 62, 132, 136, 141; correspondence 62, 65–66, 85, 123, 125, 129, 140, 143; Eaton, J., legal aid to 157; Eaton, J. resignation, reaction to 149; Eaton, M., rejected by 114, 126, 127, 179; at Hermitage 35, 194*n*7; indebtedness 146, 149; Lewis, M.A., visit to 184–185; marriage, 1st 67–68, 87–88, 126, 127; marriage, 2nd 145, 146; political setbacks 146–147; Poplar Grove home 168; post–Jackson life 145–147; Timberlake, J. relations with 110; Washington, trip to 68, 88
Donelson, Andrew Jackson (Elizabeth Randolph's son) 62
Donelson, Andrew Jackson, Jr. (AJ's grandnephew) 132, 139, 143
Donelson, Andrew Jackson, Junior, Jr. 142
Donelson, Catherine Davies (John Donelson's grandmother) 20, 145, 193*n*10
Donelson, Daniel Smith (Rachel's nephew) 35, 127, 178, 194*n*7
Donelson, Elizabeth (Rachel's sister-in-law) 42, 161
Donelson, Elizabeth Anderson Martin Randolph (Andrew Jackson Donelson's 2nd wife) 62, 132, 145–146, 156, 182
Donelson, Emily Tennessee (AJ's niece): actions, rationale behind 129; AJ, conflict with 2, 87, 175; AJ, separations from 132; AJ relations with 2, 89, 115, 126, 175, 179, 180, 181, 187, 189; AJ, value to 90, 104, 140–141, 187; as AJ's caregiver 131, 132, 136, 138, 141, 166; as aunt 141, 175, 182, 183; background and life before AJ presidency 92, 133; biographies 88–89; birth and childhood 86, 87, 175; in Calhoun, F.'s circle 115; children 62, 89, 131, 132, 136, 141, 168, 169; correspondence 106–107, 140, 143; domestic life 89; in Donelson family tree 174, 175; Eastin, Mary,

friendship with 87, 176, 177; Eaton, M., comparison to 91–92; Eaton, M., conflict with 2, 91, 105–108, 114, 118, 126, 188; Eaton, M., final encounter with 149; Eaton, M., 1st impression of 105; Eatons opposed by 130; education 87; final illness and death 140, 142–145, 146, 149, 189; as First Lady surrogate 103; health problems 87, 89, 132, 140, 142–145, 170; Jackson, S., impression of 164; marriage 67–68, 87–88, 91, 92, 126, 127, 132; physical description 131, 133; siblings 51; as surrogate First Lady 84, 85, 167, 175, 176, 182, 189; Van Buren, M. dealings with 107, 179; in Washington 89–90; Washington, trip to 68, 88–89; at White House 169; White House, banishment from 114, 126, 128, 134, 176; as White House hostess 43, 83, 126, 131, 132, 133–134, 142, 145, 168, 170, 176, 178
Donelson, John (Elizabeth and Andrew's son) 156
Donelson, Capt. John (Emily's father): AJ dealings with 30, 43, 92; background 85; children 84, 85, 175; Emily's health, concerns over 89; grandchildren 62; land given by 89; land inherited by 86; marriage 86
Donelson, John (Jack) (AJ's nephew) 43, 51
Donelson, Col. John (Rachel's father) 20, 85, 193*n*10; background 20–21; children 51, 175; death 24; estate and heirs 86; as Nashville founder 21; Rachel (daughter) relationship with 22; Tennessee, trip to 23; as vestryman 56
Donelson, John (Rachel's nephew) 35, 194*n*7
Donelson, John Samuel (Emily's son) 136, 139, 141
Donelson, Lemuel (Rachel's nephew) 60–61
Donelson, Leven (AJ's brother-in-law) 41, 43
Donelson, Mary Purnell (Emily's mother) 84, 85–86, 87, 89, 133, 136, 175
Donelson, Mary Rachel (AJ's grandniece) 132, 139
Donelson, Patrick (John Donelson's grandfather) 20, 193*n*10
Donelson, Phila Ann Lawrence 90
Donelson, Rachel (AJ's wife). *See* Jackson, Rachel Donelson (AJ's wife)
Donelson, Rachel (Emily's sister-in-law) 88

Donelson, Rachel Jackson (Emily's daughter) 141
Donelson, Rachel Stockley (AJ's mother-in-law) 20, 21, 28, 85
Donelson, Samuel (AJ's brother-in-law): AJ's dealings with 30; children 35, 43, 62, 194*n*7; death 43; guardian 43
Donelson, Samuel (Rachel's nephew) 35, 194*n*7
Donelson, Severn (AJ's brother-in-law) 42, 43, 51, 62, 161
Donelson, Stockley (AJ's brother-in-law) 29
Donelson, Stockley (Emily's brother) 89, 90
Donelson, Thomas Jefferson 142, 161, 165–166, 214*n*2
Donelson, William (AJ's brother-in-law) 43, 88, 120, 164, 168, 206*n*14
Donelson family: AJ rupture with 108; AJ supported by 51; family tree 174; Jackson-Donelson family discord 126–130; Jackson family compared to 20; in Kentucky 23–24; overview 2; religious practices 21; Tennessee, trip to 21, 22–26
dueling, practice of 36

Earl, Ralph 132
Earle, Ralph E. W. 164
Eastin, Mary Ann 174–175, 176–182, 183, 187, 189; AJ influence on 3; as AJ's ward 43; children 182; correspondence 128, 177, 179–180, 181; education 87, 175–176; marriage 2, 142, 174, 180–181, 182; at White House 132, 134, 141, 164, 176
Eastin, Rachel (Rachel Donelson Eastin's daughter) 175
Eastin, Rachel Donelson (Emily's sister) 86, 175
Eastin, Tabitha 175, 217*n*4
Eastin, William 86, 175, 176
Eaton, John Henry 69, 76; AJ, fallout and reconciliation with 155–156; AJ friendship with 96, 97, 127, 149, 151–152, 153, 203*n*30; AJ recalled by 159; as AJ's biographer 47, 83, 92; AJ's defense 111, 112, 205*n*40; AJ's presidential campaign, 1928, aid with 100; Branch, J., meeting with 122; burial site 159; cabinet appointment, controversy over 109, 121, 123; cabinet resignation of 120, 148, 149; Call, R. K., relations with 152; Clay, Henry interviewed by 78; correspondence 78, 106–107, 127–128, 154, 155; death 157, 158, 159; as Donelson, AJ creditor 146, 149; duel, challenges for 121–122, 125; Eaton, M. defended by 112; Eaton, M. influenced by 95; Eaton, M., relationship with 97–98, 100; Eaton Affair, impact on 113, 120; Elizabeth's advice to AJ according to 16; as Florida Territory Governor 149, 152–153; Harrison, W.H. backed by 155; Inaugural Ball, 1829 attended by 106; Ingham, S. confronted by 124–125; marriage, 1st 184; marriage, 2nd 91–92, 94, 100–101, 109; New York City, trip to 111; as O'Neale boarder 98; post-cabinet assignments 149; post–Jackson life 145; publications 149–150; rooms rented by 67; as Secretary of War 2, 105; as Spain ambassador 153; Spain Ambassadorship 149; Tennessee, return to 150; in U.S. Senate race, 1832 151; White House visits by 104
Eaton, Margaret (Peggy) O'Neale Timberlake: AJ dinner invitation rejected by 108; AJ friendship with 97, 98–99, 100, 101, 105, 149, 150–151, 153; AJ influence on 3, 154; AJ influenced by 120, 187; AJ meeting of 67; AJ's defense of 103, 110, 111; background and life before AJ presidency 92–101, 106; biographies 92, 93, 97, 98, 107, 150, 151, 156; cabinet breakup over 124; cabinet resignations, attitude concerning 130; Call, M., relations with 152; Call, R. attempted seduction of 98; children 96, 99, 149, 156, 157–158; death 148; divorce 159; Donelson, AJ, dealings with 126; Donelson, E., conflict with 2, 91, 105–108, 114, 118, 126, 188; Donelson, E., final encounter with 149; Donelson, E., 1st impression of 88–89, 105–106; education 93–94; elopement, foiled attempt at 94–95; Ely, E. confronted by 111–112; in Florida 152; gossip about 109; grandchildren 149, 158; health problems 150, 151–152, 157; Jackson, R. impression of 99, 110; marriage, 1st 91, 95–96; marriage, 2nd 91–92, 94, 100–101, 109; marriage, 3rd 92, 158–159; miscarriage 112; Petticoat Affair, involvement in 2; physical description 93, 106, 152; in post–Jackson years 148–159; social attacks and maligning of 78, 83, 97–98, 99, 100–101, 113, 120, 129; social ostracism of 103, 106, 114–115, 116, 117, 118, 122, 126, 127; in Spain 153–154; Tennessee, return to 150; in Washington

(post–Eaton Affair) 156–157, 159; Washington, return trips to 128, 148, 156; White House, barring from 94, 97; White House, visits to 107; widowhood 99–100
Eaton Affair (a.k.a. Petticoat Affair) 108–115, 141, 146; Eastin, M.A., role during 175, 178–180; Eaton, J., analysis 149–150; Eaton, M., at center of 105; end 148; hypothetical scenarios 188; impact 103, 189; overview 2; Senate attitude concerning 153; term 3
"Eaton Malaria" (term) 3, 117, 128, 156, 176
Edwards, Jonathan 56
Ely, Ezra Stiles 109, 110, 111, 112–113, 178–179
English Church *see* Anglican Church
Eppes, John 72, 199*n*7
Erwin, Joseph 39
Evangelical Protestants 63
Executive Mansion *see* White House
eye inflammation 80

Farquhar, Emma Yorke 31, 165–166
Farquhar, Mrs. George 163
Ferdinand VII, King of Spain 153, 154
Fields, John 48–49
Fillmore, Millard 146
First Lady, potential 77, 81
Florida Territory: annexation 2, 61, 198*n*14; governorship 57, 61–62, 63–64, 65, 123, 149, 152–153; political brawling 48; statehood 123
Fort Mims, Alabama Territory, Creek Indian massacre at 46
France, U.S. relations with 115
Franklin Hotel complex 156
Franklin House 88, 93, 94, 96–97, 99
French & Indian War 10
Fulton, John 68

Gadsby, John 88
Gadsby's hotel *see* Franklin House
Galloway, Linda 161
"General" (term) 3
Georgia, Native American attacks in 48
Gray, William 135
Green, Duff 90
Guista, Antoine 133, 134

Hall, James Crowdhill 138, 139
Hammond, Charles 76–77, 78
Harrison, William Henry 155
Harrodsburgh salts 184
Hay, Eliza 84, 85

Hayes, Samuel Jackson 164
Hays, Jane Donelson (AJ's sister-in-law) 26, 29, 42, 62
Hays, Narcissa (AJ's nephew) 62
Hays, Robert (Rachel's brother-in-law): AJ reliance on 42–43; as AJ's lawyer 30; children 62; correspondence 60; land fraud accusation against 79; marriage ceremony performed by 29; Rachel boarding with 26
Hays, Samuel Jackson 178
Hays, Stockley Donelson (AJ's nephew) 44, 62
Healy, George 171
heart attack 80, 82
Heiskell, Dr. Henry Le (sp.) 82
hemorrhoids 74
Hermitage (Jackson home): AJ convalescence at 40; AJ vacations 127, 132, 165–166, 167, 182; as center of lives 33; children 63, 87; church, land donated for 57, 74; in Civil War 172; Eatons at 149, 150–151, 156; fire, 1834 54, 65, 167–168; healing influence 80; interludes 61, 64–66, 71; Jackson, Andrew, Junior at 162; Jackson, Andrew III vacating of 173; Jackson family at 172, 181; life 170; loss 171; management 34–35, 55, 189; move to 31, 34; physicians 75, 81; as political headquarters 73–74; property adjoining 89; Washington compared to 69
"Hero" (term) 3
Hogg, Dr. Samuel 54, 75, 81, 82, 139, 142, 183
Houston, Sam 82, 156
Howard, Benjamin 125–126
Hume, William 81, 88, 168, 169
Hunnt, Henry 138, 140
Hunter, John 137
Hunters Hill (Jackson home) 31, 34, 65
Hutchings, Andrew Jackson (Little Hutchings) (Rachel's grandnephew) 51–52, 62, 132, 142, 163, 182, 183
Hutchings, Catherine Donelson (AJ's sister-in-law) 42, 51
Hutchings, John (AJ's nephew) 42, 51
Hutchings, Mary Coffee 52, 62
Hutchings, Moses 85
Hutchings, Stockley (AJ's nephew) 49
Hutchings, Thomas (Rachel's brother-in-law) 42, 85
Hutchinson children, birth order of 9, 191*n*27
Huygens, Chevalier Bangeman 119
Huygens, Madame Constantia 119

232 Index

Hyde, John Ellsworth 111
hypertension 80

Inaugural Ball, 1829 106, 114–115, 177
Inaugural Ball, 1833 183
Indian Removal Act 189
infectious diseases 49–50
Ingham, Mrs. 106, 115, 129, 130
Ingham, Samuel 123–236; AJ break with 121; bank policy development, role in 115; cabinet resignation 120, 124; criticism 150; as Eaton, M., detractor 114; Eaton, M., ostracism, role in 119; government post, departure from 130
Ireland 6, 14
Irish, fight against Scottish immigrants 7
Irish "problem" 6–7

Jackson, Andrew: absences from home 31, 34–35, 46–48, 55, 66–67, 167; adopted children 33, 42, 161; ancestry and family background 5–11; angry temperament 33, 35–36, 43–44, 56, 68, 72, 186–187; Army, resignation from 53, 61; assault and battery, conviction for 43–44; assaults against 137, 139–140; biographies 1, 47, 52, 83, 103, 120, 135, 136, 140, 176; birth 10, 11–12; British, hostility toward 14; cabinet 114, 116, 117, 118, 119, 120–122, 130; Calhoun, J., relations with 117–118; Campbell, J., dealings with 112–113; childhood and formative years 13–14, 187; correspondence 31, 32, 33, 37, 38, 48, 49, 50, 53, 56, 57, 62, 64, 65–66, 67, 74, 78–79, 82, 86, 87, 89, 99, 104, 108, 109, 110, 112–113, 121, 123, 125–126, 127–128, 129, 131, 135, 161–162, 163, 164, 165, 166, 174, 176, 179–180, 181; death 40, 149, 155, 156, 170, 171; Donelson, AJ firing considered by 126, 127–128; Donelson, AJ relations with 115, 126–127, 129–130, 140, 146–147, 180; Donelson, Emily, relations with 2, 89, 115, 126, 175, 179, 180, 181, 187, 189; Donelson family, rupture with 108; duels 26, 33, 35–41, 52, 56, 68, 72, 78–79, 186; Eastin, M.A., relations with 175, 176–177, 181; Eaton, J., defended by 111, 112, 205n40; Eaton, J., fallout and reconciliation with 155–156; Eaton, J., friendship with 96, 97, 127, 149, 151–152, 153, 203n30; Eaton, M., defended by 103, 111, 112, 119, 120, 122; Eaton, M., friendship with 97, 98–99, 100, 101, 149, 151–152, 153; Eaton, M., influenced by 95; Eaton Affair impact on 103, 105, 107, 108–115, 118, 119–120, 150, 189; education 14, 18, 19; election as president, 1828 71, 73, 76, 77, 79, 81, 100, 113; election as president, 1832 132, 151, 181, 188; family, sense of 32; fights, private 43–45, 46; finances and business dealings 33, 41; as first generation American 8, 20; in Florida 101, 135; as Florida Territory governor 57, 61–62, 63–64, 65, 152; as Franklin House boarder 96–97; funeral 141; grandchildren 166, 167; health problems 31, 40, 45, 52–55, 61, 65–66, 74–75, 130, 132, 134–136, 139, 140, 143, 166, 171, 180; homes and haunts *see under name of home*; inauguration and political trip, 1833 137–138; Ingham, S., dealings with 125; injuries 33, 38, 40, 45, 52, 74, 135, 137–138; Jackson, AJ, Jr. debts paid off by 170; Jackson, R., death impact on 103, 104–105; Jackson, S., relations with 164–165, 169; kinship ties 42–43, 51; law career 18, 19; leadership qualities 33; Lewis, W. influence on 127; marriage 28, 29–32, 41–42, 76–77; as matchmaker 141–142, 183; military exploits 3; Nashville, arrival in 25; Natchez, flight to 27, 28; Native Americans, attitude toward 1, 2, 56, 186; O'Neale, W., boarding with 105; overview and assessment of 1, 186–187; political ambitions 75–79, 80; political troubles 41; Polk, J. as supporter of 157; portraits 1; presidency success, factors affecting 102, 113, 115; as president 160; presidential campaign 66, 68, 69–70, 71–73, 75, 90, 100, 103, 123; private life 34; property provided to Donelsons by 89; public life 58–59, 65; Rachel, introduction to 18, 20, 25–26; Rachel, reaction to perceived insult against 37, 39; Rachel, relations before marriage 27, 28, 37; religion 13, 56–57, 74, 170; retirement 149, 160, 171; in Revolutionary War years 14, 15, 16; Robards, L., dealings with 19, 26; Scots-Irish traits inherited by 35, 44, 52, 126, 137, 187; in Seminole War, First 72, 96, 114, 118; as senator 66–68; slavery, attitude toward 1; smallpox and infertility 16, 41; stature, heightening of 30–31, 32, 47; Swann, T. caned by 38; teenage years 18–19; as Tennessee Militia Major General 36–37, 46; as uncle 87, 88; vacations

Index

127, 132, 135, 139, 143, 165–166, 167, 169, 182; Van Buren, M. leverage with 117; as warrior 35–41, 45–47; will 171; women, chivalrous attitude toward 2, 17, 27, 103; women, early dealings with 19
Jackson, Andrew (AJ's father) 5, 9–10, 11
Jackson, Andrew III (AJ's grandson) 167, 170, 172, 173
Jackson, Andrew Junior: adoption 33, 42, 161; at AJ's deathbed 171; as AJ's namesake 62; AJ's relationship with 50; children 165, 170, 172; correspondence 169; courtships 161–163; death 172–173; debts and money woes 170, 171–172; health problems 49–50; Hermitage fire, response to 168; inheritance 171; Jackson, Andrew III, dealings with 172; management incompetence 164–165, 167, 170; marriage 160, 163, 164, 176; post–Jackson life 145; at Rip Raps 169; travels 47, 60–61, 62, 177, 184–185; at White House 166
Jackson, Elizabeth Hutchinson (AJ's mother): advice to AJ 16, 35, 36; AJ influenced by 2, 13, 16–17, 187; birth and family background 9; death 5, 14, 16, 18; defamation against 17, 79; employment 10; English, hatred of 14; hypothetical scenarios 187–189; marriage 9; religion 13, 57, 170; in Revolutionary War years 15; slander against 77; traits 12–13; widowhood 12
Jackson, Hugh (AJ's brother) 14, 15
Jackson, Hugh (AJ's paternal grandfather) 9
Jackson, Hugh (AJ's paternal uncle) 9
Jackson, Lincoya: adoption 33, 49, 50; education 132, 209*n*1
Jackson, Rachel (Sarah Yorke Jackson's daughter) 139, 165, 166, 167, 169, 171, 172
Jackson, Rachel Donelson (AJ's wife): adopted children 33, 42, 161; AJ, duel over 2; AJ, influenced by 2, 20, 187; AJ, introduction to 18, 20, 25–26; AJ, relations before marriage 27, 28, 37; AJ's absences, attitude concerning 31, 66–67, 80; AJ's political ambitions, price paid for 75–79, 80; as aunt 50–51, 87–88, 92, 104, 136, 175, 176, 203*n*5; birth 21–22; burial site and epitaph 82, 83; Call, M., acquaintance with 104, 203*n*4; as caregiver 35, 40–41, 52–55, 74, 75; character, attacks on 71, 75, 76, 79, 81, 113; correspondence 31, 49, 50,

233

53, 56, 57, 60, 66, 78, 99, 168; defense of 77–78; Donelson, AJ, referencing of 129; Donelson, E., threatened with same fate as 106–107; in Donelson family tree 175; Eaton, M., compared to/as reflection of 103, 105; Eaton, M., impression of 99; Eaton, M., relations with 109, 110; Elizabeth, comments regarding 17; final illness and death 71, 75–76, 79–83, 92, 102–103, 130, 176, 179, 180; in Florida 63; health problems 31, 49–50, 61, 62, 64, 69, 72, 75, 80, 81; honor, aspersions against 37, 39; as hostess 30, 31, 73–74; household management by 34–35, 48–49; hypothetical scenarios 103, 187–189; legacy 102–103, 104–105, 111; marriage to AJ 28, 29–32, 41–42, 76–77; marriage to Lewis Robards 20, 24–25, 29, 76–77, 78; as mother 33, 42, 49–50, 55; Natchez, flight to 27, 28; New Orleans, trip to 47; O'Neale, R. friendship with 93, 99; plantation responsibilities 167; public life, attitude concerning 58–59, 188; religion 13, 55–57, 74, 170; restraint, influence for 35, 38, 70; separation and divorce from Lewis Robards 24–25, 26–27, 28, 29, 76, 77; support provided by 33–34; travels 47, 58–61, 62–64, 68–69, 73, 81, 99; youth and family of origin 19–22
Jackson, Robert (AJ's brother) 14, 15, 16
Jackson, Samuel (AJ's grandson) 172
Jackson, Samuel Dorsey 44
Jackson, Sarah Yorke 142, 176; AJ influence on 3; AJ influenced by 2, 187; AJ relations with 164–165, 169; as AJ's caregiver 138, 166, 171; background and family of origin 163–164; children 165, 169, 170; cousins 142; death 173; health problems 166, 167; as Hermitage mistress 165, 166, 168–169, 181; marriage 160, 163, 164; musical abilities 165; physical description 164; religion 170–171; vacations taken by 139; at White House 166, 168, 169; as White House hostess 170, 189
Jackson family: Donelson family compared to 20; at Hermitage 172; Jackson-Donelson family discord 126–130; in Revolutionary War 14, 15
Jackson lineage, preserving 165
James, Marquis 136, 176
James II, King of England 9
James VI, King of Scotland 6
Jefferson, Thomas: children 118, 177;

grandchildren 132, 146, 209n6; social hostess 84, 176, 218n7; vice president under 93
Johnson, Richard M. 119

Kendall, Amos 157
Key, Francis Scott 112, 139–140, 204n40
Key, Philip Scott 158
Kirk of Scotland *see* Presbyterian Church (Scotland)
Know Nothing Party 146
Knox, John 6
Krudener, Baron Paul de 118

Ladies Hermitage Association 173
Ladies of Washington 114, 115, 122, 189
Lafayette, Marquis de 69, 73, 74, 88, 104
Lawrence, Dr. John M. 172
Lawrence, Richard 139
Lawson, Thomas 170
lawyers, duels fought between 36
lead poisoning 45, 52, 74
Lewis, Mary Ann (William Lewis's daughter) 43, 142, 184–185
Lewis, Myra 96, 184
Lewis, William B. 156, 157, 168–169; AJ, influence with 127; AJ presidential campaign, assistance with 73; as AJ's confidante 96; children 43, 142, 177; correspondence 77, 98, 113, 127, 128, 151; marriage 184; at White House 132
Lewis, William Terrell 184
Leyburn, James 6
The Life of Major General Andrew Jackson (Eaton) 47
Lincoln, Abraham 138
liverwort 135
Livingston, Cora 178, 181, 184
Livingston, Edward 184
lockjaw 173
Lockridge, Jane (Sarah Yorke Jackson's sister) 163

Macomb, Mrs. 118
Madison, Dolley 84, 94, 95, 158, 176, 218n7
Madison, James 53, 93
malaria 135, 136
Mansion (Donelson residence) 86, 87, 88, 133, 143, 175
Maria Cristina de Borbón, Queen of Spain 153–154
Martin, Catherine (Emily's sister) 88
Martin, Elizabeth (AJ's grandniece) *see* Donelson, Elizabeth Anderson Martin

Randolph (Andrew Jackson Donelson's 2nd wife)
May, Dr. Francis 39, 40, 52, 78–79
McCorkle, Dr. Miles 81
McGary, Hugh 28
McKemie, Margaret Hutchinson (AJ's maternal aunt) 9, 12
McLane, Louis 177, 188–189
McLemore, Elizabeth Donelson (Emily's sister) 88, 110, 113, 141, 174, 182, 204n31
McLemore, John Christian 110, 112, 182
McLemore, Mary 131, 132, 141, 142, 181, 182–183
McNairy, John 19, 73
Meacham, Jon 1, 12, 156, 177
mercurous chloride (calomel) 52, 74–75
mercury poisoning 74
Mexico, U.S. relations with 115
Michigan Territory, governorship of 151
Mobile, Alabama 47
Monroe, Elizabeth (Eliza) Kortright (James Monroe's daughter) 176, 218n7
Monroe, Elizabeth (James Monroe's wife) 94, 97, 98, 176, 188, 218n7
Monroe, James: AJ campaigning for 54–55; AJ dealings with 64; appointments by 61; children 176, 218n7; correspondence 48, 53; doctor attending 138; O'Neale family, connection to 94
Montgomery, John B. 133–134
Moore, Thomas Patrick 72

Nashville, Tennessee: description 19–20; founding 21, 23; Pensacola compared to 63; political conditions 51, 196–197n26
Nashville Female Academy 87, 129, 175–176, 183
National Bank 132, 186, 189
Native Americans: attacks by 48; military forays against 36; removal 149, 189; Southern tribes 2
Navy department, fraud in 115
New Orleans 59–60, 62–63, 69
New Orleans, Battle of, 1815: martial law during 68; victory in 35, 38, 47, 73, 81
Nolte, Vincent 60
North Carolina 21, 26
Northern Ireland 7

"Old Hickory" (term) 3
O'Neale, John 93
O'Neale, Rhoda 92–93, 99, 156, 158
O'Neale, William: AJ as boarder 96–97, 99, 105; children 93; as inn and saloon

owner 92; M. elopement curtailed by 95; M. wedding attended by 101; New York City, trip to 111; tavern belonging to 68–69
Overton, John: AJ presidential campaign, assistance with 73; as AJ's dueling second 39; as AJ's guest 135; correspondence 151, 164; Lewis-Rachel Robards reconciliation arranged by 25; nephew 38; Rachel-Andrew interactions observed 26; Rachel defended 78; Robards divorce as understood by 28
Overton, Thomas 38, 39, 40

Pageot, Andrew Jackson 185
Pageot, Joseph 185
Paris, Treaty of, 1783 24
Parker, Daniel 94
Parton, James 12
Pensacola, Florida: capture 47; description 152; trips to 61–62, 63; yellow fever epidemic 52, 197n33
Petrikin, Henry 124
Petticoat Affair see Eaton Affair (a.k.a. Petticoat Affair)
Petticoat Affair (term) 3
Philadelphia as port of entry 8, 10
Phillips, Leon 156
phthisis 80
physicians, presidential 138–139
Physick, Dr. Phillip Synge 53, 137, 139, 166
plumbism 45
Pocahontas (riverboat) 73
Polk, James K.: correspondence 74, 174; as Donelson, R.J.'s godfather 141; malaria contracted by 135; as president 156–157; relatives 142, 181
Polk, Lucius 2, 142, 174, 181, 182
Polk, Mary Eastin see Eastin, Mary Ann
Polk, Sarah (James' wife) 135
Polk, Sarah Rachel (Mary Eastin Polk's daughter) 142
Pollack, Queena 97, 150, 154
Poplar Grove (Jackson home) 30, 146, 168
Potomac (Navy frigate) 107
Presbyterian Church (Scotland) 7, 9–10
Presbyterianism, evangelical 55
Presbyterians 7
presidential election, 1824 68, 69–70
presidential election, 1828 see Jackson, Andrew: election as president, 1828
presidential election, 1832 132, 151, 181, 188
presidential election, 1840 155

prison conditions in Revolutionary War 15–16
Provost, Theodosia 34
pulmonary tuberculosis deterioration 144

Quincy, Josiah 137
quinine 136

Rachel (AJ's granddaughter) 137, 139
Randolph, Emily (Margaret's granddaughter) 157, 158, 159
Randolph, John B. (Margaret Eaton's son-in-law) 155, 159
Randolph, John Chapman (Margaret's grandson) 158
Randolph, John H. Eaton (Margaret's grandson) 158, 159
Randolph, Lewis 132
Randolph, Lewis Jackson (Lewis and Elizabeth's son) 132, 209n6
Randolph, Margaret Rosa Timberlake (Margaret's daughter) 153, 155, 158, 159
Randolph, Martha Jefferson (Thomas Jefferson's daughter) 118, 177
Randolph, Mary (Margaret's granddaughter) 158
Randolph, Meriwether Lewis 146
Randolph, Robert R. 137
Reid, John 47, 60–61
Reiff, Joseph 168, 169
Remini, Robert 1, 52, 60, 78, 80, 120, 156, 167
Revolutionary War 14–16
Rip Raps (artificial island) 132, 135, 139, 143, 166, 169
Rives, John C. 172
Roane, Archibald 37
Robards, Elizabeth Lewis 25
Robards, Lewis (Rachel's first husband): AJ dealings with 19, 26, 76; Kentucky, move to 24; marriage, first 24–26, 76–77, 78; marriage, second 28; separation and divorce 26, 27–28, 76, 77
Robertson, Dr. Felix 45
Robertson, James 21, 22, 39, 45
Roosevelt, Franklin 1
Roosevelt, Theodore 1
Root, Captain 95
Rush, Richard 153

Sampayo, Duc A. de 158
Sappington, Frank 40
Saunders, Harrison 49
Scots-Irish: in America 10, 11; historic

overview 6–9; in Revolutionary War 15; traits 5, 35, 44, 52
Scottish Lowlands 5, 6
Seminole War, First (1818): AJ's performance during, criticism of 72, 96, 114, 118, 186–187; cause 48; conducting 53; English influence 14; executions 68; health hazards 61
Seminole War, Second 155
Seminoles 47–48, 153
senators, selection of 66, 198n38
Seventeenth Amendment 66, 98, 198n38, 203n36
Sevier, John 33, 41
Shelby, Isaac 54
ship fever (epidemic typhus) 16
Sim, Thomas 138–139
Singleton, Angela 178
slavery, AJ practice of 186
slaves: AJ's inheritance including 171; fornication with 26; at Hermitage 35, 48–49, 50; from Hermitage 68; at White House 134
smallpox 16, 41
Smith, Miss Mary 162
Society Ladies of Washington 114, 115, 122, 189
Southern Indian tribes 2
Spain: ambassadorship of 149, 153, 154; civil war (Carlist Rebellion) 153; Florida Territory ceded by 61, 198n14; Minister to Kingdom of 153, 154; war, potential 61
Springdale (Donelson residence) 89, 90
"The Star-Spangled Banner" (U.S. national anthem) 158
states' rights 114
sugar of lead 52, 138
surrogate First Ladies 84–85, 133, 175, 176, 182, 189
Swann, Thomas 38, 39, 42
Swartwout, Samuel 74, 112

Tallahasee 152
tariff 114, 132
Tennessee 22–26, 36, 98, 203n36
Tennessee Militia, Major General of 36–37, 46
Tennessee State Constitutional Convention 30
tetanus 173
Texas, U.S. annexation of 146
That Eaton Woman (Phillips) 156
Timberlake, John Bowie: children 157–158; death 99–100; Eaton, J., relations with 110; Eaton, M. influenced by 95–96; funds stolen from 137, 211n27; at sea 97, 99, 112; setbacks suffered by 96, 97
Timberlake, Mary Virginia (Margaret's daughter) 96, 153, 157–158
Timberlake, Peggy (Margaret) O'Neale *see* Eaton, Margaret (Peggy) O'Neale Timberlake
Toplovich, Ann 27
Towson, General 121–122
Trist, Nicholas 125, 128
Truman, Harry 1
Trump, Donald 1
tuberculosis 80, 143–144, 157, 184
Tulip Grove (formerly Poplar Grove) (Jackson home) 30, 146, 168
Tutt, Charles Pendleton 76
Tyler, John 123, 157
Tyler, Letitia 188

Ulster, drought affecting 8
Ulster Plantation, Northern Ireland 5, 6, 7, 8, 9
Union, indissolubility of 114
United States, foreign relations 115
United States senators, appointment *versus* election of 98, 203n36

Van Buren, Abraham 178
Van Buren, Martin 135, 153, 181; cabinet resignation 120; Calhoun, J. as rival 118; correspondence 121, 131; as Donelson, AJ, creditor 146; Eaton, J., relations with 154–155; Eaton Affair, involvement 107, 117, 118, 124, 130, 179; inauguration 170; official dinners hosted by 117; as president 154–155, 178; as vice president 151; White House visits 104
Vaughan, Sir Charles 118
Virginia boundaries 21

Walker, Dr. James Monroe 183
Wallace, Dr. James 142
War of American Independence 14–16
War of 1812 14, 47, 53, 58, 59, 94, 95
Ward, Edward 74, 161
Warren, Elizabeth 79
Warren, John 138
Washington, George 24, 41
Washington, D.C. 60–61, 68–70, 93, 135
Waxhaw Indians 10, 11
Waxhaw region 10–11, 14–15
West Point (United States Military Academy) 51, 67, 90, 93, 172
Wetherill, Mrs. Mordecai 163

White House: burning 94; guests 141, 156–157; hostesses 170, 178, 189 (*see also* Donelson, Emily Tennessee (AJ's niece); life 132, 136, 140–142; meals 133–134; weddings 142, 181, 184, 185
white male suffrage 186
Wilkinson, James 44
William I, King of England 9, 191*n*26

women, AJ influence on 3
Woodbury, Levi 139
Wynn, Hannah 28

yellow fever 52, 197*n*33
Yorke, Mary Haines 163
Yorke, Peter 163
Young Hickory (Booraem) 18

www.ingramcontent.com/pod-product-compliance
Lightning Source LLC
Chambersburg PA
CBHW032038300426
44117CB00009B/1108